ADOBE AFTER EFFECTS CC BEGINNERS GUIDE

BY NATHAN CLARK

Chapter 1 Introduction

After Effects CC is an application that allows you to create dynamic, visually stunning motion graphics and cinematic visual effects. This application can be used to create 2D and 3D animation that allows you to also create dynamic text animation using the many typography tools within After Effects.

It can also be used to apply nondestructive effects to video, using various tinting and adjustment methods, isolating objects from their background using rotoscoping technology, and correcting for camera shake by utilizing cutting-edge stabilization features.

After Effects also integrates with several other Creative Suite applications, such as Photoshop for animating 3D layers, Premiere Pro with shared effects and copy and paste support, and Flash Professional for creating engaging web animation sequences. Learning Objectives

After completing the instructions in this book, you will be able to: Import and organize footage• Create, arrange, and composite layers in a composition• Modify and animate layer properties• Add effects and modify effect properties• Preview those changes• Render and export your project•

Chapter 2 Workspaces

Planning your work

Correct project settings, preparation of footage, and initial composition settings can help you to avoid errors and unexpected results when rendering your final output movie. Before you begin, think about the kind of work you intend to do in After Effects and the kind of output you plan to create. After you have planned your project and made some basic decisions about project settings, you are ready to start importing footage and assembling compositions from layers based on that footage.

The best way to ensure that your movie is suitable for a specific medium is to render a test movie and view it using the same type of equipment as your audience. It's best to do such tests before you have completed the difficult and time-consuming parts of your work, to uncover problems early.

Aharon Rabinowitz provides an article on the Creative COW website about planning your project with the final delivery specifications in mind.

For more information about encoding and compression options, see this FAQ entry: "FAQ: What is the best format for rendering and exporting from After Effects?"

Storyboards and scripts (screenplays)

Your movie or video production project often starts with the pre-production tasks of writing a script (screenplay) and creating storyboards, which then effectively guide you through your production (shooting) and post-production (editing, soundtrack, visual effects, and so on) stages.

You can use Adobe Story to collaboratively write and manage screenplays and dynamically generate shooting scripts, shooting schedules, character lists, shot lists, and more from your script using metadata. You can also generate specific metadata-based reports during the editing phase from Adobe Story. Adobe Photoshop and Adobe Illustrator help you create storyboards based on your script for shooting your movie or video.

Acquiring, choosing, and preparing footage

Before importing footage, first decide which media and formats to use for your finished movies, and then determine the best settings for your source material. Often, it's best to prepare footage before importing it into After Effects.

For example, if you want an image to fill your composition frame, configure the image in Adobe Photoshop so that the image size and pixel aspect ratio match the composition size and pixel aspect ratio. If the image is too large when you import it into After Effects, you increase the memory and processor requirements of the compositions that use it. If the image is too small, you lose image quality when you scale it to the desired size. See Pixel aspect ratio and frame aspect ratio.

If you can shoot footage with consistent lighting and colors—and otherwise prevent the need to do tedious utility work in post-production—then you have more time for creative work.

Workspaces

If possible, use uncompressed footage or footage encoded with lossless compression. Lossless compression produces better results for operations, such as keying and motion tracking because the compression is reversible, whereas lossy compression discards some data that cannot be restored (generation loss). Certain kinds of compression—such as the compression used in MPEG-2 or MPEG-4 camera formats—are especially bad for color keying, because they discard the subtle differences in color that you depend on for good bluescreen or greenscreen keying. It's often best to wait until the final rendering phase to use compression other than lossless compression. See Keying introduction and resources.

If possible, use footage with a frame rate that matches that of your output, so that After Effects doesn't have to use frame blending or similar methods to fill in missing frames. See Frame rate.

The kind of work that you do in After Effects and the kind of output movie that you want to create can even influence how you shoot and acquire your footage. For example, if you know that you want to animate using motion tracking, consider shooting your scene in a manner that optimizes for motion tracking—for example, using tracking markers. See Motion tracking workflows.

Also consider shooting at a larger frame size than what you need for final delivery if you want "head-room" for post-production, whether for fake pans and zooms, or for stabilization.

Project settings

Project settings fall into three basic categories: how time is displayed in the project, how color data is treated in the project, and what sampling rate to use for audio. Of these settings, it is important to think about the color settings before you do much work in your project, because they determine how color data is interpreted as you import footage files, how color calculations are performed as you work, and how color data is converted for final output. See Color managementand Timecode and time display units .

If you enable color management for your project, the colors that you see are the same colors that your audience see when they view the movie that you create.

Note: Click the color depth indicator at the bottom of the Project panel to open the Project Settings dialog box. Alt-click (Windows) or Option-click (Mac OS) to cycle through color bit depths: 8 bpc, 16 bpc, and 32 bpc. See Color depth and high dynamic range color.

Composition settings

After you prepare and import footage items, you use these footage items to create layers in a composition, where you animate and apply effects. When you create a composition, specify composition settings such as resolution, frame size, and pixel aspect ratio for your final rendered output. Although you can change composition settings at any time, it's best to set them correctly as you create each composition to avoid unexpected results in your final rendered output. For example, the composition frame size should be the image size in the playback medium. See Composition settings.

If you are rendering and exporting a composition to more than one media format, always match the pixel dimensions for your composition to the largest pixel dimensions used for your output. Later, you can use output modules in the Render Queue panel to encode and export a separate version of the composition for each format. See Output modules and output module settings.

Performance, memory, and storage considerations

If you work with large compositions, make sure that you configure After Effects and your computer to maximize performance. Complex compositions can require a large amount of memory to render, and the rendered movies can take a large amount of disk space to store. Before you attempt to render a three-hour movie, make sure that you have the disk space available to store it. See Storage requirements for output files .

Workspaces

If your source footage files are on a slow disk drive (or across a slow network connection), then performance is affected. When possible, keep the source footage files for your project on a fast local disk drive. Ideally, you have three drives: one for source footage files, one from which the application runs, and one for rendered output.

For more information, see Improve performance and Memory & Multiprocessing preferences .

Planning for playback on computer monitors and mobile devices

When you create a movie for playback on a computer or a mobile device—whether downloaded from the Web, played from a media drive, or streamed from a site—specify composition settings, render settings, and output module settings that keep file size low without compromising on the intended delivery quality. Consider that a movie with a high data rate may not play well on older devices. Similarly, a large movie may take a long time to download over a slower data network.

When rendering your final movie, choose a file type and encoder appropriate for the final media. The corresponding decoder must be available on the system used by your intended audience; otherwise they will not be able to play the movie. Common codecs (encoders/decoders) include the codecs installed with media players such as Flash Player, Windows Media Player, and QuickTime Player.

Adobe Media Encoder CC offers presets that contain predefined settings for various platforms and formats for mobile devices, broadcast, cinema, web video, and so on. For more details about Media Encoder presets, see Using the Preset Browser .

For more information on rendering and exporting in After Effects, see Basics of rendering and exporting.

The article Exporting for the Web and mobile devices covers some important tips related to exporting your videos for Web and mobile devices.

For more information about encoding and compression options for After Effects, see this FAQ entry: "FAQ: What is the best format for rendering and exporting from After Effects?"

Mobile devices

Many of the considerations for creating movies for playback on mobile devices, such as mobile phones and tablets, are similar to the considerations for creating movies for playback on computers—but the limitations are even more extreme. Because the amount of storage (disk space) and processor power can vary for mobile phones, file size and data rate for movies must be even more tightly controlled.

Screen dimensions, video frame rates, and color gamuts vary greatly from one mobile device to another.

Use these tips when shooting video for mobile devices:

•Tight shots are better. It's hard to see a face on a tiny screen unless it's shot in relative close-up.

Light your subjects well, and keep them separated from the background; keep the colors and brightness values between background and subject different.

Avoid excessive zooming and rolling, which hinder temporal compression schemes.

Because stable (non-shaky) video is easier to compress, shoot video with a tripod to minimize the shaking of the camera.

Avoid using auto-focus and auto-exposure features. When these features engage, they change the appearance of all of the pixels in an image from one frame to the next, making compression using interframe encoding schemes less efficient.

Use these tips when working in After Effects (for mobile devices):

•Use a lower frame rate (12-24 fps) for mobile devices.

Workspaces

Use motion-stabilization tools and noise-reduction or blur effects before rendering to final output, to aid the compressor in reducing file size.

Match the color palette to the mobile devices that you are targeting. Mobile devices, in general, have a limited color gamut.

Consider using cuts and other fast transitions instead of zooming in and out or using fades and dissolves. Fast cuts also make compression easier.

Cross-platform project considerations

After Effects project files are compatible with Mac OS and Windows operating systems, but some factors—mostly regarding the locations and naming of footage files and support files—can affect the ease of working with the same project across platforms.

Project file paths

When you move a project file to a different computer and open it, After Effects attempts to locate the project's footage files as follows: After Effects first searches the folder in which the project file is located; second, it searches the file's original path or folder location; finally, it searches the root of the directory where the project is located.

If you are building cross-platform projects, it's best if the full paths have the same names on Mac OS and Windows systems. If the footage and the project are on different volumes, make sure that the appropriate volume is mounted before opening the project and that network volume names are the same on both systems.

It's best to store footage in the same folder as the project file or in another folder within that folder. Here's a sample hierarchy:

/newproject/project_file.aep

/newproject/source/footage1.psd

/newproject/source/footage2.avi

You can then copy the new project folder in its entirety across platforms, and After Effects properly locates all the footage.

Use the Collect Files feature to gather copies of all the files in a project into a single folder. You can then move the folder ▪ containing the copied project to the other platform. See Collect files in one location.

File-naming conventions

Name your footage and project files with the appropriate filename extensions, such as .mov for QuickTime movies and .aep for After Effects projects. For using files on the Web, be sure that filenames adhere to applicable conventions for extensions and paths.

Supported file types

Some file types are supported on one platform but not others. See Supported import formatsand Supported output formats.

Resources

Ensure that all fonts, effects, codecs, and other resources are available on both systems. Such resources are often plug-ins.

Workspaces

If you use a native After Effects effect in a project on one operating system, the effect still works on the other operating system to which you've transferred your project. However, some third-party effects and other third-party plug-ins may not continue to operate, even if you have versions of these plug-ins on the target system. In such cases, you may need to reapply some third-party effects.

Setup and installation

Installing the software

Before installing Adobe After Effects software, review the complete system requirements .

In addition to the full version of Adobe After Effects, you can also install additional copies on additional computers to use as After Effects render engines to assist with network rendering.

Installing a render-only instance of Adobe After Effects CC

Before you start:

If you have installed Creative Cloud applications on two computers, sign out of one of them by opening any of the applications and choosing Sign Out from the Help menu.

You can sign back into Creative Cloud on this computer after the render-only instances of After Effects are installed.

To install a render-only instance of After Effects CC, do the following:

Go to the product page to download and install After Effects CC.

When the installation is complete, start After Effects.

Choose Sign Out from the Help menu.

Quit After Effects.

Create and place the ae_render_only_node.txt file as described in this blog post.

Limitations of the trial version

The trial version of After Effects includes all of the codecs that are included with the full version of After Effects. This means that you can import and export to all of the supported file formats using the trial version.

The trial version of After Effects also includes the Keylight plug-in, mocha-AE, mocha shape, Cycore (CC) effects, and Color Finesse.

If your installation of After Effects is missing some third-party components, contact your system administrator to ensure that all licensed components have been installed correctly.

Activate the software

A single-user retail license activation supports two computers. For example, you can install the software on a desktop computer at work and on a laptop computer at home.

For more information on product licensing and activation, see the Read Me file or go to the Adobe website.

Workspaces

General user interface items

Activate a tool

The Tools panel can be displayed as a toolbar across the top of the application window or as a normal, dockable panel.

Note: *Controls related to some tools appear only when the tool is selected in the Tools panel.*

Click the button for the tool. If the button has a small triangle at its lower-right corner, hold down the mouse button to view the hidden tools. Then, click the tool you want to activate.

Press the keyboard shortcut for the tool. (Placing the pointer over a tool button displays a tool tip with the name and keyboard shortcut for the tool.)

To cycle through hidden tools within a tool category, repeatedly press the keyboard shortcut for the tool category. (For example, press the Q key repeatedly to cycle through the pen tools.)

To momentarily activate a tool, hold down the key for the desired tool; release the key to return to the previously active tool. (This technique does not work with all tools.)

To momentarily activate the Hand tool, hold down the spacebar, the H key, or the middle mouse button. (The middle mouse button does not activate the Hand tool under a few circumstances, including when the Unified Camera tool is active.)

To pan around in the Composition, Layer, or Footage panel, drag with the Hand tool. Hold Shift, too, to pan faster.

To show or hide panels most relevant to the active tool, click the panel button 🖵 if available. For example, clicking this button when a paint tool is active opens or closes the Paint and Brushes panels. Select the Auto-Open Panels option in the Tools panel to automatically open the relevant panels when certain tools are activated.

Open panel, viewer, and context menus

Panel menus provide commands relative to the active panel or frame. Viewer menus provide lists of compositions, layers, or footage items that can be shown in the viewer, as well as commands for closing items and locking the viewer. Context menus provide commands relative to the item that is *context-clicked*. Many items in the After Effects user interface have associated context menus. Using context menus can make your work faster and easier.

To open a panel menu, click the button ◄▪ in the upper-right corner of the panel.

To open a viewer menu, click the name of the active composition, layer, or footage item in the viewer tab.

To open a context menu, right-click (Windows) or Control-click (Mac OS). This action is sometimes referred to as context-clicking.

Columns

The Project, Timeline, and Render Queue panels contain columns.

To show or hide columns, right-click (Windows) or Control-click (Mac OS) a column heading (or choose Columns from the panel menu), and select the columns that you want to show or hide. A check mark indicates that the column is shown.

Workspaces

Note: In general, the search and filter functions in the Project and Timeline panels only operate on the content of columns that are shown.

To reorder columns, select a column name and drag it to a new location.

To resize columns, drag the bar next to a column name. Some columns cannot be resized.

To sort footage items in the Project panel, click the column heading. Click once more to sort them in reverse order.

Search and filter in the Timeline, Project, and Effects & Presets panels

The Project, Timeline, and Effects & Presets panels each contain search fields that you can use to filter items in the panel.

To place the insertion point in a search field, click in the search field.

To place the insertion point in the search field for the active panel, choose File > Find or press Ctrl+F (Windows) or Command+F (Mac OS).

To clear the search field, click the ▣ button that appears to the right of the text in the search field.

When you type in the search field, the list of items in the panel is filtered, showing some items and hiding others. Only items with entries that match the search query that you've typed are shown. The folders, layers, categories, or property groups that contain the matched items are also shown, to provide context.

In general, only text in columns that are shown is searched for this filtering operation. For example, you may need to show the Comments column to search and filter by the contents of comments. (See Columns.)

If one or more layers are selected in a composition, the filtering operation in the Timeline panel only affects selected layers. In this case, unselected layers are not filtered out (hidden) if they don't match the search query. However, if no layers are selected in the composition, the filtering operation applies to all layers in the composition. This behavior matches that for showing and hiding of layer properties by pressing their property shortcut keys. (See Show or hide properties in the Timeline panel.)

Clearing the search field and ending the search causes expanded folders and property groups to collapse (close). Therefore, it's easier to work with the items that are found by the filter operation if you operate on them before you clear the search field and end the search.

If the text that you type in the search field in the Project or Timeline panel contains spaces, the spaces are treated as and-based operators. For example, typing dark solid matches footage items or layers named Dark Red Solid and Dark Gray Solid. In the Effects & Presets panel, spaces are treated as space characters in the search field. For example, typing change color matches the Change Color effect, but not the Change To Color effect.

Project, Timeline, and Effects & Presets panels accept or-based searching. In an or-based search, a comma denotes an or, with and-based operators taking precedence over or-based ones. For example, sometimes the name of the property that determines the amount for a blur effect is Amount, sometimes it is Blurriness, and sometimes it is Blur Radius. If you search for Amount, Blurriness, Radius, then you will see the equivalent values for all of your blur effects.

When you type in a search field, recent search strings that match your input appear.

This search method also allows a way to save items you use often via a menu that opens when you click the search icon in the search field. The search menu consists of two lists, separated by a divider. The top list contains the six most recent searches, with the most recent one at the top. The bottom list contains saved search items. As you type, the top list filters to show matching terms.

To save a search item, Shift-click it in the top list of the search menu. Up to ten items may be saved.

To delete a saved search item from either list, hover the mouse over the item to highlight it, and then press Delete or Backspace.

Workspaces

See this video on the Video2Brain website to learn about the features for searching and filtering in panels.

Examples of searches in the Project panel

To show only footage items for which the name or comment contains a specific string, start typing the string.

To show only footage items for which the source file is missing, type the entire word missing. (This search works whether or not the File Path column is shown, which is an exception to the general rule that only shown columns are searched.)

To show only unused footage items, type the entire word unused.

To show only used footage items, type the entire word used.

To show only Cineon footage items, type Cineon with the Type column shown.

Examples of searches in the Timeline panel

To show only layers and properties for which the name or comment contains a specific string, type the string. For example, type starch to show pins created by the Puppet Starch tool.

To show only properties that have an expression that uses a specific method, type the method name.

To show only layers with a specific label, type the label name. (See Color labels for layers, compositions, and footage items.)

Click the swatch for a label to see the context menu that lists the label names. Alternatively, drag the right edge of the ▪ Label column heading to expand the column to read the label names.

Scroll or zoom with the mouse wheel

You can use the mouse wheel to zoom in the Timeline, Composition, Layer, and Footage panels. You can use the mouse wheel to scroll in the Timeline, Project, Render Queue, Flowchart, Effect Controls, Metadata, and Effects & Presets panels.

To zoom into the center of the panel, or into the feature region when tracking, roll the mouse wheel forward.

To zoom out of the center of the panel, or out of the feature region when tracking, roll the mouse wheel backward.

To zoom into the area under the pointer, hold down Alt (Windows) or Option (Mac OS) as you roll the mouse wheel forward. In the Timeline, Footage, and Layer panels, this action zooms in time when the pointer is over the time navigator or time ruler.

To zoom out of the area under the pointer, hold down Alt (Windows) or Option (Mac OS) as you roll the mouse wheel backward. In the Timeline, Footage, and Layer panels, this action zooms in time when the pointer is over the time navigator or time ruler.

To scroll vertically, roll the mouse wheel forward or backward.

To scroll horizontally, hold down Shift as you roll the mouse wheel backward or forward. In the Timeline, Footage, and Layer panels, Shift-rolling backward moves forward in time and vice versa when the pointer is over the time navigator or time ruler.

You can scroll or zoom with the mouse wheel in a panel even if it is not currently active, as long as the pointer is over it.

Undo changes

You can undo only those actions that alter the project data. For example, you can undo a change to a property value, but you cannot undo the scrolling of a panel or the activation of a tool.

Workspaces

You can sequentially undo as many as 99 of the most recent changes made to the project.

To avoid wasting time undoing accidental modifications, lock a layer when you want to see it but do not want to modify it.

To undo the most recent change, choose Edit > Undo [action] or Ctrl-Z

To undo a change and all changes after it, choose Edit > History, and select the first change that you want to undo.

To revert to the last saved version of the project, choose File > Revert. All changes made and footage items imported since you last saved are lost. You cannot undo this action.

After Effects user interface tips

Use ClearType text anti-aliasing on Windows. ClearType makes the outlines of system text, such as menus and dialog boxes, easier to read. See Windows Help for information on how to enable ClearType text anti-aliasing.

To show tool tips, select the Show Tool Tips preference (Edit > General > Preferences (Windows) or After Effects > Preferences > General (Mac OS)).

Use a workspace that contains the Info panel, and leave that panel in front of other panels in its panel group whenever possible. The Info panel shows messages about what After Effects is doing, information about items under the pointer, and much more.

Use context menus.

Use keyboard shortcuts.

Working with After Effects and other applications

Working with Adobe Bridge and After Effects

Use Adobe Bridge to run animation presets; run cross-product workflow automation scripts; view and manage files and folders; organize your files by assigning keywords, labels, and ratings to them; search for files and folders; and view, edit, and add metadata.

To open Adobe Bridge from After Effects, choose File > Browse In Bridge.

To reveal a file in Adobe Bridge, select a file in the Project panel and choose File > Reveal In Bridge.

To use Adobe Bridge to browse for animation presets, choose Animation > Browse Presets.

Adobe Bridge is part of the Creative Cloud suite of applications and can be downloaded and installed through Creative Cloud. See the help documentation and the Adobe Bridge CC product page for more information.

See this video to get an overview of Adobe Bridge CC.

Working with Photoshop and After Effects

If you use Photoshop to create still images, you can use After Effects to bring those still images together and make them move and change. In After Effects, you can animate an entire Photoshop image or any of its layers. You can even animate individual properties of Photoshop images, such as the properties of a layer style. If you use After Effects to create movies, you can use Photoshop to refine the individual frames of those movies.

Workspaces

Comparative advantages for specific tasks

The strengths of After Effects are in its animation and automation features. This means that After Effects excels at tasks that can be automated from one frame to another. For example, you can use the motion tracking features of After Effects to track the motion of a microphone boom, and then automatically apply that same motion to a stroke made with the Clone Stamp tool. In this manner, you can remove the microphone from every frame of a shot, without having to paint the microphone out by hand on each frame.

In contrast, Photoshop has excellent tools for painting and drawing.

Deciding which application to use for painting depends on the task. Paint strokes in Photoshop directly affect the pixels of the layer. Paint strokes in After Effects are elements of an effect, each of which can be turned on or off or modified at any time. If you want to have complete control of each paint stroke after you've applied it, or if you want to animate the paint strokes themselves, use the After Effects paint tools. If the purpose of applying a paint stroke is to permanently modify a still image, use the Photoshop paint tools. If you are applying several paint strokes by hand to get rid of dust, consider using the Photoshop paint tools.

The animation and video features in Photoshop include simple keyframe-based animation. After Effects uses a similar interface, though the breadth and flexibility of its animation features are far greater.

After Effects can also automatically create 3D layers to mimic the planes created by the Photoshop Vanishing Point feature.

Exchanging still images

After Effects can import and export still images in many formats, but you will usually want to use the native Photoshop PSD format when transferring individual frames or still image sequences between After Effects and Photoshop.

When importing or exporting a PSD file, After Effects can preserve individual layers, masks, layer styles, and most other attributes. When you import a PSD file into After

Effects, you can choose whether to import it as a flattened image or as a composition with its layers separate and intact.

It is often a good idea to prepare a still image in Photoshop before importing it into After Effects. Examples of such preparation include correcting color, scaling, and cropping. It is often better for you to do something once to the source image in Photoshop than to have After Effects perform the same operation many times per second as it renders each frame for previews or final output.

By creating your new PSD document from the Photoshop New File dialog box with a Film & Video preset, you can start with a document that is set up correctly for a specific video output type. If you are already working in After Effects, you can create a new PSD document that matches your composition and project settings by choosing File > New > Adobe Photoshop File.

Exchanging movies

You can also exchange video files, such as QuickTime movies, between Photoshop and After Effects. When you open a movie in Photoshop, a video layer is created that refers to the source footage file. Video layers allow you to paint nondestructively on the movie's frames, much as After Effects works with layers with movies as their sources. When you save a PSD file with a video layer, you save the edits that you made to the video layer, not edits to the source footage itself.

You can also render a movie directly from Photoshop. For example, you can create a QuickTime movie from Photoshop that can then be imported into After Effects.

Color

After Effects works internally with colors in an RGB (red, green, blue) color space. Though After Effects can convert CMYK images to RGB, you should do video and animation work in Photoshop in RGB.

Workspaces

If relevant for your final output, it is better to ensure that the colors in your image are broadcast-safe in Photoshop before you import the image into After Effects. A good way to do this is to assign the appropriate destination color space—for example, SDTV (Rec. 601)—to the document in Photoshop. After Effects performs color management according to color profiles embedded in documents, including imported PSD files.

Working with Animate CC and After Effects

If you use Adobe Animate (formerly called Flash Professional) to create video or animation, you can use After Effects to edit and refine the video. For example, from Adobe Animate, you can export animations and applications as QuickTime movies, .mp4, and other standard video formats. You can then use After Effects to edit and refine the video.

If you use After Effects to edit and composite video, you can then use Animate to publish that video.

Animate and After Effects use separate terms for some concepts that they share in common. The following table lists the differences between the terms used in the two applications:

After Effects	Animate
Composition	Movie Clip
Composition frame (Composition panel)	Stage
Project panel	Library panel
Project files	FLA files
Render and export a movie	Publish SWF file

Additional resources

The following articles provide additional information about using Animate and After Effects together:

Richard Harrington and Marcus Geduld provide an excerpt, "Flash Essentials for After Effects Users", of their book After Effects for Flash | Flash for After Effects on the Peachpit website. In this chapter, Richard and Marcus explain Animate in terms that an After Effects user can understand.
http://www.peachpit.com/articles/article.aspx?p=1350895

Richard Harrington and Marcus Geduld also provide "After Effects Essentials for Flash Users", another excerpt from their book After Effects for Flash | Flash for After Effects. In this chapter, Richard and Marcus explain After Effects in terms that an Animate user can understand.
http://www.peachpit.com/articles/article.aspx?p=1350894

Robert Powers provides a video tutorial on the Slippery Rock NYC website that shows the basics of using After Effects from the perspective of someone who is familiar with Animate.

Exporting QuickTime video from Animate

If you create animations or applications with Animate, you can export them as QuickTime movies using the File > Export > Export Movie command in Animate. For a Animate animation, you can optimize the video output for animation. For an Animate application, Animate renders video of the application as it runs, allowing the user to manipulate it. This lets you capture the branches or states of your application that you want to include in the video file.

Importing and publishing video in Animate

When you import a movie file into Animate, you can use various techniques, such as scripting or Animate components, to control the visual interface that surrounds your video. For example, you might include playback controls or other graphics. You can also add graphic layers on top of the movie for composite results.

Composite graphics, animation, and video

Workspaces

Animate and After Effects each include many capabilities that allow you to perform complex compositing of video and graphics. Which application you choose to use will depend on your personal preferences and the type of final output you want to create.

Animate is the more web-oriented of the two applications, with its small final file size. Animate also allows for run-time control of animation. After Effects is oriented toward video and film production, provides a wide range of visual effects, and is generally used to create video files as final output.

Both applications can be used to create original graphics and animation. Both use a timeline and offer scripting capabilities for controlling animation programmatically. After Effects includes a larger set of effects.

Both applications allow you to place graphics on separate layers for compositing. These layers can be turned on and off as needed. Both also allow you to apply effects to the contents of individual layers.

In Animate, composites do not affect the video content directly; they affect only the appearance of the video during playback in Flash Player. In contrast, when you composite with imported video in After Effects, the video file you export actually incorporates the composited graphics and effects.

Because all drawing and painting in After Effects is done on layers separate from any imported video, it is always non-destructive. Animate has both destructive and nondestructive drawing modes.

Importing SWF files into After Effects

Animate has a unique set of vector art tools that make it useful for a variety of drawing tasks not possible in After Effects or Adobe® Illustrator®. You can import SWF files into After Effects to composite them with other video or render them as video with additional creative effects. Interactive content and scripted animation are not retained. Animation defined by keyframes is retained.

Each SWF file imported into After Effects is flattened into a single continuously rasterized layer, with its alpha channel preserved. Continuous rasterization means that graphics stay sharp as they are scaled up. This import method allows you to use the root layer or object of your SWF files as a smoothly rendered element in After Effects, allowing the best capabilities of each tool to work together.

Working with Adobe Premiere Pro and After Effects

Adobe Premiere Pro is designed to capture, import, and edit movies. After Effects is designed to create motion graphics, apply visual effects, composite visual elements, perform color correction, and perform other post-production tasks for movies.

You can easily exchange projects, compositions, sequences, tracks, and layers between After Effects and Adobe Premiere Pro:

You can create text template compositions in After Effects where you can edit the source text in Premiere Pro. See Live Text Templates.

You can import an Adobe Premiere Pro project into After Effects. See Import an Adobe Premiere Pro project.

You can export an After Effects project as an Adobe Premiere Pro project. See Export an After Effects project as an Adobe Premiere Pro project .

You can copy and paste layers and tracks between After Effects and Adobe Premiere Pro. See Copy between After Effects and Adobe Premiere Pro.

You can render and replace After Effects compositions in Premiere Pro to speed up compositions that take a long time to render. (See Render and Replace After Effects compositions in Adobe Premiere Pro .)

Workspaces

If you have Adobe Premiere Pro, you can do the following:

Use Adobe Dynamic Link to work with After Effects compositions in Adobe Premiere Pro. A dynamically linked composition appears as a clip in Adobe Premiere Pro.

Use Adobe Dynamic Link to work with Adobe Premiere Pro sequences in After Effects. A dynamically linked sequence appears as a footage item in After Effects.

Start After Effects from within Premiere Pro and create a new composition with settings that match the settings of your Premiere Pro project.

Select a set of clips in Adobe Premiere Pro and convert them to a composition in After Effects.

For information on using Dynamic Link with After Effects and Premiere Pro, see Dynamic Link and After Effects and Dynamic Link sections in Adobe Premiere Pro Help.

Working with Adobe Media Encoder and After Effects

You can use Adobe Media Encoder to export video from After Effects. Use Adobe Media Encoder to encode formats like H.264, MPEG-2, and WMV. Other formats, are available in Adobe Media Encoder, but not in After Effects. For example, the DNxHD format is available in Adobe Media Encoder, but not in After Effects.

You can add After Effects project files to a watch folder in Adobe Media encoder, and the composition is automatically added to the encoding queue Adobe Media Encoder. See the Import files with Watch folder section in Adobe Media Encoder for detailed information.

For details about using Adobe Media Encoder with After Effects, see Render and export with Adobe Media Encoder.

See this tutorialto learn how to export After Effects compositions using Adobe Media Encoder.

Edit in Adobe Audition

While working in After Effects, you can use the more comprehensive audio-editing capabilities of Adobe Audition to fine-tune your audio. You can use the Edit in Adobe Audition command to start Adobe Audition from within After Effects.

If you edit an audio-only file (for example, a WAV file) in Adobe Audition, you change the original file. If you edit a layer that contains both audio and video (for example, an AVI file), you edit a copy of the source audio file.

Select the layer that contains the audio that you want to edit. The item must be of a type that is editable in Adobe Audition.

Choose Edit > Edit In Adobe Audition to open the clip in Edit view in Adobe Audition.

Edit the file, and then do one of the following:

If you're editing an audio-only layer, choose File > Save to apply your edits to the original audio file. You can also choose File > Save As to apply your edits to a copy of the audio file. If you choose File > Save As, import the copy of the file into After Effects.

If you're editing a layer that contains both audio and video, choose File > Save As. After you save the file, import it into After Effects. Then, add it to the composition, and mute the original audio in the audio-video clip by deselecting the Audio switch in the Timeline panel.

Note: Any effects applied to audio in After Effects aren't included in the copy that is sent to Adobe Audition.

Tutorials and resources about using Adobe Audition to modify audio from After Effects can be found on this post from the After Effects Region of Interest blog.

Workspaces

Sync Settings

When you work on multiple computers, managing and syncing preferences among the computers can be time-consuming, complex, and error-prone.

The Sync Settings feature in After Effects enables you to sync preferences and settings via Creative Cloud. For example, if you use two computers, the Sync Settings feature makes it easy for you to keep those settings synchronized across these two computers.

The synchronization takes place via your Adobe Creative Cloud account. Settings are uploaded to your Creative Cloud account and then are downloaded and applied on the other computer. You can also synchronize settings from another Creative Cloud account. After Effects creates a user profile on your computer and uses it to synchronize settings to and from the associated Creative Cloud account.

You can initiate the synchronization manually; it does not happen automatically and it cannot be scheduled.

Synchronize your settings

To initiate the synchronization, choose Edit > [your Adobe ID] > Sync Settings Now (Windows) or After Effects > [your Adobe ID] > Sync Settings Now.

You can also synchronize the settings on the Start screen. Click **SYNC SETTINGS >
Sync Now** [your Adobe ID] on the screen to initiate the synchronization.

Download Settings: Synchronize Settings from Creative Cloud to your computer;
overwrite the local version with the Creative Cloud version of settings.

Upload Settings: Synchronize settings from this local computer to Creative Cloud.

Progress and details about the synchronization is displayed in the Info panel
(Window > Info).

Restart After Effects to apply downloaded preferences after using Sync Settings .

By default, the Adobe ID associated with the license for the product is used to
synchronize the preferences. To use a different Adobe ID to synchronize the
settings, from the Edit menu (Windows) or After Effects menu (Mac OS), choose
[your Adobe ID] > Use Settings From a Different Account. Enter the Adobe ID and
password.

Alternatively, on the Start screen, click **SYNC SETTINGS > Use Settings from a
Different Account**.

Managing synchronization

Workspaces

Clear Settings

Select Edit > [your Adobe ID] > Clear Settings (Windows) or After Effects [your Adobe ID] > Clear Settings (Mac OS), to clear all settings and reset them to the default state. Clear Settings also resets the token that is used to indicate the user's settings that was used to sync the settings.

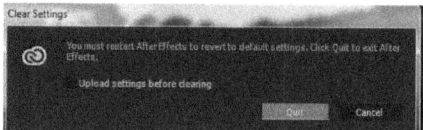

Click Quit to clear the current preferences, and close After Effects. When the application is launched again, default preferences are set.

Manage Sync Settings

To change the settings for the Sync Settings feature (Windows):

Click Edit > [your Adobe ID] > Manage Sync Settings

Click Edit > Preferences > Sync Settings

To change the settings for the Sync Settings feature (Mac OS):

Click After Effects > [your Adobe ID] > Manage Sync Settings

Click After Effects > Preferences > Sync Settings

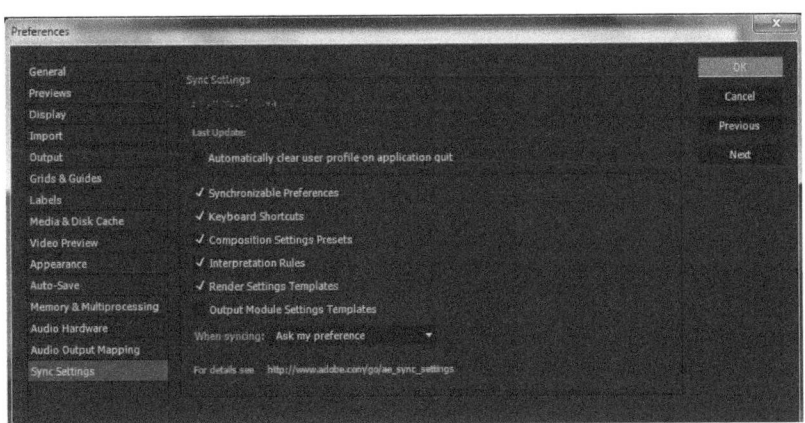

Preferences

| General |
| Previews |
| Display |
| Import |
| Output |
| Grids & Guides |
| Labels |
| Media & Disk Cache |
| Video Preview |
| Appearance |
| Auto-Save |
| Memory & Multiprocessing |
| Audio Hardware |
| Audio Output Mapping |
| Sync Settings |

Sync Settings

Last Update:

Automatically clear user profile on application quit

✓ Synchronizable Preferences
✓ Keyboard Shortcuts
✓ Composition Settings Presets
✓ Interpretation Rules
✓ Render Settings Templates
  Output Module Settings Templates

When syncing: Ask my preference

For details see   http://www.adobe.com/go/ae_sync_settings

OK
Cancel
Previous
Next

You can change the following settings in the settings dialog:

Automatically clear user profile on application quit Enable this option to clear the user profile when you quit After Effects. On next launch, preferences are fetched from the default Adobe ID used to license the product.

Workspaces

Select the preferences to synchronize.

Synchronizable Preferences

Keyboard Shortcuts

Composition Settings Presets

Interpretation Rules

Render Settings Templates

Output Module Settings Templates

Note: Synchronizable preferences refer to preferences that are not dependent on computer or hardware settings.

Note: Keyboard shortcuts created for Windows synchronize only with Windows and Mac OS keyboard shortcuts synchronize only with Mac OS.

Choose one of the following options from the drop-down menu to instruct After Effects when to synchronize the settings :

Ask my preference

Always Upload Settings

Always Download Settings

Note: The Sync Settings feature does not synchronize files that are manually placed in the preferences folder location.

Workspaces, panels, and viewers

Workspaces and panels

Adobe video and audio applications provide a consistent, customizable user interface. Although each application has its own set of panels, you move and group panels in the same way in each application.

The main window of a program is the *application window*. Panels are organized in this window in an arrangement called a *workspace*.

Each application includes several predefined workspaces that optimize the layout of panels for specific tasks. You can also create and customize your own workspaces by arranging panels in the layout that best suits your working style for specific tasks.

You can drag panels to new locations, move panels into or out of a group, place panels alongside each other, and undock a panel so that it floats in a new window above the application window. As you rearrange panels, the other panels resize automatically to fit the window.

Workspaces

Example workspace

A Application window B Grouped panels C Individual panel

To increase the available screen space, use multiple monitors. When you work with multiple monitors, the application window appears on the main monitor, and you place floating windows on the second monitor. Monitor configurations are stored in the workspace.

Workspaces are stored in XML files in the preferences folder. With some caveats regarding monitor size and layout, these workspaces can be moved to another computer and used there.

(Windows) [drive]:\Users\[user_name]\AppData\Roaming\Adobe\After Effects\[version]\ModifiedWorkspaces

(Mac OS) [drive]/Users/[user_name]/Library/Preferences/Adobe/After Effects/[version]/ModifiedWorkspaces See this video tutorial about workspaces by Andrew Devis on the Creative Cow website for more details.

Stacked panel layout

Customize your workspace by grouping panels the way you want to. In a panel group, you can arrange panels in both stacked and tabbed states.

You can expand and collapse stacked panels with a single mouse-click on the panel header. For more information, see Working with stacked panels .

Customizing workspaces

Choose a workspace

You can access custom or default workspaces with a single click in the new workspace bar. The workspace bar occupies the right side of the Tools panel. You can customize the width of the bar by dragging the vertical divider between the tool and the workspace bars.

Workspaces

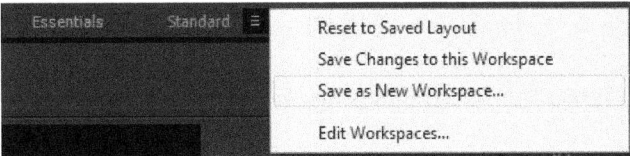

The workspaces that do not fit in the available space display in the chevron menu (>>) on the workspace bar.

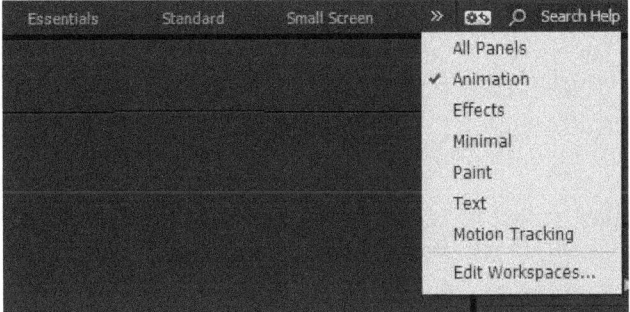

When you move the Tools panel from its position, the Workspace menu replaces the workspace bar.

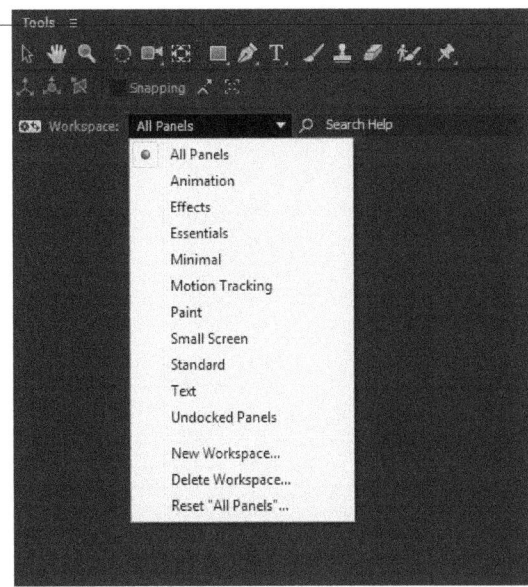

Note: Choose **Window > Workspace > Edit Workspaces** or click the chevron menu *(>>) on the workspace bar to display the* **Edit Workspaces** *dialog box. You can select a workspace and reorder workspaces.*

Workspaces

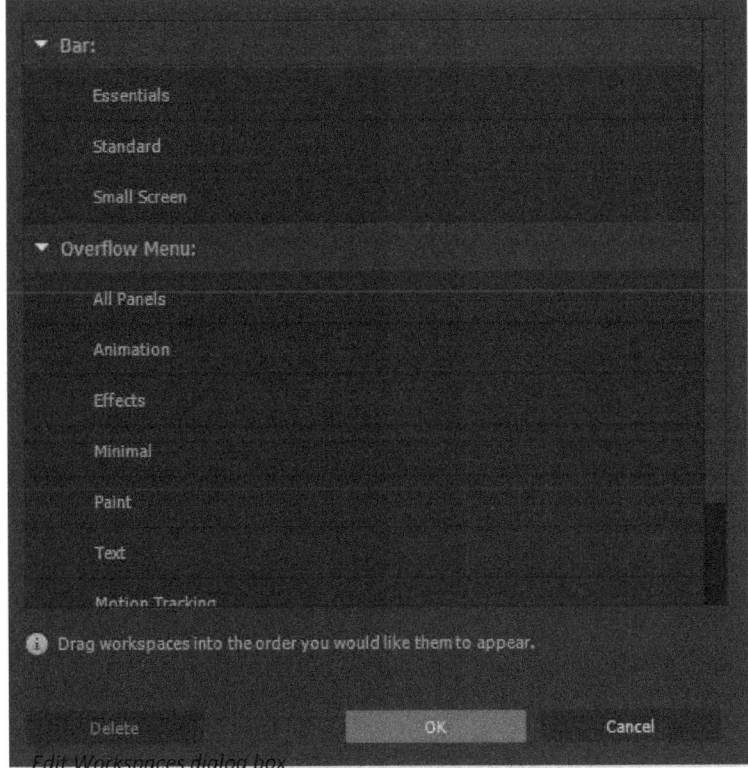

Edit Workspaces dialog box

Choose a workspace

Choose Window > Workspace, and select the desired workspace.

Choose a workspace from the Workspace menu in the Tools panel.

If the workspace has a keyboard shortcut assigned, press Shift+F10, Shift+F11, or Shift+F12.

To assign a keyboard shortcut to the current workspace, choose Window > Assign Shortcut To [Workspace Name] Workspace.

Save, reset, or delete workspaces

Save a custom workspace

As you customize a workspace, the application tracks your changes, storing the most recent layout. To store a specific layout more permanently, save a custom workspace. Saved custom workspaces appear in the Workspace menu, where you can return to and reset them.

Arrange the frames and panels as desired, and then choose Window > Workspace > New Workspace. Type a name for the workspace, and click OK.

Note: *(After Effects, Premiere Pro) If a project saved with a custom workspace is opened on another system, the application looks for a workspace with a matching name. If the application cannot find a match (or the monitor configuration doesn't match), it uses the current local workspace.*

Reset a workspace

Reset the current workspace to return to its original, saved layout of panels.

Choose Window > Workspace > Reset *workspace name.*

Workspaces

Delete a workspace

Choose Window > Workspace >Delete Workspace.

Choose the workspace you want to delete, and then click OK.

Note: You cannot delete the currently active workspace.

Dock, group, or float panels

You can dock panels together, move them into or out of groups, and undock them so they float above the application window. As you drag a panel, *drop zones*—areas onto which you can move the panel—become highlighted. The drop zone you choose determines where the panel is inserted, and whether it docks or groups with other panels.

Docking zones

Docking zones exist along the edges of a panel, group, or window. Docking a panel places it adjacent to the existing group, resizing all groups to accommodate the new panel.

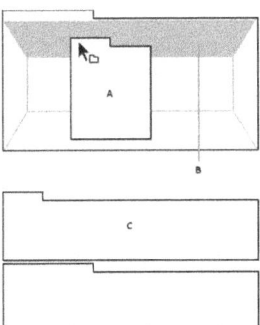

Dragging panel (A) onto docking zone (B) to dock it (C)

Grouping zones

Grouping zones exist in the middle of a panel or group, and along the tab area of panels. Dropping a panel on a grouping zone stacks it with other panels.

Workspaces

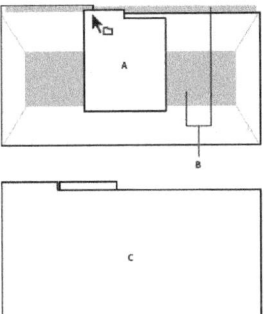

Dragging panel (A) onto grouping zone (B) to group it with existing panels (C)

Dock or group panels

If the panel you want to dock or group is not visible, choose it from the Window menu.

Do one of the following:

To move an individual panel, drag the gripper area in the upper-left corner of a panel's tab onto the desired drop zone.

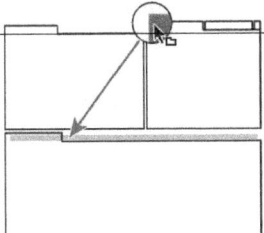

Drag panel gripper to move one panel

To move an entire group, drag the group gripper in the upper-right corner onto the desired drop zone.

Workspaces

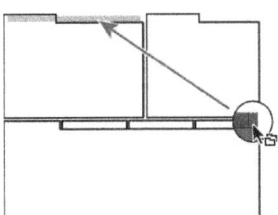

Drag group gripper to move entire group

The application docks or groups the panel, according to the type of drop zone.

Undock a panel in a floating window

When you undock a panel in a floating window, you can add panels to the window and modify it similarly to the application window. You can use floating windows to use a secondary monitor, or to create workspaces like the workspaces in earlier versions of Adobe applications.

Select the panel you want to undock (if it's not visible, choose it from the Window menu), and then do one of the following:

Choose Undock Panel or Undock Frame from the panel menu. Undock Frame undocks the panel group.

Hold down Ctrl (Windows®) or Command (Mac OS®), and drag the panel or group from its current location. When you release the mouse button, the panel or group appears in a new floating window.

Drag the panel or group outside the application window. (If the application window is maximized, drag the panel to the Windows taskbar.)

Maximize or restore panel groups

Double-click the active panel's tab, or in the fallow area of the tab well of a panel group to maximize or restore that panel group. You can also press the ` (accent grave) key with the mouse pointer over that panel group to maximize or restore a panel group.

Resize panel groups

To quickly maximize a panel beneath the pointer, press the ` (accent grave) key. (The accent grave is the unshifted ◦ character under the tilde, ~, on standard US keyboards.) Press the key again to return the panel to its original size.

When you drag the divider between panel groups, all groups that share the divider are resized.

Do either of the following:

To resize either horizontally or vertically, position the pointer between two panel groups. The pointer becomes
a double arrow ↔ .

To resize in both directions at once, position the pointer at the intersection between three or more panel groups. The pointer becomes a four-way arrow ✛ .

Hold down the mouse button, and drag to resize the panel groups.

Workspaces

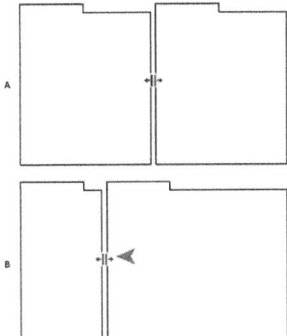

Dragging divider between panel groups to resize them horizontally

*A Original group with resize pointer **B** Resized groups*

Open, close, and show panels and windows

Even if a panel is open, it may be out of sight, beneath other panels. Choosing a panel from the Window menu opens it and brings it to the front of its group.

When you close a panel group in the application window, the other groups resize to use the newly available space. When you close a floating window, the panels within it close, too.

To open or close a panel, choose the panel from the Window menu.

To close a panel or window, click its Close button × . If you accidentally close a panel, choose the panel from the Window menu, and the panel will be displayed again.

To open or close a panel, use its keyboard shortcut.

If a frame contains multiple panels, place the pointer over a tab and roll the mouse scroll wheel forward or backward to change which panel is active.

If a frame contains more grouped panels than can be shown at once, drag the scroll bar that appears above the tabs.

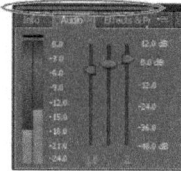

Scroll bar for showing tabs of other panels

Workspaces

Viewers

A *viewer* is a panel that can contain multiple compositions, layers, or footage items, or multiple views of one such item.

The Composition, Layer, Footage, Flowchart, and Effect Controls panels are viewers.

Locking a viewer prevents the currently displayed item from being replaced when you open or select a new item. Instead, when a viewer is locked and a new item is opened or selected, After Effects creates a new viewer panel for that item. If you select the item from the viewer menu of a locked viewer, a new viewer isn't created; the existing viewer is used.

Instead of housing multiple items in a single viewer and using the viewer menu to switch between them, you can choose to open a separate viewer for each open composition, layer, or footage item. When you have multiple viewers open, you can arrange them by docking or grouping them, like any other panels.

For example, you can create one Composition viewer each for different 3D views (Top, Bottom, Back, Front, custom views) so that you can maximize each of the views with the ` (accent grave) keyboard shortcut, which maximizes or restores the panel under the pointer.

To create a custom workspace with multiple viewers, ensure that all viewers are unlocked before you save the workspace.

Locked viewers are associated with a specific project context and are therefore not saved in the preferences file.

To create a new viewer, choose New from the viewer menu. (See Open panel, viewer, and context menus.)

To lock or unlock a viewer, choose Locked from the viewer menu, or click the Toggle Viewer Lock ⬚ button.

To lock the current viewer, split the current frame, and create a new viewer of the same type in the new frame, press Ctrl+Alt+Shift+N (Windows) or Command+Option+Shift+N (Mac OS).

To cycle forward or backward through the items in the viewer menu list for the active viewer, press Shift+period (.) or Shift+comma (,).

Edit this, look at that (ETLAT) and locked Composition viewers

If a Composition viewer is locked, the Timeline panel for another composition is active, and the Composition viewer for the active composition is not shown, then most commands that affect views and previews operate on the composition for which the viewer is shown.

For example, pressing the numpad 0 can start a preview for the composition visible in a locked Composition viewer rather than the composition associated with the active Timeline panel.

This behavior facilitates a working setup sometimes referred to as edit-this-look-at-that (ETLAT). The most common scenario in which this behavior is useful is the scenario in which you make a change in the Timeline panel for a nested (upstream) composition and want to preview the result of the change in a containing (downstream) composition.

Note: ETLAT behavior works for keyboard shortcuts for zooming, fitting, previewing, taking and viewing snapshots, showing channels, showing and hiding grids and guides, and showing the current frame on a video preview device.

To prevent this behavior, unlock the Composition viewer or show the Composition viewer for the composition that you want to view or preview.

See this video on the Video2Brain website to learn about the improvements in ETLAT (edit-this-look-at-that) workflow.

Workspaces

Use the Adobe Color Themes extension

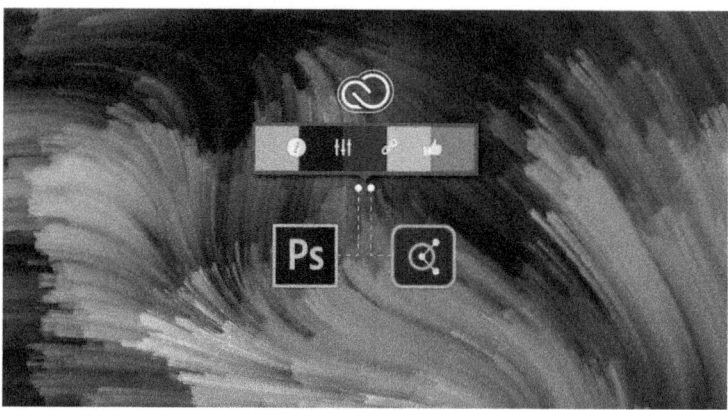

The Adobe Color service helps you choose harmonious and appealing color combinations for your After Effects compositions. Adobe Color is integrated right within After Effects in the form of an extension that lets you create, save, and access your color themes. You can also explore the many public color themes available on Adobe Color and filter them in several ways: Most Popular, Most Used, Random, themes you've published, or themes you've appreciated in the past. Once you've found a theme that you like; you can edit it and save it to your themes, or add it to your swatches in After Effects.

Aside from After Effects, the Adobe Color Themes extension is currently available in two other Creative Cloud desktop applications: Adobe InDesign and Adobe Photoshop. Themes saved to Creative Cloud libraries from within these desktop apps, mobile apps such as Capture CC, or using the Adobe Color website are accessible seamlessly in After Effects.

Access the Adobe Color Themes panel

In After Effects, select Window > Extensions > Adobe Color Themes.

Workspaces

Explore color themes

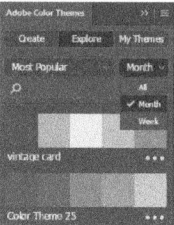

Explore themes

Click the Explore tab in the Adobe Color Themes panel. By default, the Explore tab displays all public color themes.

If necessary, filter the color themes by a category and a timeframe. Use the search bar if you're looking for a specific theme.

Create and save a color theme

Click the Create tab in the Adobe Color Themes panel.

Select the color rule on which you want to base the theme: Analogous, Monochromatic, Triad, Complementary, Compound, Shades, or Custom.

Analogous Uses colors that are adjacent on the color wheel. Analogous colors usually blend well with one another and are harmonious and pleasing to the eye.

Workspaces

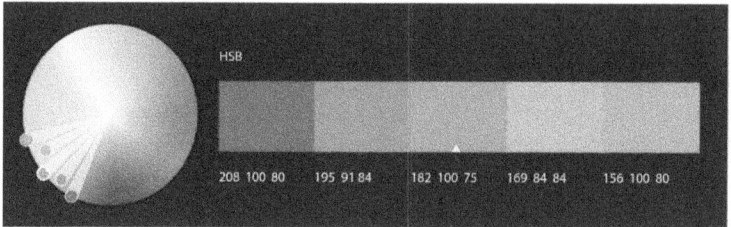

Example: Analogous color rule

Monochromatic Uses variations in saturation and brightness of a single color. When you use this color rule, you're presented with five colors sharing the same hue (example: H:182) but different saturation and brightness values. Monochromatic colors go well together and produce a soothing effect.

Workspaces

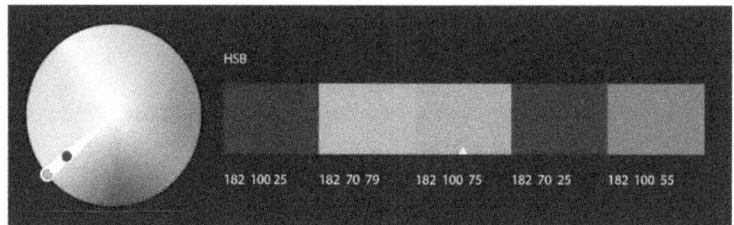

Example: Monochromatic color rule

Triad Uses colors evenly spaced around three equidistant points on the color wheel. When you use this color rule, you're presented with two colors with the same hue but different saturation and brightness values from the first point on the color wheel (example: HSB: 182, 90, 45 & HSB: 182, 100, 75), two from the second point on the color wheel (HSB: 51, 90, 55 & HSB: 51, 95, 45), and one color from the third point (HSB: 321, 90, 79). Triadic colors tend to be contrasting—albeit not as contrasting as complementary colors—while still retaining harmony when used together.

Workspaces

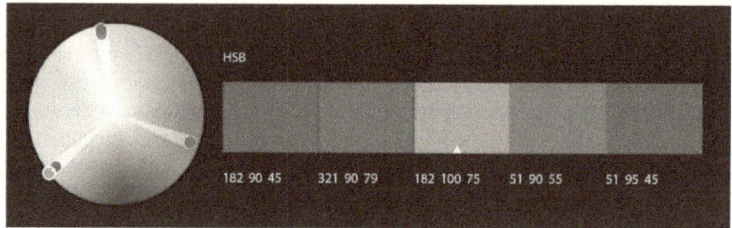

Example: Triad color rule

Complementary Uses colors opposite to each other on the color wheel. When you use this color rule, you are presented with two colors with the same hue as the base color (example: HSB: 182, 100, 45 & HSB: 182, 90, 100), the base color itself (HSB: 182, 100, 75), and two colors with the same hue from the opposite point on the color wheel (HSB: 23, 100, 45 & HSB: 23, 100, 75). Complementary colors provide high contrast and tend to stand out when used together.

Workspaces

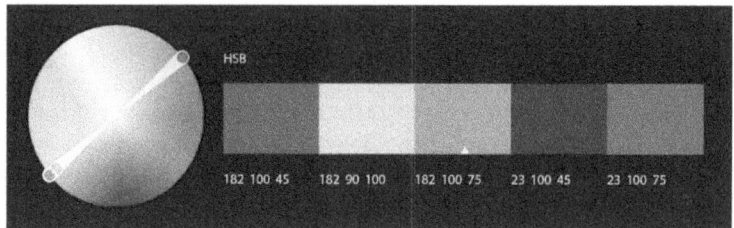

Example: Complementary color rule

Compound Uses a mix of complementary and analogous colors. When you use this color rule, you are presented with two colors with the same hue that are adjacent (analogous) to the base color (example: HSB: 214, 90, 95 & HSB: 214, 60, 35), the base color itself (HSB: 182, 100, 75), and two colors opposite to the base color (complementary) but adjacent to each other (HSB: 15, 75, 78 & HSB: 6, 90, 95). Compound color themes have the same strong visual contrast as complementary color themes, but they have less pressure.

Workspaces

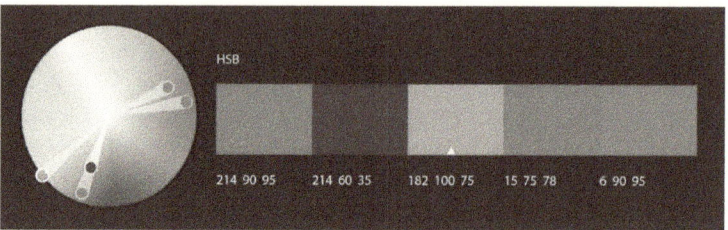

HSB

214 90 95   214 60 35   182 100 75   15 75 78   6 90 95

Example: Compound color rule

Shades Uses five colors—all sharing the same hue (example: H: 182) and saturation (S: 100) but different brightness values.

Workspaces

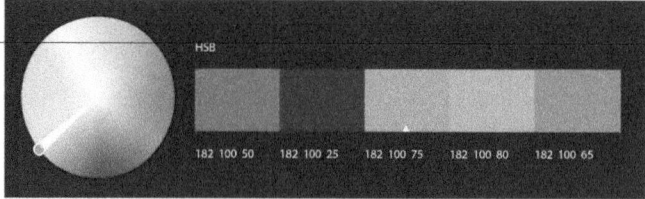

Shades color rule

Custom Lets you manually select the colors on the color wheel in your palette without any rules controlling them.

Workspaces

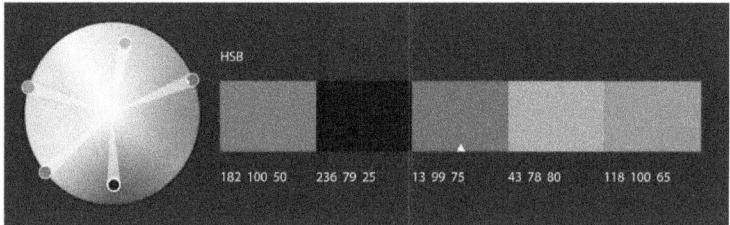

Custom color rule

Now, choose a base color by clicking the little triangle corresponding to a color in the theme you're editing. Based upon the color rule selected, a color theme is automatically built around the base color.

Choose a base color

While a color is selected, you can adjust it either using the color wheel or by changing its value in one of the following ⬡ color systems: CMYK, RGB, LAB, HSB, or HEX.

Enter a name for the new color theme. Click Save.

Choose the Creative Cloud library to which you want to save the theme.

Workspaces

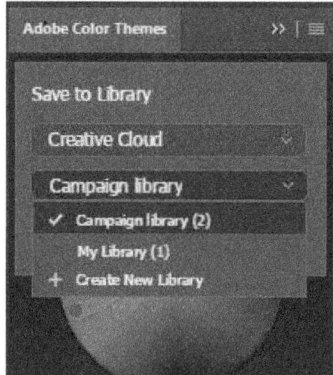

Save the new theme to a library

Click Save.

Note: *Depending on whether you're logged in using your Adobe ID or your enterprise credentials, different sets of libraries may be available for saving themes. Select Help > Manage My Account to check the credentials with which you're logged in. If you land at the authentication screen for your organization when you select this option, you're logged in using your enterprise credentials.The same email ID may be associated with an Adobe ID as well as an enterprise ID.*

Access themes saved to your libraries

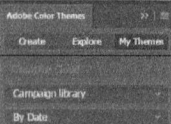

Access your themes

In the Adobe Color Themes panel, click the My Themes tab.

Select the Creative Cloud library from which you want to access the color theme.

If necessary, select a sorting parameter/order for the listed themes: By Date, By Name, or By Quantity; ascending or descending.

See also

Color basics

Adobe Capture CC FAQ

Create inspiring color themes with Adobe Color CC

Dynamic Link and After Effects

Note: For more information on compatibility when using dynamic link between various versions of Premiere Pro and After Effects see the KB article, Using Dynamic Link between various versions of Premiere Pro and After Effects .

Workspaces

From an expert: Creative Dynamic Link workflows with Premiere Pro and After Effects

From an expert: Creative Dynamic Link workflows with Premiere Pro and After Effects

About Dynamic Link

In the past, sharing media assets among post-production applications required you to render and export your work from one application before importing it into another. This workflow was inefficient and time-consuming. If you wanted to change the original asset, you rendered and exported the asset again. Multiple rendered and exported versions of an asset consume disk space, and they can lead to file-management challenges.

Dynamic Link offers an alternative to this workflow. You can create dynamic links between After Effects and Adobe Premiere Pro. Creating a dynamic link is as simple as importing any other type of asset. Dynamically linked assets appear with unique icons and label colors to help you identify them. Dynamic links are saved in projects generated by these applications.

Create and link to After Effects compositions with Dynamic Link

You can create new After Effects compositions, and dynamically link to them from Adobe Premiere Pro. You can also dynamically link to existing After Effects compositions from Adobe Premiere Pro.

Create a composition from clips in Adobe Premiere Pro

You can replace selected clips in Adobe Premiere Pro with a dynamically linked After Effects composition based on those clips. The new composition inherits the sequence settings from Adobe Premiere Pro.

Open Premiere Pro and select the clips you want to replace.

Right-click any of the selected clips.

Select Replace With After Effects Composition.

After Effects opens (if it is not already open) and a new linked composition is created.

Create a dynamically linked composition from Adobe Premiere Pro

Creating a new dynamically linked composition from Adobe Premiere Pro launches After Effects. After Effects then creates a project and composition with the dimensions, pixel aspect ratio, frame rate, and audio sample rate of the originating project. (If After Effects is already running, it creates a composition in the current project.) The new composition name is based on the Adobe Premiere Pro project name, followed by Linked Comp [x].

In Adobe Premiere Pro, choose File > Adobe Dynamic Link > New After Effects Composition. In the 2014 version of Premiere Pro, you can import compositions using Media Browser. See the following sections in Premiere Pro for more information:

Import files with Media Browser

Adobe Dynamic Link

If the After Effects Save As dialog box appears, enter a name and location for the After Effects project, and click Save.

When you create a dynamically linked After Effects composition, the composition duration is set to 30 seconds. To ▪ change the duration, select the composition in After Effects, choose Composition > Composition Settings. Click the Basic tab, and specify a new value for Duration.

Workspaces

Link to an existing composition

For best results, match composition settings (such as dimensions, pixel aspect ratio, and frame rate) to the settings in the Adobe Premiere Pro.

Do one of the following:

In Adobe Premiere Pro, choose File > Adobe Dynamic Link > ImportAfter Effects Composition. Choose an After Effects project file (.aep), and then choose one or more compositions.

In Adobe Premiere Pro, choose an After Effects project file and click Open. Then choose a composition in the displayed dialog box and click OK.

Drag one or more compositions from the After Effects Project panel to the Adobe Premiere Pro Project panel.

Drag an After Effects project file into the Premiere Pro Project panel. If the After Effects project file contains multiple compositions, the Import Composition dialog box opens.

Note: *You can link to a single After Effects composition multiple times in a single Adobe Premiere Pro project.*

Modify a dynamically linked composition in After Effects

Use the Edit Original command in Adobe Premiere Pro to modify a linked After Effects composition. Once the composition is open in After Effects, you can change the composition without having to use the Edit Original command again.

Select the After Effects composition in Adobe Premiere Pro, or choose a linked clip in the Timeline, and choose Edit > Edit Original.

Change the composition in After Effects. Then, switch back to Adobe Premiere Pro to view your changes.

The changes made in After Effects appear in Adobe Premiere Pro. Adobe Premiere Pro stops using any preview files rendered for the clip before the changes.

Note: You can change the name of the composition in After Effects after creating a dynamic link to it from Adobe Premiere Pro. Adobe Premiere Pro does not update the linked composition name in the Project panel. Adobe Premiere Pro does retain the dynamic link, however.

Delete a dynamically linked composition or clip

You can delete a linked composition from an Adobe Premiere Pro project at any time, even if the composition is used in a project.

You can delete linked clips from the timeline of an Adobe Premiere Pro sequence or timeline at any time.

In Adobe Premiere Pro, select the linked composition or clip and press the Delete key.

Create a linked sequence in Adobe Premiere Pro with Dynamic Link

Link to a new sequence

Creating an Adobe Premiere Pro sequence from After Effects launches Adobe Premiere Pro. Adobe Premiere Pro then creates a project and sequence with the dimensions, pixel aspect ratio, frame rate, and audio sample rate of the originating project. (If Adobe Premiere Pro is already running, it creates a sequence in the current project.)

In After Effects, choose File > Adobe Dynamic Link > New Premiere Pro Sequence.

Workspaces

Link to an existing sequence

For best results, match sequence settings and project settings in Adobe Premiere Pro (such as dimensions, pixel aspect ratio, and frame rate) to those settings in the After Effects project.

Do one of the following:

In After Effects, choose File > Adobe Dynamic Link > Import Premiere Pro Sequence. Choose an Adobe Premiere Pro project, and then choose one or more sequences.

Drag one or more sequences from the Adobe Premiere Pro Project panel to the After Effects Project panel.

Dynamic Link performance

A linked clip can refer to a complex source composition. Actions you perform on the source composition require additional processing time depending on the complexity. After Effects applies the actions and make the final data available to Adobe Premiere Pro using the global performance cache and the persistent disk cache features. These features improve the After Effects performance by using the cached frames when Premiere Pro requests the frames.

To reduce playback delays, do one of the following:

Take the linked composition offline

Disable a linked clip to temporarily stop referencing a composition

Replace the dynamically linked composition with the rendered file using the Render and Replace feature in Premiere Pro (Clip > Render And Replace).

If you commonly work with complex source compositions, increase your RAM or upgrade to a faster processor.

Note: *A linked After Effects composition will not support Render Multiple Frames Simultaneously multiprocessing. See Improve performance by optimizing memory, cache, and multiprocessing settings.*

Export to Adobe Media Encoder

To encode After Effects compositions, you must add the item to the encoding queue in Adobe Media Encoder, and then select encoding presets or create your own custom settings for rendering. In After Effects, you can add a composition to Media Encoder queue using one of the following options:

File > Export > Add to Media Encoder Queue

Composition > Add to Media Encoder Queue

When you add a composition or project to Adobe Media Encoder queue, After Effects launches Adobe Media Encoder with the compositions listed in the queue.

Creating a Basic Animation Using Effects and Presets

Use Adobe Bridge to preview and import footage items.

Work with the layers of an imported Adobe Illustrator file.

Apply drop-shadow and emboss effects.

Apply a text animation preset.

Adjust the time range of a text animation preset.

Precompose layers.

Apply a dissolve transition effect.

Adjust the transparency of a layer.

Render an animation for broadcast use.

Getting started

, you will become more familiar with the Adobe After Effects project workflow. You'll learn new ways to accomplish basic tasks as you create a simple identification graphic for a fictional travel show called "Travel Europe" on the fictional Destinations cable network. You will animate the travel show ID so that it fades to become a watermark that can appear in the lower right corner of the screen during other TV programs. Then you'll export the ID for use in broadcast output.

First, take a look at the final project files to see what you'll be doing.

Make sure the following files are in the Lessons/Lesson02 folder on your hard disk, or download them from your Account page at www.peachpit.com now:

In the Assets folder: destinations_logo.ai, ParisRiver.jpg

In the Sample_Movie folder: Lesson02.mov

Open and play the Lesson02.mov sample movie in QuickTime Player to see what you will create in this lesson. When you are done, quit QuickTime Player. You may delete this sample movie from your hard disk if you have limited storage space.

When you begin the lesson, restore the default application settings for After Effects. See "Restoring default preferences" on page 2 for more information.

Start After Effects, and then immediately hold down Ctrl+Alt+Shift (Windows) or Command+Option+Shift (Mac OS) to restore default preferences settings. When prompted, click OK to delete your preferences.

Close the Start window.

After Effects opens to display a blank, untitled project.

Choose File > Save As > Save As.

In the Save As dialog box, navigate to the Lessons/Lesson02/Finished_Project folder.

Name the project **Lesson02_Finished.aep**, and then click Save.

Importing footage using Adobe Bridge

In Lesson 1, you chose File > Import > File to import footage. However, After Effects offers another, more powerful, more flexible way to import footage for a composition: Adobe Bridge. You can use Adobe Bridge to organize, browse, and locate the assets you need to create content for print, web, television, DVD, film, and mobile devices. Adobe Bridge keeps native Adobe files (such as PSD and PDF files) as well as non-Adobe application files available for easy access. You can drag assets into your layouts, projects, and compositions as needed; preview your assets; and even add metadata (file information) to assets to make files easier to locate.

Adobe Bridge is not automatically installed with After Effects CC. You'll need to install it separately. If Bridge is not installed, you'll be prompted to install it when you choose File > Browse In Bridge.

In this exercise, you will jump to Adobe Bridge to import the still image that will serve as the background of your composition.

Tip

You can use Adobe Bridge separately to manage your files. To open Adobe Bridge directly, choose Adobe Bridge from the Start menu (Windows) or double-click the Adobe Bridge icon in the Applications / Adobe Bridge folder (Mac OS).

Choose File > Browse In Bridge. If you receive a message about enabling an extension to Adobe Bridge, click Yes.

Adobe Bridge opens, displaying a collection of panels, menus, and buttons.

Click the Folders tab in the upper left corner of Adobe Bridge.

In the Folders panel, navigate to the Lessons/Lesson02/Assets folder. Click the arrows to open nested folders. You can also double-click folder thumbnail icons in the Content panel.

⬤ Note

We're using the Essentials workspace, which is the default workspace in Bridge.

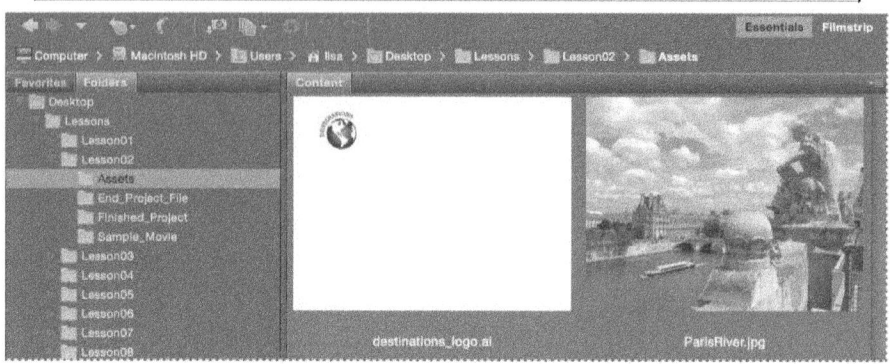

The Content panel updates interactively. For example, when you select the Assets folder in the Folders panel, thumbnail previews of the folder's contents appear in the Content panel. Adobe Bridge displays previews of image files such as those in PSD, TIFF, and JPEG formats, as well as Illustrator vector files, multipage Adobe PDF files, QuickTime movie files, and more.

▶ Tip

To prioritize different information in Adobe Bridge, change the workspace: Choose Window > Workspace, and then select a workspace. See Adobe Bridge Help to learn about customizing Adobe Bridge.

Drag the thumbnail slider at the bottom of the Adobe Bridge window to enlarge the thumbnail previews.

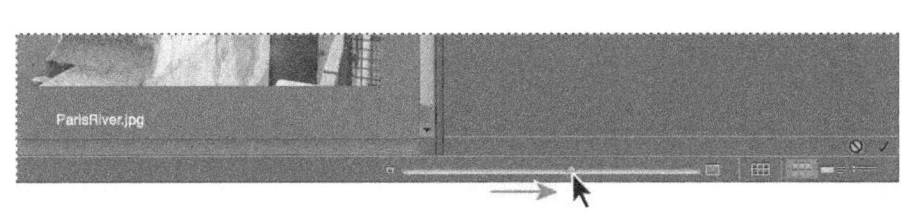

Select the ParisRiver.jpg file in the Content panel, and notice that it appears in the Preview panel as well. Information about the file, including its creation date, bit depth, and file size, appears in the Metadata panel.

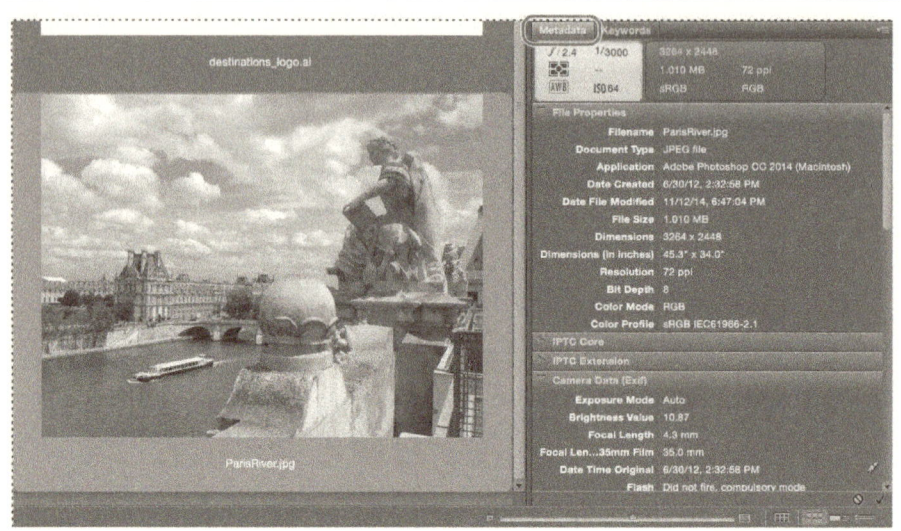

Double-click the ParisRiver.jpg thumbnail in the Content panel to place the file in your After Effects project. Alternatively, you can drag the thumbnail into the Project panel in After Effects.

Return to After Effects, if you're not already there.

You can close Adobe Bridge if you'd like. You won't be using it again during this lesson.

Creating a new composition

Following the After Effects workflow you learned in Lesson 1, the next step to building the travel show ID is to create a new composition. In Lesson 1, you created the composition based on footage items that were selected in the Project panel. You can also create an empty composition, and then add your footage items to it.

Create a new composition by doing one of the following:

Click the Create A New Composition button () at the bottom of the Project panel.

Choose Composition > New Composition.

Press Ctrl+N (Windows) or Command+N (Mac OS).

In the Composition Settings dialog box, do the following:

Name the composition **Destinations**.

Choose NTSC D1 from the Preset pop-up menu. NTSC D1 is the resolution for standard-definition television in the United States and some other countries. This preset automatically sets the width, height, pixel aspect ratio, and frame rate for the composition to NTSC standards.

In the Duration field, type **300** to specify 3 seconds.

Click OK.

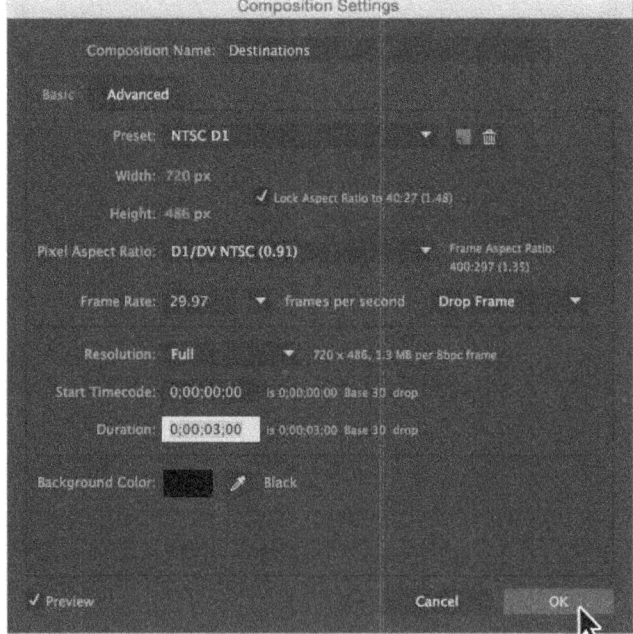

After Effects displays an empty composition named Destinations in the Composition panel and in the Timeline panel. Now, you'll add the background.

Drag the ParisRiver.jpg footage item from the Project panel to the Timeline panel to add it to the Destinations composition.

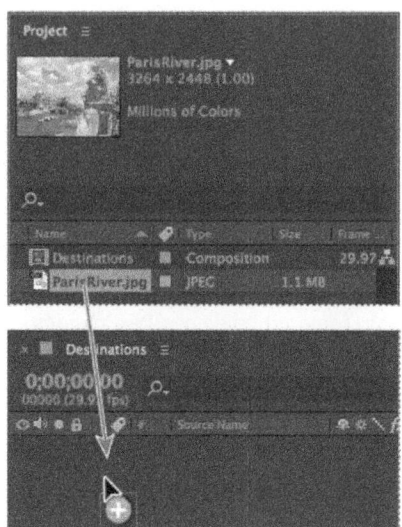

The keyboard shortcut for fitting a layer to a composition is Ctrl+Alt+F (Windows) or Command+Option+F (Mac OS).

With the ParisRiver layer selected in the Timeline panel, choose Layer > Transform

Fit To Comp to scale the background image to the dimensions of the composition.

Importing the foreground element

Your background is now in place. The foreground object you'll use is a layered vector graphic that was created in Illustrator.

Choose File > Import > File.

In the Import File dialog box, select the destinations_logo.ai file in the Lessons/Lesson02/Assets folder. (The file appears as destinations_logo if file extensions are hidden.)

Select Composition from the Import As menu, and then click Import or Open.

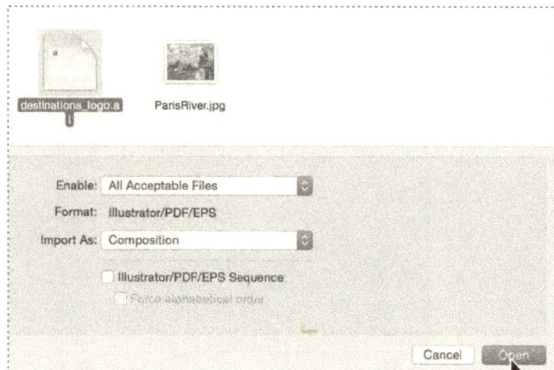
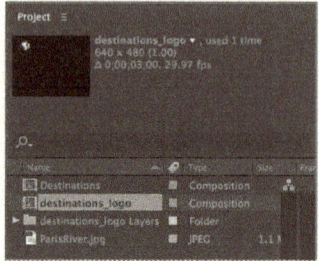

The Illustrator file is added to the Project panel as a composition named destinations_logo. A folder named destinations_logo Layers also appears. This folder contains the three individual layers of the Illustrator file. Click the triangle to open the folder and see its contents if you like.

Drag the destinations_logo composition file from the Project panel into the Timeline panel above the ParisRiver layer.

You should now see both the background image and the logo in the Composition panel and in the Timeline panel.

Working with imported Illustrator layers

The destinations_logo graphic was created in Illustrator; your job in After Effects is to add text and animate it. To work with the layers of the Illustrator file independently of the background footage, you'll open the destinations_logo composition in its own Timeline and Composition panels.

Double-click the destinations_logo composition in the Project panel. The composition opens in its own Timeline and Composition panels.

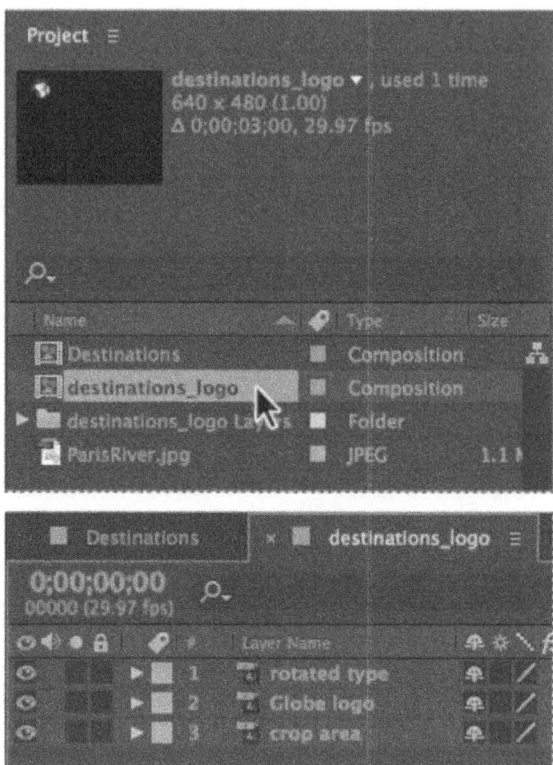

Select the Horizontal Type tool (T) in the Tools panel, and click in the Composition panel.

Type **TRAVEL EUROPE**, all capital letters, and then select all of the text you just entered.

In the Character panel, select a sans serif typeface such as Myriad Pro, and change the font size to **24** pixels. Click the eyedropper in the Character panel, and click the rotated "Destinations" text on the logo to select the green color. After Effects applies it to the text you typed. Leave all other options in the Character panel at their defaults.

Note

If the Character panel isn't open, choose Window > Character. You may need to expand the width of the panel to see the eyedropper.

You'll learn more about working with text in Lesson 3, "Animating Text."

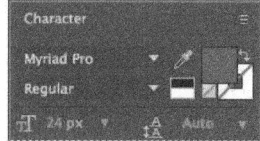

⊳ **Tip**

Choose View > Show Grid to make the nonprinting grid visible to help you position objects. Choose View > Show Grid again to hide the grid later.

Select the Selection tool (▶), and then drag the text in the Composition panel to position it as it appears in the following figure. Notice that when you switch to the Selection tool, the generic Text 1 layer name in the Timeline panel changes to TRAVEL EUROPE, the text you typed.

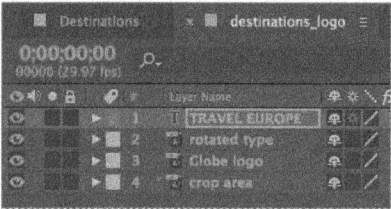

Applying effects to a layer

Now you will return to the main composition, Destinations, and apply an effect to the destinations_logo layer. This will apply the effect to all of the layers nested in the destinations_logo composition.

Click the Destinations tab in the Timeline panel, and then select the destinations_logo layer.

The effect you create next will be applied only to the logo elements, not to the background image of the river.

Choose Effect > Perspective > Drop Shadow.

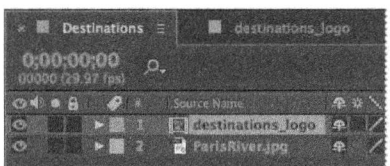 

A soft-edged shadow appears behind the nested layers of the destinations_logo layer—the logo graphic, the rotated type, and the words *travel Europe*—in the Composition panel. You can customize the effect using the Effect Controls panel, which appears in front of the Project panel when you apply an effect.

Applying and controlling effects

You can apply or remove an effect at any time. Once you've applied effects to a layer, you can temporarily turn off one or all of the effects in the layer to concentrate on another aspect of your composition. Effects that are turned off do not appear in the Composition panel, and typically aren't included when the layer is previewed or rendered.

By default, when you apply an effect to a layer, the effect is active for the duration of the layer. However, you can make an effect start and stop at specific times, or make the effect more or less intense over time. You'll learn more about creating animation using keyframes or expressions in Lesson 5, "Animating a Multimedia Presentation," and Lesson 6, "Animating Layers."

You can apply and edit effects on adjustment layers just as you do with other layers. Note, however, that when you apply an effect to an adjustment layer, the effect is applied to all layers below it in the Timeline panel.

Effects can also be saved, browsed, and applied as animation presets.

In the Effect Controls panel, reduce the drop shadow's Distance to **3** and increase its Softness to **4**. You can set these values by clicking the field and typing the number or by dragging the blue value.

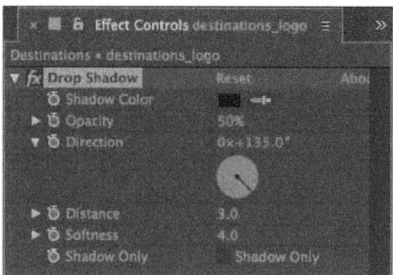

The drop shadow is nice, but the logo will stand out even more if you apply an emboss effect. You can use either the Effect menu or the Effects & Presets panel to locate and apply effects.

Click the Effects & Presets tab to open the panel. Then click the triangle next to Stylize to expand the category.

With the destinations_logo layer selected in the Timeline panel, drag the Color Emboss effect into the Composition panel.

The Color Emboss effect sharpens the edges of objects in the layer without suppressing the original colors. The Effect Controls panel displays the Color Emboss effect and its settings below the Drop Shadow effect.

 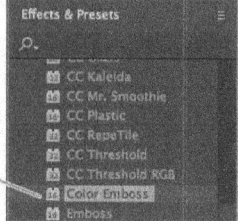 

Choose File > Save to save your work.

Applying an animation preset

You've positioned the logo and applied some effects to it. It's time to add some animation!
You will learn several ways to animate text in <u>Lesson 3</u>; for now, you'll use a simple
animation preset that will fade the words *travel Europe* onto the screen next to the logo.
You'll need to work in the destinations_logo composition so that you can apply the
animation to only the TRAVEL EUROPE text layer.

Click the destinations_logo tab in the Timeline panel, and select the TRAVEL EUROPE layer.

Move the current-time indicator to 1:10, which is the point at which you want the text to
start fading in.

In the Effects & Presets panel, choose Animation Presets > Text > Blurs.

Drag the Bullet Train animation preset onto the TRAVEL EUROPE layer in the Timeline panel or over the words *travel Europe* in the Composition panel. Don't worry about the text disappearing—you're looking at the first frame of the animation, which happens to be blank.

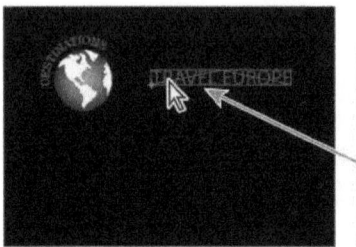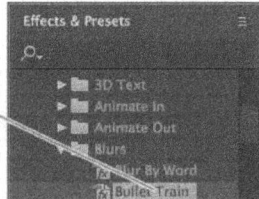

Click a blank area of the Timeline panel to deselect the TRAVEL EUROPE layer, and then drag the current-time indicator to 2:00 to manually preview the text animation. The text appears, letter by letter, until the words *travel Europe* are fully onscreen at 2:00.

Precomposing layers for a new animation

The travel show ID is coming along nicely, and you're probably eager to preview the complete animation. Before you do, however, you'll add a dissolve to all of the logo elements except the words *travel Europe*. To do this, you need to precompose the other three layers of the destinations_logo composition: rotated type, Globe logo, and crop area.

Precomposing is a way to nest layers within a composition. Precomposing moves the layers to a new composition, which takes the place of the selected layers. When you want to change the order in which layer components are rendered, precomposing is a quick way to create intermediate levels of nesting in an existing hierarchy.

Shift-click to select the rotated type, Globe logo, and crop area layers in the destinations_logo Timeline panel.

Choose Layer > Pre-compose.

In the Pre-compose dialog box, name the new composition **Dissolve_logo**. Make sure the Move All Attributes Into The New Composition option is selected. Then click OK.

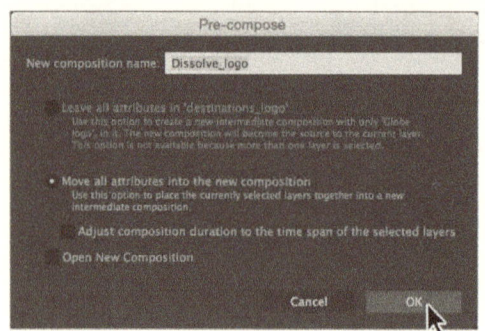

The three layers are replaced in the destinations_logo Timeline panel with a single layer, Dissolve_logo. This new, precomposed layer contains the three layers that you selected in step 1. You can apply the dissolve effect to it without affecting the TRAVEL EUROPE text layer and its Bullet Train animation.

Make sure the Dissolve_logo layer is selected in the Timeline panel, and press the Home key or drag the current-time indicator to go to 0:00.

▶ **Tip**

To locate the Dissolve – Vapor preset quickly, type **vap** in the search box in the Effects & Presets panel.

In the Effects & Presets panel, choose Animation Presets > Transitions – Dissolves, and then drag the Dissolve – Vapor animation preset onto the Dissolve_logo layer in the Timeline panel or onto the Composition panel.

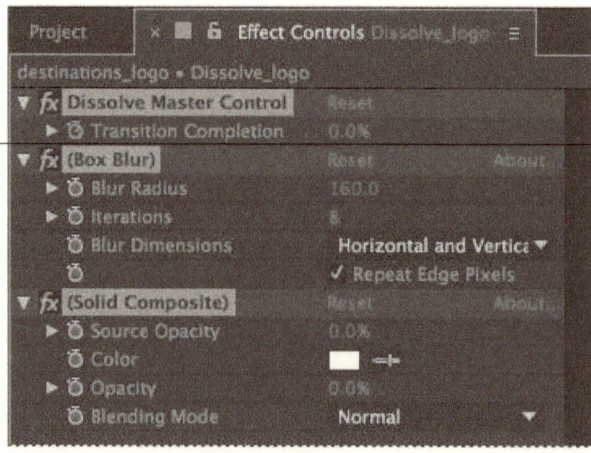

The Dissolve – Vapor animation preset includes three components—a master dissolve, a box blur, and a solid composite, all of which appear in the Effect Controls panel. The default settings are fine for this project.

Choose File > Save.

Previewing the effects

It's time to preview all of the effects together.

Click the Destinations tab in the Timeline panel to switch to the main composition. Press the Home key or drag the current-time indicator to make sure you're at the beginning of the time ruler.

Make sure the Video switch (⊙) is selected for both layers in the Destinations Timeline panel.

Click the Play button (▶) in the Preview panel, or press the spacebar, to watch the preview. Press the spacebar to stop playback at any time.

Adding transparency

Many TV stations display logos semitransparently in the corner of the frame to emphasize the brand. You'll reduce the opacity of the ID so that it can be used this way.

Still in the Destinations Timeline panel, go to 2:24.

Select the destinations_logo layer, and press T to display its Opacity property. By default, the Opacity is 100%—fully opaque. Click the stopwatch icon (⏱) to set an Opacity keyframe at this point in time.

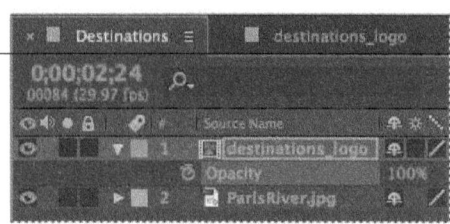 

Press the End key or drag the current-time indicator to go to the end of the time ruler (2:29), and change the Opacity to **40%**. After Effects adds a keyframe.

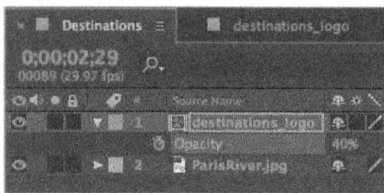 

The logo appears, the words *travel Europe* fly in, and it all fades to 40% opacity.

Click the Play button (▶) in the Preview panel, press the spacebar, or press 0 on your numeric keypad to preview your composition. Press the spacebar to stop playback when you're done.

Choose File > Save to save your project.

Rendering the composition

You're ready to prepare your travel show ID for output. When you create output, the layers of a composition and each layer's masks, effects, and properties are rendered frame by frame into one or more output files or, in the case of an image sequence, into a series of consecutive files.

Making a movie from your final composition can take a few minutes or many hours, depending on the composition's frame size, quality, complexity, and compression method. When you place your composition in the Render Queue, it becomes a render item that uses the render settings assigned to it.

After Effects provides a variety of formats and compression types for rendering output; the format you choose depends on the medium from which you'll play your final output or on the requirements of your hardware, such as a video-editing system.

● **Note**

For more about output formats and rendering, see Lesson 14, "Rendering and Outputting."

You'll render and export the composition so that it can be broadcast on television.

Note

For output to final-delivery formats, you can use Adobe Media Encoder, which is installed when you install After Effects. You'll learn about Adobe Media Encoder in <u>Lesson 14</u>, "<u>Rendering and Outputting</u>."

Do one of the following to add the composition to the Render Queue:

Select the Destinations composition in the Project panel, and choose Composition

Add To Render Queue. The Render Queue panel opens automatically.

Choose Window > Render Queue to open the Render Queue panel, and then drag the Destinations composition from the Project panel onto the Render Queue panel.

Choose Panel Group Settings > Maximize Panel Group from the Render Queue panel menu so that the panel fills the application window.

▶ **Tip**

The keyboard shortcut for the Maximize Panel Group command is the accent grave character (`), which shares a key with the tilde character (~).

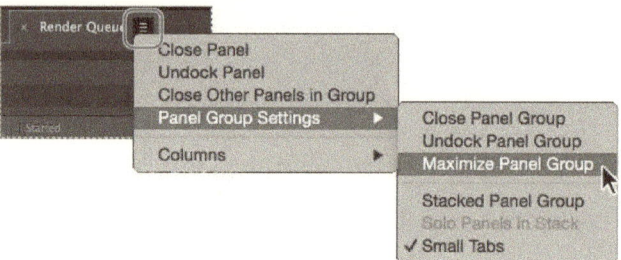

Click the triangle to expand the Render Settings options. By default, After Effects renders compositions with Best Quality and Full Resolution. The default settings are fine for this project.

Click the triangle to expand the Output Module options. By default, After Effects uses lossless compression to encode the rendered composition into a movie file, which is fine for this project. But you need to identify where to save the file.

Click the blue words *Not Yet Specified* next to the Output To pop-up menu.

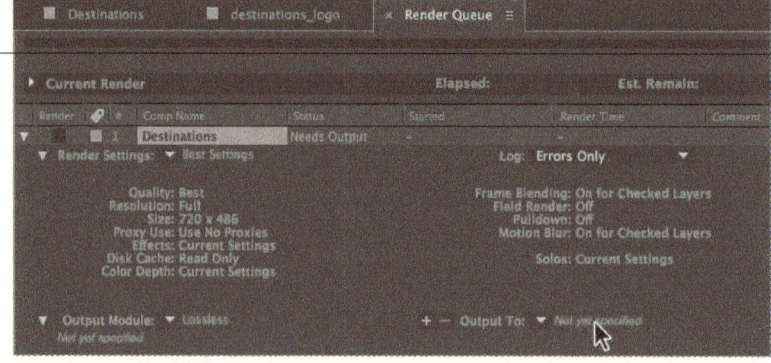

In the Output Movie To dialog box, accept the default movie name (Destinations), select the Lessons/Lesson02/Finished_Project folder for the location, and then click Save.

Back in the Render Queue panel, click the Render button.

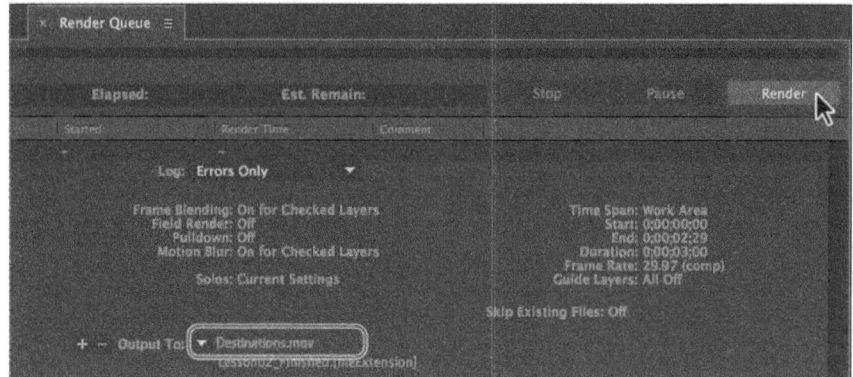

After Effects displays a progress bar in the Render Queue panel as it encodes the file, and issues an audio alert when all items in the Render Queue have been rendered and encoded.

When the movie is complete, choose Panel Group Settings > Restore Panel Group Size from the Render Queue panel menu to restore your workspace.

If you want to see your final product, double-click the Destinations.avi or Destinations.mov file in the Lessons/Lesson02/Finished_Project folder to open it in Windows Media Player or QuickTime, and then play the file.

Close the project file, and then quit After Effects. Congratulations. You've created a travel show ID suitable for broadcast.

Review questions

1. How do you use Adobe Bridge to preview and import files?

2. What is *precomposing*?

3. How do you customize an effect?

4. How do you modify the transparency of a layer in a composition?

Review answers

1. Choose File > Browse In Bridge to jump from After Effects to Adobe Bridge. If Bridge isn't installed, you'll be prompted to download and install it. In Bridge, you can search for and preview image assets. When you locate the asset you want to use in an After Effects project, double-click it, or drag it to the Project panel.

2. *Precomposing* is a way to nest layers within a composition. Precomposing moves the layers to a new composition, which takes the place of the selected layers. When you want to change the order in which layer components are rendered, precomposing is a quick way to create intermediate levels of nesting in an existing hierarchy.

3. After you apply an effect to a layer in a composition, you can customize its properties in the Effect Controls panel. This panel opens automatically when you

apply the effect, or you can open it at any time by selecting the layer with the effect and choosing Window > Effect Controls.

<u>4.</u> To modify the transparency of a layer, reduce its opacity. Select the layer in the Timeline panel, press T to reveal its Opacity property, and enter a value lower than 100%.

Animating Text

Create and animate text layers.

Stylize text using the Character and Paragraph panels.

Apply and customize text animation presets.

Preview animation presets in Adobe Bridge.

Install fonts using Adobe Typekit.

Animate text using keyframes.

Animate layers using parenting.

Edit and animate imported Adobe Photoshop text.

Use a text animator group to animate selected characters on a layer.

Getting started

Adobe After Effects offers many ways to animate text. You can animate text layers by manually creating keyframes in the Timeline panel, using animation presets, or using expressions. You can even animate individual characters or words in a text layer. In this lesson, you'll employ several different animation techniques, including some that are unique to text, while you design the opening title credits for an animated documentary called *Road Trip*. You'll also take advantage of Adobe Typekit to install a font for use in your project.

As in other projects, you'll begin by previewing the movie you're creating, and then you'll open After Effects.

Make sure the following files are in the Lessons/Lesson03 folder on your hard disk, or download them from your Account page at www.peachpit.com now:

In the Assets folder: background_movie.mov, car.ai, compass.swf, credits.psd

In the Sample_Movie folder: Lesson03.mov

Open and play the Lesson03.mov sample movie to see the title credits you will create in this lesson. When you're done, quit QuickTime Player. You may delete this sample movie from your hard disk if you have limited storage space.

As you start the application, restore the default settings for After Effects. See "Restoring default preferences" on page 2.

Start After Effects, and then immediately hold down Ctrl+Alt+Shift (Windows) or Command+Option+Shift (Mac OS) to restore default preferences settings. When prompted, click OK to delete your preferences.

Close the Start window.

After Effects opens to display a blank, untitled project.

Choose File > Save As > Save As, and navigate to the Lessons/Lesson03/Finished_Project folder.

Name the project **Lesson03_Finished.aep**, and then click Save.

Importing the footage

You need to import two footage items to begin this lesson.

Double-click an empty area of the Project panel to open the Import File dialog box.

Navigate to the Lessons/Lesson03/Assets folder on your hard disk, Ctrl-click (Windows) or Command-click (Mac OS) to select both the background_movie.mov and compass.swf files, and then click Import or Open.

After Effects can import several file formats including Adobe Photoshop and Adobe Illustrator files, as well as QuickTime and AVI movies. This makes After Effects an incredibly powerful application for compositing and motion graphics work.

Creating the composition

Now, you'll create the composition.

Press Ctrl+N (Windows) or Command+N (Mac OS) to create a new composition.

In the Composition Settings dialog box, name the composition

Road_Trip_Title_Sequence, choose NTSC DV from the Preset menu, and set the Duration to **10:00**, which is the length of the background movie. Then click OK.

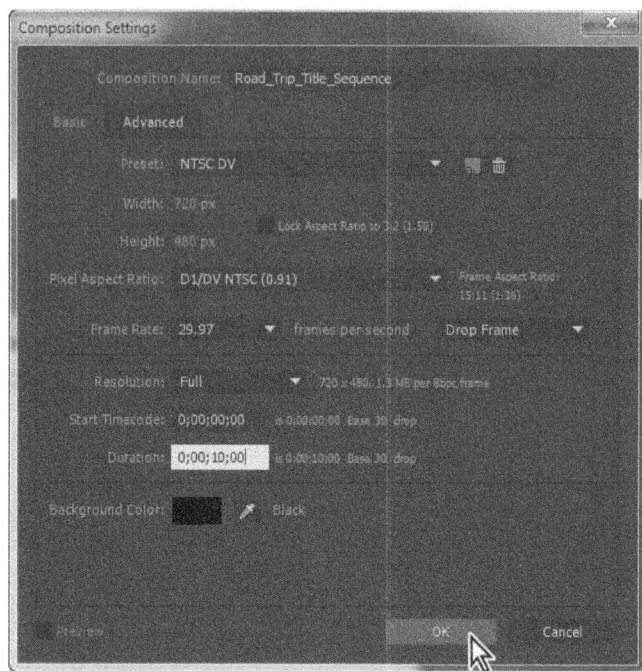

Drag the background_movie.mov and compass.swf footage items from the Project panel
to the Timeline panel. Arrange the layers so that compass.swf is above
background_movie.mov in the layer stack.

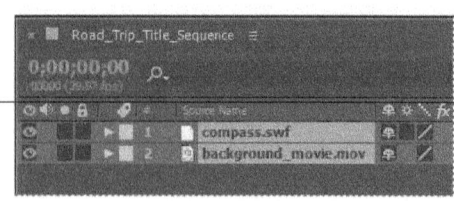

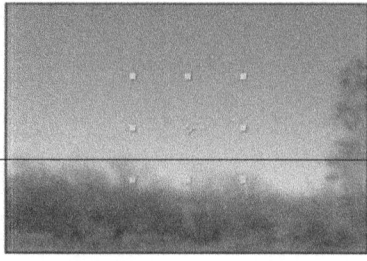

Choose File > Save.

You're ready to add the title text to the composition.

About text layers

In After Effects, you can add text with flexibility and precision. The Tools, Character, and Paragraph panels contain a wide range of text controls. You can create and edit horizontal or vertical text directly on the screen in the Composition panel, and quickly change the font, style, size, and color of the text. You can apply changes to individual characters and set formatting options for entire paragraphs, including alignment, justification, and word-wrapping. In addition to all of these style features, After Effects provides tools for easily animating specific characters and properties, such as text opacity and hue.

After Effects uses two types of text: point text and paragraph text. Use *point text* to enter a single word or line of characters; use *paragraph text* to enter and format text as one or more paragraphs.

In many ways, text layers are just like any other layers in After Effects. You can apply effects and expressions to text layers, animate them, designate them as 3D layers, and edit the 3D text while viewing from multiple angles. As with layers imported from Illustrator, text layers are continuously rasterized, so when you scale the layer or resize the text, it retains crisp, resolution-independent edges. The two main differences between text layers and other layers are that you cannot open a text layer in its own Layer panel and you can animate the text in a text layer using special text-animator properties and selectors.

Installing a font using Typekit

Hundreds of fonts are available through Adobe Typekit, which is included with an Adobe Creative Cloud membership. You'll use Typekit to install a font that will work well for the title text. When you install a Typekit font on your system, it's available in any application.

Choose File > Add Fonts From Typekit.

After Effects opens the Adobe Typekit page in your default browser.

Make sure you're signed in to Creative Cloud. If not, click Sign In at the top of the screen, and then enter your Adobe ID.

You can browse fonts on the Adobe Typekit website, but because there are so many, it's often more efficient to filter them or to search for a specific font. You'll filter fonts to see those that meet your requirements.

Make sure the My Library tab is selected so you'll see all the fonts.

Choose Sort By Name from the pop-up menu in the upper right corner. Then, on the right side of the page, click the Sans Serif button in the Classification area and both the Web and Sync buttons in the Availability area. In the Properties area, select the buttons for medium weight, medium width, low contrast, and standard capitalization.

Typekit displays several fonts that meet the requirements you specified. You'll preview the fonts to see which one looks best.

Type **Road Trip** in the sample text field, and move the slider to decrease the sample text size so you can see the full title.

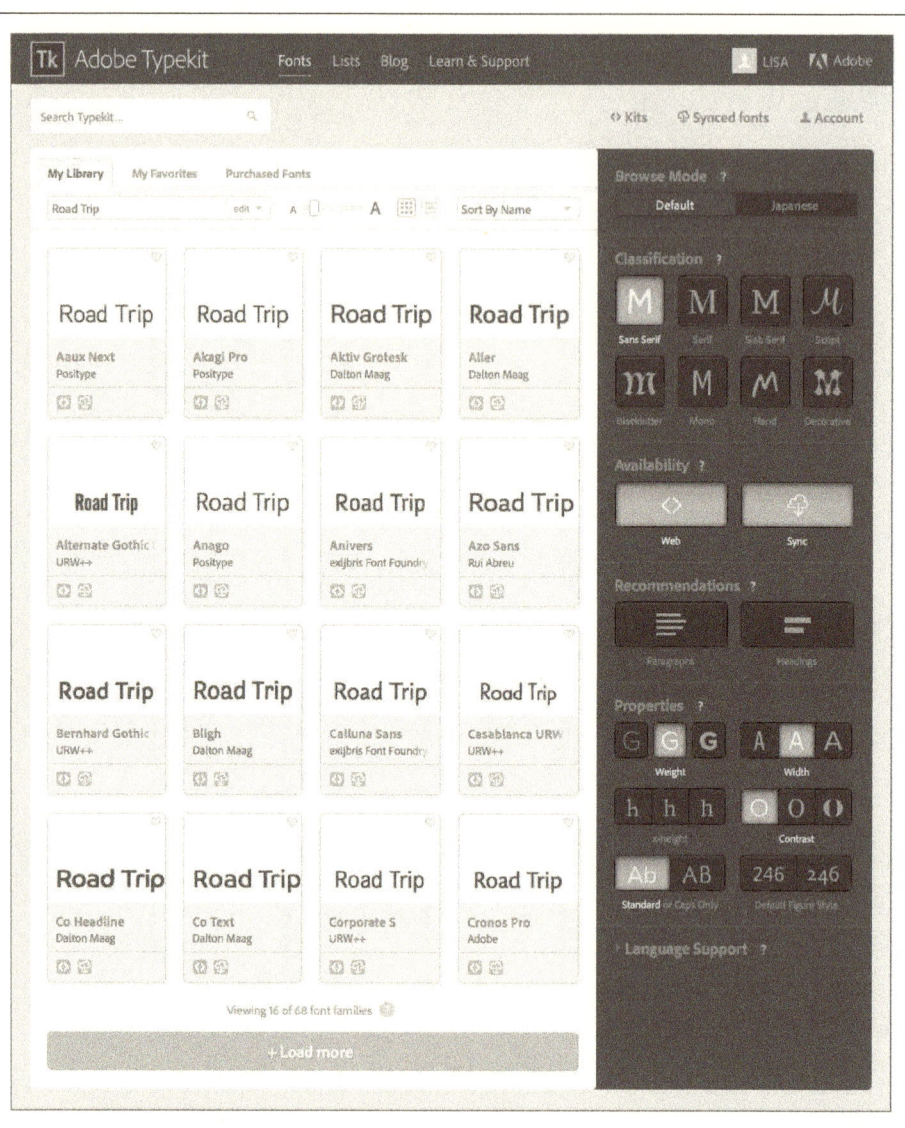

Using your own text as the sample text lets you get a feel for how a font will work in your project. Calluna Sans will work nicely.

Hover your mouse over Calluna Sans until you see a green overlay. Then click +Use Fonts. (If you don't see Calluna Sans, click +Load More until you do, or choose a different font.)

If you click the font name without clicking +Use Fonts, you'll see sample text for all the fonts in the selected family, as well as additional information about the font.

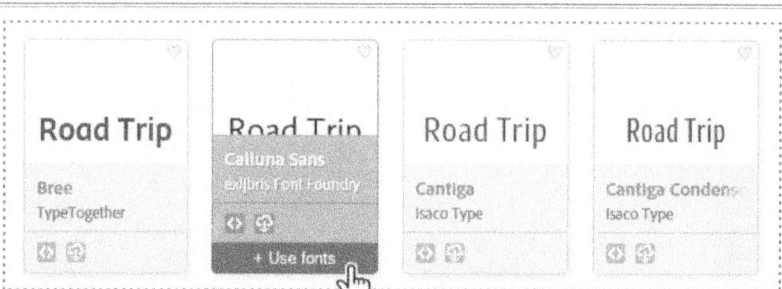

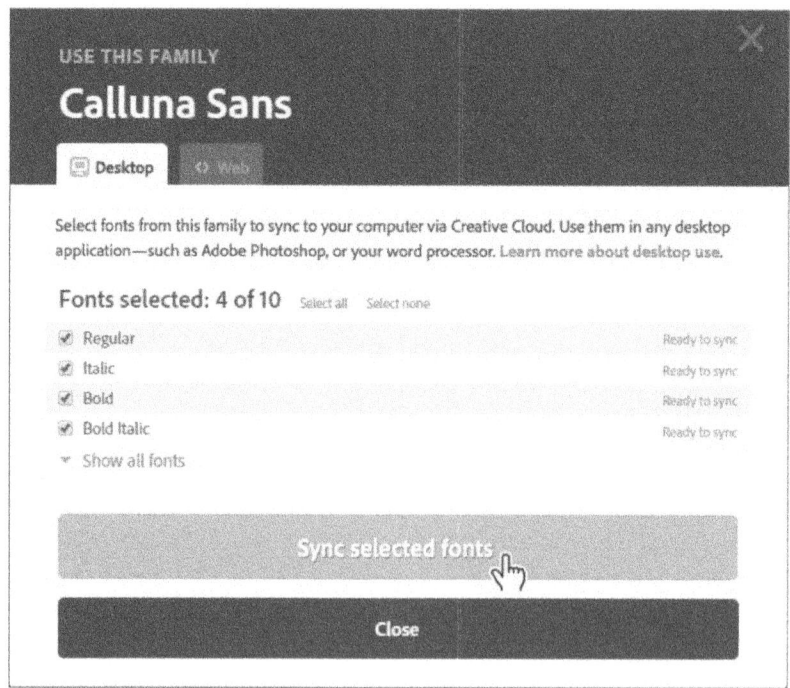

Click Sync Selected Fonts. If the Creative Cloud application isn't running on your computer, click Launch The Creative Cloud Application to start it.

The selected fonts are automatically added to your system and are then available in any application, including After Effects.

Creating and formatting point text

When you enter point text, each line of text is independent—the length of a line increases or decreases as you edit the text, but it doesn't wrap to the next line. The text you enter appears in a new text layer. The small line through the I-beam marks the position of the text baseline.

In the Tools panel, select the Horizontal Type tool (T).

Note

If you press Enter or Return on the regular keyboard instead of on the numeric keypad, you'll begin a new paragraph.

Click anywhere in the Composition panel, and type **Road Trip**. Then press Enter on the numeric keypad to exit text-editing mode and to select the text layer in the Composition panel. Or, you can select the layer name to exit text-editing mode.

Using the Character panel

The Character panel provides options for formatting characters. If text is highlighted, changes you make in the Character panel affect only the highlighted text. If no text is highlighted, changes you make in the Character panel affect the selected text layers and the text layers' selected Source Text keyframes, if any exist. If no text is highlighted and no text layers are selected, changes you make in the Character panel become the new defaults for the next text entry.

Choose Window > Workspace > Text to display only those panels you need while working with text.

Tip

To open the panels individually, choose Window > Character or Window > Paragraph. To open both panels, select the Horizontal Type tool, and then click the Toggle The Character And Paragraph Panels button in the Tools panel.

Select the Road Trip text layer in the Timeline panel.

In the Character panel, choose Calluna Sans from the Font Family menu.

Choose Bold from the Font Style menu.

Set the Font Size to **90** pixels.

Leave all other options at their default settings.

 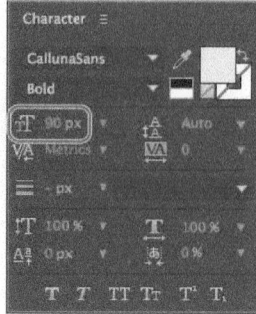

Using the Paragraph panel

Use the Paragraph panel to set options that apply to an entire paragraph, such as alignment, indentation, and leading. For point text, each line is a separate paragraph. You can use the Paragraph panel to set formatting options for a single paragraph, multiple paragraphs, or all paragraphs in a text layer. You just need to make one adjustment in the Paragraph panel for this composition's title text.

In the Paragraph panel, click the Center Text button (≣). This aligns horizontal text to the center of the layer, not to the center of the composition.

Note

Your screen may look different, depending on where you started typing.

 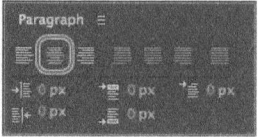

Leave all other options at their default settings.

Positioning the type

To precisely position layers, such as the text layer you're working on now, you can display rulers, guides, and grids in the Composition panel. These visual reference tools don't appear in the final rendered movie.

Make sure the Road Trip text layer is selected in the Timeline panel.

Choose Layer > Transform > Fit To Comp Width. This scales the layer to fit to the width of the composition.

Now you can position the text layer using a grid.

Choose View > Show Grid and then View > Snap To Grid.

Using the Selection tool (▶), drag the text up in the Composition panel until the base of the letters sits on the horizontal gridline in the center of the composition. Press Shift after you start dragging to constrain the movement and help you position the text.

When the layer is in position, choose View > Show Grid again to hide the grid.

This project isn't destined for broadcast TV, so it's okay that the title extends beyond the title-safe and action-safe areas of the composition at the beginning of the animation.

Click Essentials in the Workspace bar at the top of the application window to return to the Essentials workspace. (Click the double arrows to see Essentials if it doesn't fit in the Workspace bar.)

Choose File > Save to save your project.

Using a text animation preset

Now you're ready to animate the title. The easiest way to do that is to use one of the many animation presets that come with After Effects. After applying an animation preset, you can customize it and save it to use again in other projects.

Press the Home key or go to 0:00 to make sure the current-time indicator is at the beginning of the time ruler.

After Effects applies animation presets from the current time.

Select the Road Trip text layer.

Browsing animation presets

You already applied an animation preset using the Effects & Presets panel in Lesson 2, "Creating a Basic Animation Using Effects and Presets." But what if you're not sure which animation preset you want to use? To help you choose the right animation preset for your projects, you can preview them in Adobe Bridge.

Choose Animation > Browse Presets. Adobe Bridge opens, displaying the contents of the After Effects Presets folder.

In the Content panel, double-click the Text folder, and then the Blurs folder.

Click to select the first preset, Blur By Word. Adobe Bridge plays a sample of the animation in the Preview panel.

Select a few other presets, and watch them in the Preview panel.

Preview the Evaporate preset, and then double-click its thumbnail preview. Alternatively, you can right-click (Windows) or Control-click (Mac OS) the thumbnail and choose Place In After Effects CC 2015.

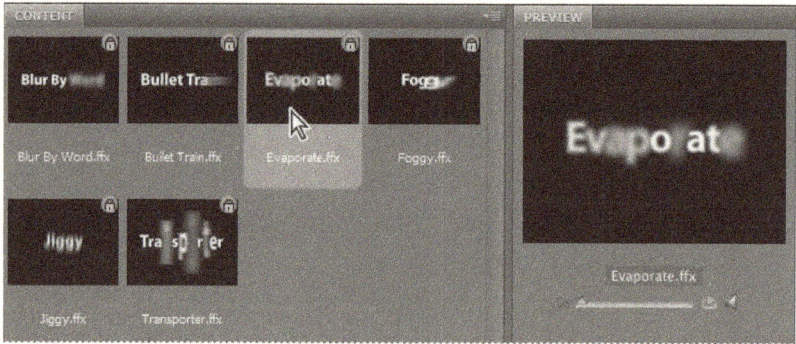

After Effects applies the preset to the selected layer, which is the Road Trip layer, but nothing appears to change in the composition. This is because at 0:00, the first frame of the animation, the letters haven't yet evaporated.

Previewing a range of frames

Now, preview the animation. Although the composition is 10 seconds long, you need to preview only the first few seconds, since that is where the text animation occurs.

In the Timeline panel, move the current-time indicator to 3:00, and press N to set the end bracket of the work area.

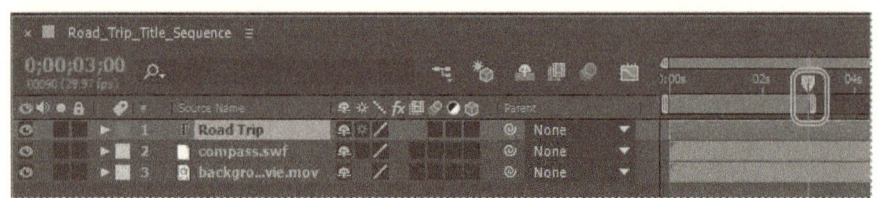

Press the spacebar to watch a preview of the animation.

  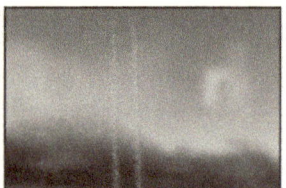

The letters appear to evaporate into the background. It looks great—but you want the letters to fade in and remain onscreen, not disappear. You'll customize the preset to suit your needs.

Press the spacebar to stop the preview, and then press the Home key to move the current-time indicator back to 0:00.

Customizing an animation preset

After you apply an animation preset to a layer, all of its properties and keyframes are listed in the Timeline panel. You'll use those properties to customize the preset.

Select the Road Trip text layer in the Timeline panel, and press U.

▶ Tip

If you press U twice (UU), After Effects displays all modified properties for the layer, instead of only the animated properties. Press the U key again to hide all the layer's properties.

The U key, sometimes referred to as the *Überkey*, is a valuable keyboard shortcut that reveals all the animated properties of a layer.

Click the Offset property name to select both of its keyframes.

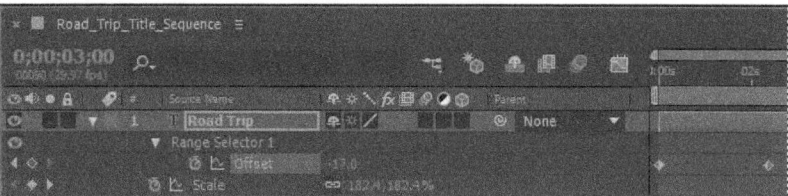

The Offset property specifies how much to offset the start and end of the selection.

Choose Animation > Keyframe Assistant > Time-Reverse Keyframes.

The Time-Reverse Keyframes command switches the order of the two Offset keyframes so that the letters are invisible at the beginning of the composition, and then emerge into view.

Drag the current-time indicator from 0:00 to 3:00 to manually preview the animation you edited.

 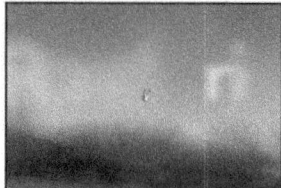 

The letters now fade into, rather than disappear from, the composition.

Press U to hide the layer's properties.

Press the End key to move the current-time indicator to the end of the time ruler, and then press **N** to set the end bracket of the work area.

Choose File > Save to save your project.

Animating with scale keyframes

The text layer was scaled to nearly 200% when you applied the Fit To Comp Width command to it earlier in this lesson. Now, you'll animate the layer's scale so that the type gradually shrinks down to its original size.

In the Timeline panel, move the current-time indicator to 3:00.

Select the Road Trip text layer, and press the S key to reveal its Scale property.

Click the stopwatch icon (⏱) to add a Scale keyframe at the current time (3:00).

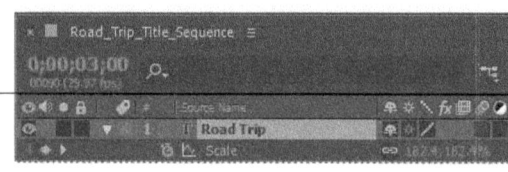 

Move the current-time indicator to 5:00.

Reduce the layer's Scale values to **100**, **100%**. After Effects adds a new Scale keyframe at the current time.

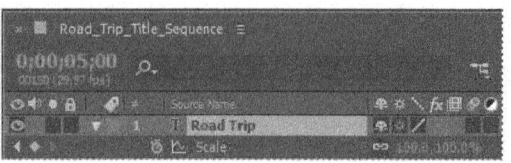 

Previewing the scale animation

Now you'll preview the change.

Move the current-time indicator to 5:10, and press N to set the end of the work area. The scale animation ends shortly before 5:10.

Press the spacebar to preview the animation from 0:00 to 5:10. The movie title fades in and then scales to a smaller size.

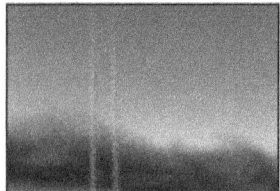  

Press the spacebar to stop playback after you've viewed the animation.

Adding Easy Ease

The beginning and end of the scale animation are rather abrupt. In nature, nothing comes to an absolute stop. Instead, objects ease into and out of starting and stopping points.

Right-click (Windows) or Control-click (Mac OS) the Scale keyframe at 3:00, and choose Keyframe Assistant > Easy Ease Out. The keyframe becomes a left-pointing icon.

Right-click (Windows) or Control-click (Mac OS) the Scale keyframe at 5:00, and choose Keyframe Assistant > Easy Ease In. The keyframe becomes a right-pointing icon.

Watch another preview. Press the spacebar to stop it when you're done.

Choose File > Save.

Animating using parenting

The next task is to make it appear as if the virtual camera is zooming away from the composition. The text scale animation you just applied gets you halfway there, but you need to animate the scale of the compass as well. You could manually animate the compass layer, but it's easier to take advantage of parenting relationships in After Effects.

Press the Home key, or drag the current-time indicator to the beginning of the time ruler.

In the Timeline panel, click the Parent pop-up menu for the compass layer, and choose 1. Road Trip.

This sets the Road Trip text layer as the parent of the compass layer, which in turn becomes the child layer.

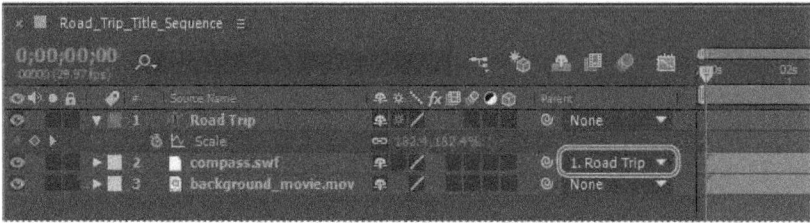

As the child layer, the compass layer inherits the Scale keyframes of its parent layer (Road Trip). Not only is this a quick way to animate the compass, but it also ensures that the compass scales at the same rate and by the same amount as the text layer.

In the Timeline panel, move the compass layer above the Road Trip text layer.

Note

When you move the compass layer, its parent becomes 2. Road Trip, because Road Trip is now the second layer.

Move the current-time indicator to 9:29, so you can clearly see the compass in the Composition panel.

In the Composition panel, drag the compass so that its anchor point is over the dot in the letter *i* in the word *trip*. Alternatively, you can select the compass layer in the Timeline panel, press P to reveal its Position property, and then enter **124, −62**.

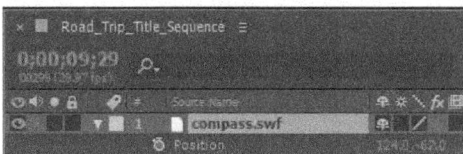 

Move the current-time indicator from 3:00 to 5:00 to manually preview the scaling.

Both the text and the compass scale down in size, so that it appears that the camera is moving away from the scene.

Press the Home key to return to 0:00, and drag the work area end bracket to the end of the time ruler.

Select the Road Trip layer in the Timeline panel, and press S to hide its Scale property. If you entered Position values for the compass, select the compass layer, and press P to hide the Position property, too. Then choose File > Save.

About parent and child layers

Parenting assigns one layer's transformations to another layer, called a *child layer*. Creating a parenting relationship between layers synchronizes the changes in the parent layer with the corresponding transformation values of the child layers, except opacity. For example, if a parent layer moves 5 pixels to the right of its starting position, then the child layer also moves 5 pixels to the right of its starting position. A layer can have only one parent, but a layer can be a parent to any number of 2D or 3D layers within the same composition. Parenting layers is useful for creating complex animations such as linking the movements of a marionette or depicting the orbits of planets in the solar system.

For more on parent and child layers, see After Effects Help.

Animating imported Photoshop text

If all text animations involved just two short words, such as *road trip,* life would be easy. But in the real world, you may often have to work with longer blocks of text, and they can be tedious to enter manually. Fortunately, you can import text from Photoshop or Illustrator. You can preserve text layers, edit them, and animate them in After Effects.

Importing text

Some of the remaining text for this composition is in a layered Photoshop file, which you'll import now.

Double-click an empty area in the Project panel to open the Import File dialog box.

Select the credits.psd file in the Lessons/Lesson03/Assets folder. Choose Composition – Retain Layer Sizes from the Import As menu, and then click Import or Open.

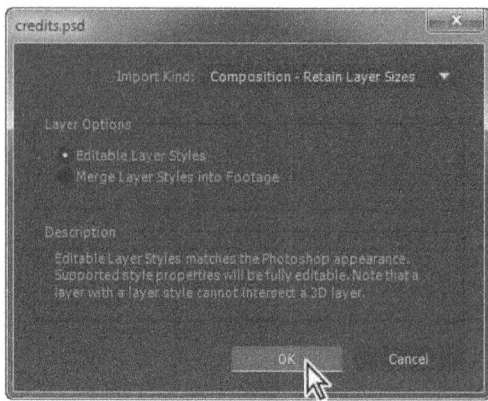

In the Credits.psd dialog box, select Editable Layer Styles, and click OK.

After Effects can import Photoshop layer styles, retaining the appearance of the layers you're importing. The imported file is added as a composition to the Project panel; its layers are added in a separate folder.

Drag the credits composition from the Project panel into the Timeline panel, placing it at the top of the layer stack.

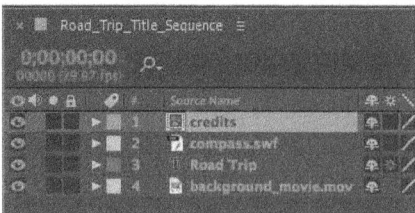 

Because you imported the credits.psd file as a composition with layers intact, you can work on it in its own Timeline panel, editing and animating its layers independently.

Editing imported text

The text you imported isn't currently editable in After Effects. You'll change that so that you can control the type and apply animations. And if you have a sharp eye, you've noticed some typos in the imported text. So, first you'll clean up the type.

Double-click the credits composition in the Project panel to open it in its own Timeline panel.

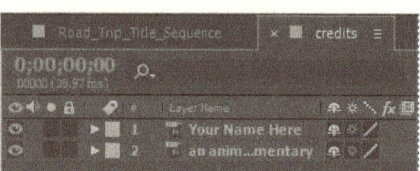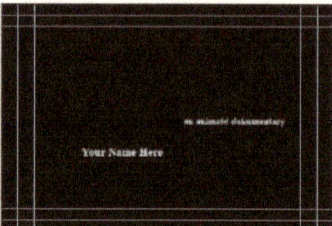

Shift-click to select both layers in the credits Timeline panel, and choose Layer > Convert To Editable Text. (Click OK if you see a warning about missing fonts.)

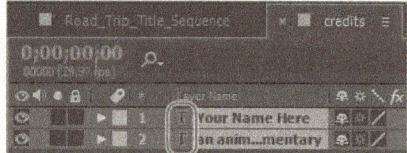

Now the text layers can be edited, and you can fix the typos.

Deselect both layers, and then double-click layer 2 in the Timeline panel to select the text and automatically switch to the Horizontal Type tool (T).

Type an *e* between the *t* and *d* in the word *animated.* Then change the *k* to a *c* in *documentary.*

⚫ **Note**

The layer name does not change in the Timeline panel when you correct the spelling in the layer. This is because the original layer name was created in Photoshop. To change a layer's name, select it in the Timeline panel, press Enter or Return, type the new name, and press Enter or Return again.

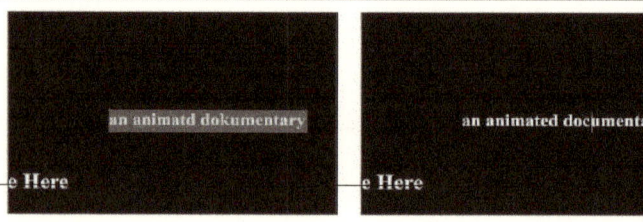

Switch to the Selection tool (↖) to exit text-editing mode.

Shift-click to select both layers in the Timeline panel.

If the Character panel isn't open, choose Window > Character to open it.

Choose the same typeface you used for the words *Road Trip*: Calluna Sans. Leave all other settings as they are.

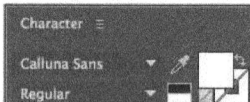

Click an empty area of the Timeline panel to deselect both layers. Then select layer 2 again.

In the Character panel, click the Fill Color box. Then, in the Text Color dialog box, select a shade of green, and click OK. We used R=66, G=82, B=42.

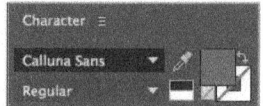

Animating the subtitle

You want the letters of the subtitle—*an animated documentary*—to fade onscreen from left to right under the movie title. The easiest way to do this is to use another text animation preset.

Go to 5:00 in the timeline. At that point, the title and the compass have finished scaling to their final size.

Select the subtitle layer (layer 2) in the Timeline panel.

Press Ctrl+Alt+Shift+O (Windows) or Command+Option+Shift+O (Mac OS) to jump to Adobe Bridge.

Navigate to the Presets/Text/Animate In folder.

Select the Fade Up Characters animation preset, and watch it in the Preview panel. This effect works well to reveal the text gradually.

Double-click the Fade Up Characters preset to apply it to the subtitle layer in After Effects.

With the subtitle layer selected in the Timeline panel, press UU to see the properties modified by the animation preset. You should see two keyframes for Range Selector 1 Start: one at 5:00, and one at 7:00.

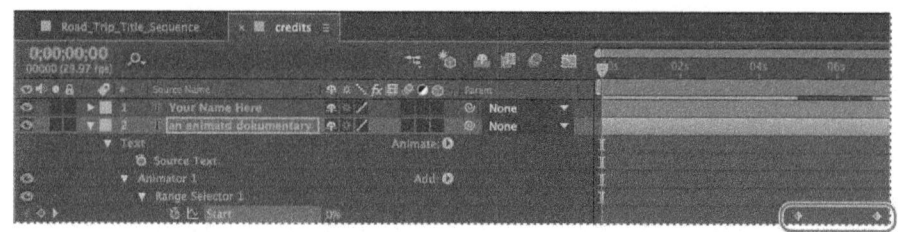

You still have a lot of animation to do in this composition, so you will speed up the effect by 1 second.

Go to 6:00, and then drag the second Range Selector 1 Start keyframe to 6:00.

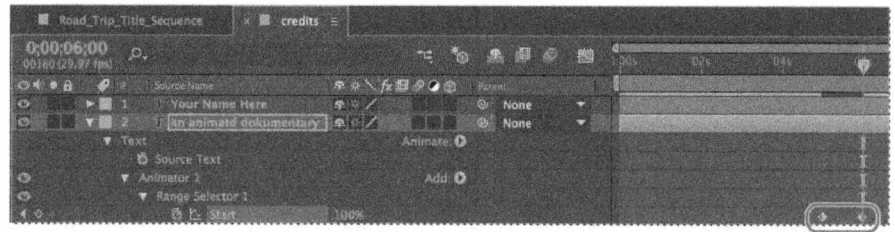

Drag the current-time indicator across the time ruler between 5:00 and 6:00 to see the letters fade in.

When you're done, select the subtitle layer, and press U to hide the modified properties. Then choose File > Save to save your work.

Animating type tracking

Next, you'll animate the appearance of the director's name in the composition using a text animation tracking preset. By animating tracking, you can make words seem to expand outward as they appear onscreen from a central point.

Customizing placeholder text

Currently, the director's name is simply a layer with placeholder text—*Your Name Here.*

Before you animate it, change it to your own name.

Still working in the credits timeline in the Timeline panel, select the Your Name Here layer.

● Note

It doesn't matter where the current-time indicator is located when you edit the text of this layer. Currently, the text is onscreen for the duration of the composition. That will change once you animate it.

Select the Horizontal Type tool (T), and then replace *Your Name Here* in the Composition panel with your own name. Use a first, middle, and last name so that you have a nice long string of text to animate. Click the layer name when you're done. The layer name doesn't change, because it was named in Photoshop.

Applying a tracking preset

Now you will animate the director's name with a tracking preset so that it starts to appear onscreen shortly after the words *an animated documentary* are fully visible in the composition.

Go to 7:10.

Select the Your Name Here layer in the Timeline panel.

Jump to Adobe Bridge, and go to the Presets/Text/Tracking folder. Double-click the Increase Tracking preset to apply it to the Your Name Here layer in After Effects.

Tip

If you're tired of jumping to Adobe Bridge and don't care to preview the preset, simply type **Increase Tracking** in the search box of the Effects & Presets panel. Then double-click the effect to apply it to the selected layer in the Timeline panel.

Drag the current-time indicator across the time ruler between 7:10 and 9:10 to manually preview the tracking animation.

Customizing the tracking animation preset

The text expands, but you want the letters to be so close initially that they're on top of each other, and then to expand to a reasonable, readable distance apart. The animation should also occur faster. You'll adjust the Tracking Amount to achieve both goals.

Select the Your Name Here layer in the Timeline panel, and press UU to reveal the properties that were modified.

Go to 7:10.

Under Animator 1, change the Tracking Amount to **–5** so that the letters are squeezed together.

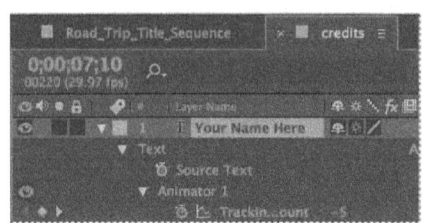

Click the Go To Next Keyframe arrow (▸) for the Tracking Amount property, and then change the value to **0**.

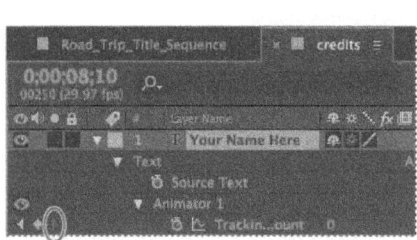

Drag the current-time indicator across the time ruler between 7:10 and 8:10. The letters expand as they appear onscreen, and stop animating at the last keyframe.

Animating text opacity

You'll take the animation of the director's name a little further by having it fade onscreen as the letters expand. To do this, you'll animate the layer's Opacity property.

Select the Your Name Here layer in the credits timeline.

Press T to reveal only the layer's Opacity property.

Go to 7:10, and set the Opacity to **0%**. Then click the stopwatch icon (🕙) to set an Opacity keyframe.

Go to 7:20, and set the Opacity to **100%**. After Effects adds a second keyframe. Now the letters of the director's name should fade in as they expand onscreen.

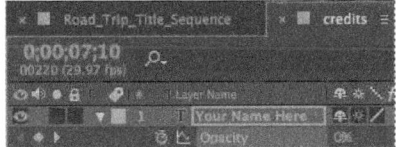 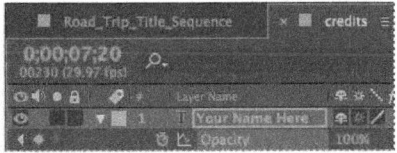

Drag the current-time indicator across the time ruler between 7:10 and 8:10 to see the letters of the director's name fade in as they spread out.

Right-click (Windows) or Control-click (Mac OS) the ending Opacity keyframe, and choose Keyframe Assistant > Easy Ease In.

Choose File > Save.

Using a text animator group

Text animator groups let you animate individual letters within a block of text in a layer. You'll use a text animator group to animate only the characters in your middle name without affecting the tracking and opacity animation of the other names in the layer.

In the Timeline panel, go to 8:10.

Hide the Opacity property for the Your Name Here layer. Then expand the layer to see its Text property group name.

Next to the Text property name, click the Animate pop-up menu, and choose Skew.

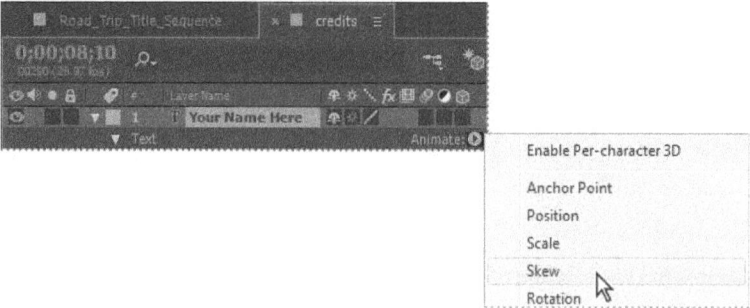

A property group named Animator 2 appears in the layer's Text properties.

About text animator groups

A text animator group includes one or more *selectors* and one or more *animator properties*. A selector is like a mask—it specifies which characters or section of a text layer you want an animator property to affect. Using a selector, you can define a percentage of the text, specific characters in the text, or a specific range of text.

Using a combination of animator properties and selectors, you can create complex text animations that would otherwise require painstaking keyframing. Most text animations require you to animate only the selector values—not the property values. Consequently, text animators use a small number of keyframes even for complex animations.

For more about text animator groups, see After Effects Help.

Select Animator 2, press Enter or Return, and rename it **Skew Animator**. Then press Enter or Return again to accept the new name.

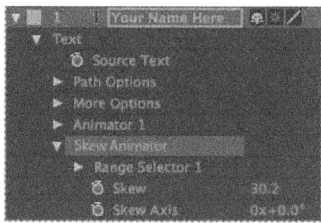

Now you're ready to define the range of letters that you want to skew.

Expand the Skew Animator's Range Selector 1 properties.

Each animator group includes a default range selector. Range selectors constrain the animation to particular letters in the text layer. You can add additional selectors to an animator group, or apply multiple animator properties to the same range selector.

While watching the Composition panel, drag the Skew Animator's Range Selector 1 Start value up (to the right) until the left selector indicator (⌐) is just before the first letter of your middle name (the *B* in *Bender*, in this example).

Drag the Skew Animator's Range Selector 1 End value down (to the left) until its indicator (⊮) is just after the last letter of your middle name (the *r* in *Bender*, in this example) in the Composition panel.

Now, any properties that you animate with the Skew Animator will affect only the middle name that you selected.

Skewing the range of text

Now, make that middle name shake and shimmy by setting Skew keyframes.

Drag the Skew Animator's Skew value left and right, and notice that only the middle name sways. The other names in the line of text remain steady.

Set the Skew Animator's Skew value to **0**.

Go to 8:05, and click the stopwatch icon (⏱) for Skew to add a keyframe to the property.

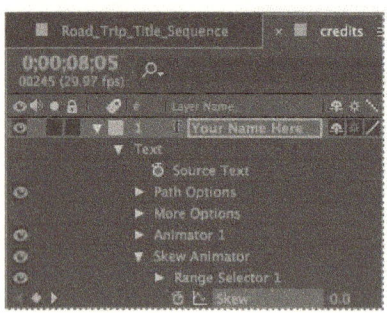 

Go to 8:08, and set the Skew value to **50**. After Effects adds a keyframe.

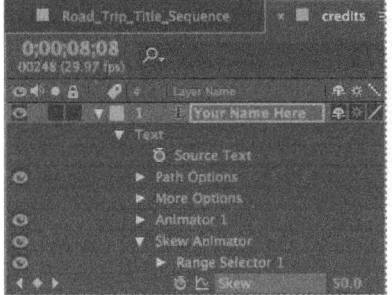 

Go to 8:15, and change the Skew value to –50. After Effects adds another keyframe.

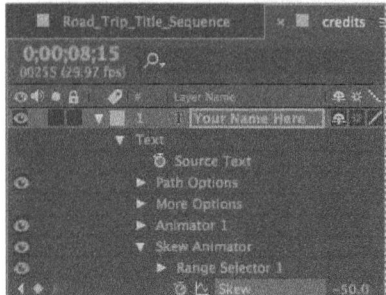 

Go to 8:20, and change the Skew value to 0 to set the final keyframe.

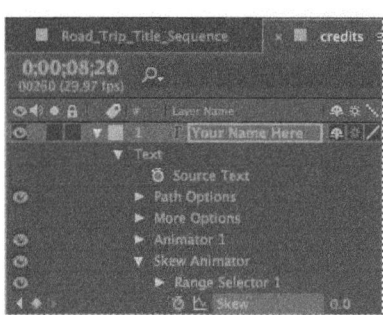 

Click the Skew property name to select all of the Skew keyframes. Then choose Animation > Keyframe Assistant > Easy Ease to add an Easy Ease to all keyframes.

Drag the current-time indicator across the time ruler from 7:10 to 8:20 to see how the director's name fades in and expands onscreen, and the middle name rocks side to side while the other names are unaffected.

Hide the properties for the Your Name Here layer in the Timeline panel.

To quickly remove all text animators from a text layer, select the layer in the Timeline panel, and choose Animation > Remove All Text Animators. To remove only one animator, select its name in the Timeline panel, and press Delete.

Select the Road_Trip_Title_Sequence tab to open its timeline.

Press Home, or go to 0:00, and then preview the entire composition.

Press the spacebar to stop playback, and then choose File > Save to save your work.

Animating a layer's position

You've used several text animation presets to dazzle your audience. But for a simpler effect, you can animate the Transform properties for a text layer, just as you can any other layer.

Currently, your name appears onscreen, but there's no context for it. You'll add the words "directed by," animating them so that they move into position as your name is appearing onscreen.

In the Road_Trip_Title_Sequence Timeline panel, go to 9:29, the end of the project.

At this point, all the other text is onscreen, so you can position the "directed by" line accurately.

Select the Horizontal Type tool.

Make sure no layers are selected, and then click in the Composition panel. Make sure you're clicking in an area that doesn't overlap an existing text layer.

Type **directed by**.

Select the directed by layer. Then, in the Character panel, choose Minion Pro from the Font Family menu.

Choose Regular for the Font Style, and set the Font Size to 20 pixels.

In the Character panel, click the Fill Color box. Then, in the Text Color dialog box, select white, and click OK. Leave all other options at their default settings.

Select the Selection tool, and then drag the directed by layer so that the text is centered over your name.

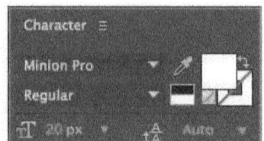

Press P to display the layer's Position property. Click the stopwatch icon to create an initial keyframe for the layer.

Go to 7:00, the point where "documentary" has just finished appearing and your name hasn't yet started to appear.

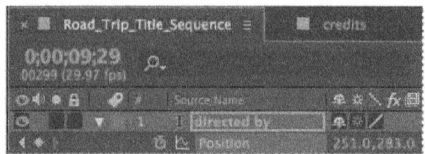 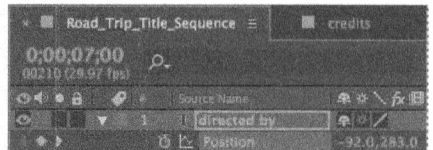

Drag the directed by layer off the left edge of the Composition window. Press the Shift key as you drag to create a straight path.

Preview the animation, and then hide the Position property.

It's simple, but effective. The text moves in from the left side and stops in its final position above your name. To make the text's entrance a little more interesting, you'll add a car graphic that will appear to be dragging the text onscreen.

Timing layer animations

You'll animate a simple car graphic so that the text appears to trail behind the car onscreen. The words should follow the car and come to rest above your name, while the car continues to fly off screen. The timing will require some adjustment, in order to keep the text and the car in sync.

First, you'll import the car graphic and add it to your composition.

Double-click an empty area in the Project panel to open the Import File dialog box.

In the Lessons/Lesson03/Assets folder, select the car.ai file, choose Composition – Retain Layer Sizes from the Import As menu, and then click Import or Open.

Drag the car composition from the Project panel to the top of the layer stack in the Road_Trip_Title_Sequence Timeline panel.

Go to 6:25, just before the directed by text begins moving.

Select the car layer, and press P to reveal its Position property.

Drag the car off the left of the Composition window, so that it overlaps the directed by text.

Click the stopwatch icon for the layer's Position property to create an initial keyframe.

Go to 9:29, the end of the composition.

Drag the car off the right side of the Composition window. The car shouldn't be visible on the screen. Hold down the Shift key as you drag to create a straight path.

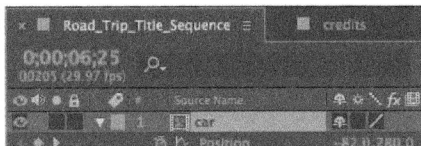 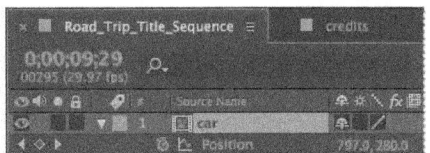

Manually preview the animation from 6:25 to 9:29.

The text trails the car, but the car picks up speed too quickly so it's not obvious that it's dragging the text. You'll need to make an adjustment to its timing to slow the car down until the text is in place.

Go to 8:29.

Move the car immediately to the right of the text.

Preview the animation again.

The timing is better, but now the car overlaps the text at the beginning. One more adjustment should do the trick.

Go to 7:19.

Pull the car forward, just ahead of the text.

Preview the animation again.

Now the car is clearly pulling the text, and it speeds up to roll off the screen before the composition finishes. If you'd like to more precisely control the animation, you can add more keyframes.

Hide the properties for all layers, and then choose File > Save to save your work.

Adding motion blur

Motion blur is the blur that occurs as an object moves. You'll apply motion blur to finesse the composition and make the movement look more natural.

In the Timeline panel, click the Motion Blur switch (⊘) for each layer *except* the background_movie and credits layers.

Now you'll apply motion blur to the layers in the credits composition.

Switch to the credits Timeline panel, and enable motion blur for both layers.

Switch back to the Road_Trip_Title_Sequence Timeline panel, and select the Motion Blur switch for the credits layer. Then click the Enable Motion Blur button (⊘) at the top of the Timeline panel so that you can see the motion blur in the Composition panel.

Preview the entire, completed animation.

Choose File > Save.

Optimize projects

This chapter examines in close detail how image data flows through an After Effects project. It's full of the information you need to help you make the most of After Effects.

Sometimes you take the attitude of a master chef—you know what can be prepped and considered "done" before the guests are in the restaurant and it's time to cook the meal. At other times, you're more like a programmer, iso-lating and debugging elements of a project, even creating controlled tests to figure out how things are working. This chapter helps you both artistically and technically (as if it's possible to separate the two).

After Effects CS6 received the most substantial perfor-mance increase of any single upgrade thanks to Global Performance Cache, a scheme to preserve more individual render data indefinitely, not just when it's buffered into the RAM cache. This addition doesn't obviate the need for a solid understanding of how to work with multiple compositions and when to precomp, nor for specific strate-gies to optimize render time. It does, however, cut down on a good deal of redundancy on the After Effects side of the equation, leaving it up to you to avoid the possibility of PEBKAC (Problem Exists Between Keyboard and Chair).

Work With Multiple Comps and Projects

It's easy to lose track of stuff when projects get compli-cated. This section demonstrates

how and why to work with some kind of project template

how to keep a complex, multiple-composition pipeline organized shortcuts to help maintain orientation within the proj-ect as a whole.

These tips are especially useful if you're someone who understands compositing but sometimes finds After Effects disorienting.

Precomping and Composition Nesting

Precomping is often regarded as the major downside of working in After Effects, because vital information is hid-den from the current comp's timeline in a nested comp. Artists may sometimes let a composition become unwieldy, with dozens of layers, rather than bite the bullet and send a set of those layers into a precomp. Yet precomping is both an effective way to organize the timeline and a key to problem solving and optimization in After Effects. Motion graphics comps can involve the animation and coordina-tion of hundreds of animated elements. In a visual effects context, however, if your main composition has more than 20 or so layers, you're not precomping effectively, making work way less efficient overall.

Typically, precomping is done by selecting the layers of

a composition that can sensibly be grouped together,

and choosing Precompose from the Layer menu

(**Ctrl+Shift+C/Cmd+Shift+C**). Two options appear (the

second option is grayed out if multiple layers have been

selected): to leave attributes (effects, transforms, masks,

paint, blending modes) in place, or transfer them into the

new composition.

Why Precomp?

Precomping prevents a composition from containing too many layers to manage in one timeline, but it also lets you do the following:

Reuse a set of elements.

Fix render order problems. For example,

masks are always applied before effects in a given layer, but a precomp can contain an effect so that the mask in the master comp follows that effect in the render order.

Organize a project by grouping interrelated elements.

Precomping is the action of selecting a set of layers in a master composi-tion and assigning it to a new subcomp, which becomes a layer in the master comp. Closely related to this is *composition nesting*, the act of placing one already created composition inside of another.

project is reopened at a later time on the same system.

Cache Work Area in Background

One reward for making effective use of precomping is the ability to then save the entire precomp to the disk cache for immediate playback. This happens automatically when you preview the master sequence containing the precomp in question, but you can also select the precomp in the Project panel or open its timeline and choose Composition > Cache Work Area in Background to make After Effects immediately pre-render it in the background. As explained later in the chapter, the resulting cache remains available even if the

rd: Pre-compose by Jeff Almasol (http://aescripts.com/ rd-pre-compose/) displays a dialog to precomp one or more layers, just like the regular After Effects dialog, but adds the ability to trim the precomp to the selected layer's dura-tion, including trim handles.

The 04_comp_templates folder and project on the disc contain relevant example comps.

Specify an element or set of layers as completed (and even pre-render them, as discussed later in this chapter).

Many After Effects artists are already comfortable with the idea of precomping but miss that last point. As you read through this, think about the advantages of considering an element finished, even if only for the time being.

the Project Panel: think of it as a File System

How do you like to keep your system organized— tidy folders for everything or files strewn across the desktop? Personally, I'm always happiest with a project that is well organized, even if I'm the only one likely to ever work on it. When sharing with others, however, good organization becomes essential. The Project panel mirrors your file system (whether it's Explorer or Finder), and keeping it well organized and tidy can clarify your thought process regarding the project itself.

I know, I know, eat your vegetables, clean your room. Imag-ine that the person next opening your project is you, but with a case of amnesia. Actually, that basically is you after a sufficient period of time.

Figure 4.1 shows a couple of typical project templates containing multiple compositions to create one final shot, although these could certainly be adapted for a group of similar shots or a sequence. When you need to return to a project over the course of days or weeks, this level of orga-nization can be a lifesaver.

Here are some ideas to help you create your own comp template:

Create folders, such as Source, Precomps, and Refer-ence, **to group specific types of elements.**

Use numbering to reflect comp and sequence order so that it's easy to see the order in the Project panel.

Create a unique Final Output comp that has the format and length of the final shot, particularly if the format is at all different from what you're using for work (because it's scaled, cropped, or uses a different frame rate or color profile).

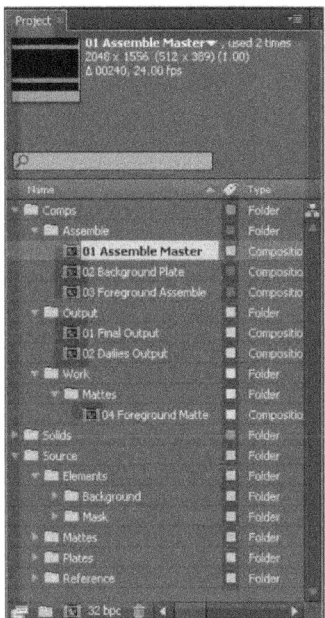
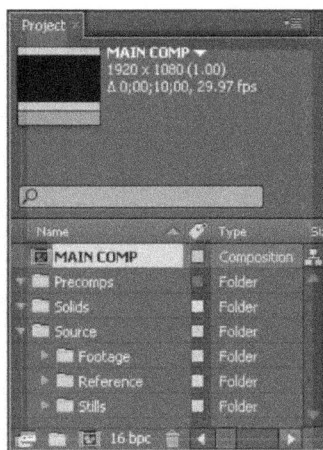

Working Foundations

Figure 4.1 A complex project such as a shot for a feature film might be generically organized (left) to include numbering that reflects pipeline order and multiple output comps with no actual edits, just the necessary set-tings. At minimum (right), you should have Source and Precomps folders, as well as a Reference folder, to keep things tidy.

with the Timeline panel displayed to enable it.

Use guide layers and comments as needed to help artists set up the comp (**Figure 4.2**).

Organize Source folders for all footage, broken down as is most logical for your project.

Place each source footage clip into a precomp. Why? Unexpected changes to source footage—where it is replaced for some reason—are easier to handle without causing some sort of train wreck.

The basic organization of master comp, source comp, and render comp seems useful on a shot of just about any complexity, but the template can include a lot more than that: custom expressions, camera rigs, color management settings, and recurring effects setups.

Manage Multiple Comps from the timeline

Ever had that "where am I?" feeling when working with a series of nested comps? That's where Mini-Flowchart, or

Miniflow, comes in. Access it via in the Timeline panel, or simply tap the **Shift** key

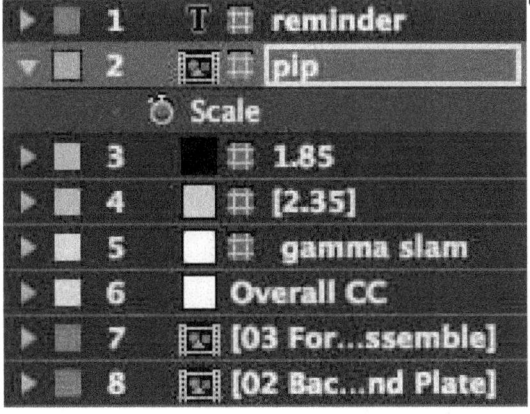

Figure 4.2 Here is a series of non-rendering guide layers to define action areas and color.

If nothing else, a locked, untouch-able Final Output comp prevents losing a render to an incorrectly set work area (because you were edit-ing it for RAM previews).

Miniflow (**Figure 4.3**) shows only the nearest neighbor comps, but click on the flow arrows at either end and you navigate up or down one level in the hierarchy. Click on any arrows or items in between the ends and that level is brought forward. You're even free to close all compositions (**Ctrl+Alt+W/Cmd+Opt+W**) and reopen only the ones you need using this feature.

Figure 4.3 By default, the comp order is shown flowing right to left. The reason for this is probably that if you open subcomps from a master comp, the tabs open to the right; however, you may want to choose Flow Left to Right in Mini-flow's panel menu instead.

Arrange Project Items into Folders (http://aescripts.com/arrange-project-items-into-folders/) looks for project items with a matching prefix and groups them together in a folder. Load Project or Template at Startup (http://aescripts.com/load-project-at-startup/) loads a project or template each time you start After Effects—this can really help if you need several people in a studio to follow a certain organizational style. Both scripts are by Lloyd Alvarez.

The Always Preview This View toggle 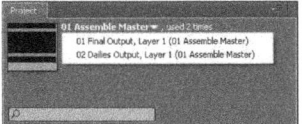 lets you work entirely in a precomp but switch automatically to the master comp (if this is on in that comp) when previewing.

What about cases where you'd like to work in the Timeline panel of a subcomp while seeing the result in the master comp? The Lock icon ⬚ at the upper left of the Composition viewer lets you keep that Composition viewer forward while you open another composition's Timeline panel and close its view panel. Lock the master comp and double-click a nested comp to open its Timeline panel; as you make adjustments, they show up in the master comp.

Ctrl+Alt+Shift+N (Cmd+Opt+Shift+N) creates two Compo-sition viewers side by side, and locks one of them, for any artist with ample screen real estate who wants the best of both worlds.

To locate a comp in the Project panel, you can

select an item in the Project panel; click the caret to see where the item is used, along with the number of times, if any, the item is used in a comp (**Figure 4.4**)

Figure 4.4 Click the caret next to the total number of times an item is used to see a list of where it is used.

context-click an item in the Project panel and choose Reveal in Composition; choose a composition and that comp is opened with the item selected

context-click a layer in the timeline and choose Reveal Layer Source in Project to highlight the item in the Project panel

context-click in the empty area of a timeline—and choose Reveal Composition in Project to highlight the comp in the Project panel (**Figure 4.5**)

type the name of the comp in the Project panel search field.

Ways to Break the Pipeline

Precomping solves problems, but it can also create more problems—or at least inconveniences. Here are a few ways that render order can go wrong:

Some but not all properties are to be precomped, but others must stay in the master comp? With precomping it's all-or-nothing, leaving you to rearrange properties manually.

Changed your mind? Restoring precomped layers to the master composition is a manual (and thus error-prone) process, due to the difficulty of maintaining proper dependencies between the two (for example, if the nested comp has also been scaled, rotated, and retimed).

Do the layers being precomped include blending modes or 3D layers, cameras, or lights? Their behavior changes depending on the Collapse Transformations setting (detailed in the next section).

Is there motion blur, frame blending, or vector artwork in the subcomp? Switches in the master composition affect their behavior, as do settings on each individual nested layer, and this relationship changes depending on whether Collapse Transformations is toggled on.

Layer timing (duration, In and Out points, frame rate) and dimensions can differ from the master comp. When this is unintentional, mishaps happen: Layers end too soon or are cropped inside the overall frame, or keyframes in the precomp fall between those of the master, wreaking havoc on tracking data, for example.

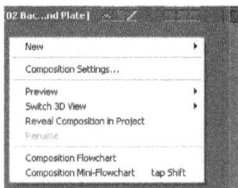

Figure 4.5 Find the empty area below the layers in the timeline and context-click; you can reveal the current comp in the Project panel.

You may already know that a double-click opens a nested comp, and **Alt**–double-click (**Opt**–double-click) reveals it in the Layer viewer.

The script preCompToLayerDur.jsx from Dan Ebberts (found on the book's disc) starts a precomped layer at frame 1 even if the layer to be precomped is trimmed to a later time.

107

True Comp Duplicator (http:// aescripts.com/true-comp-duplicator/) was created by Brennan Chapman to address the biggest bugbear of working with nested comps in After Effects—in a node-based app, you can duplicate an entire nested tree and all of the components are unique, but duplicate a comp in After Effects and its subcomps are the same as in the source. This script can reside in a panel ready to create an entire new hierarchy. Highly recommended.

Figure 4.6 The nested comp has a blue background and the leg of the letter "p" extends outside its boundaries (top); a simple quick fix is to enable Collapse Transformations, and the boundaries of the nested comp are ignored (bottom).

Are you duplicating a comp that contains subcomps? The comp itself is new and completely independent, but the nested comps are not (see Script on this page).

No wonder people avoid precomping. But there is hope if you recognize any difficulty and know what to do, so that inconveniences don't turn into deal-killers.

Boundaries of Time and Space

Each composition in After Effects contains its own fixed timing and pixel dimensions. This adds flexibility for animation but if anything reduces it for compositing. Most other compositing applications such as Nuke and Shake have no built-in concept of frame dimensions or timing and assume that the elements match the plate, as is often the case in visual effects work.

Therefore it is helpful to take precautions:

Make source compositions longer than the shot is ever anticipated to be, so that if it changes, timing is not inadvertently truncated.

Enable Collapse Transformations for the nested com-position to ignore its boundaries (**Figure 4.6**).

Add the Grow Bounds effect if Collapse Transforma-tions isn't an option (see sidebar on next page).

Collapse Transformations is the most difficult of these to get your head around, so it's worth a closer look.

Collapse Transformations

189

In After Effects, when a comp is nested in another comp, effectively becoming a layer, the ordinary behavior is for the nested comp to render completely before the layer is animated, blended, or otherwise adjusted (with effects or masks) in the master comp.

However, there are immediate exceptions. Keyframe interpolations, frame blending, and motion blur are all affected by the settings (including frame rate and timing) of the master comp—they are calculated according to its settings (which can become tricky; see the next section). 3D position data and blending modes, on the other hand, are not passed through unless Collapse Transformations is enabled. Enable the toggle and it is almost as if the pre-composed layers reside in the master comp—but now any 3D camera or lighting in the subcomp is overridden by the camera and lights in the master comp.

Not only that, but layers with Collapse Transformations lose access to blending modes—presumably to avoid con-flicts with those in the subcomp. Now here comes the trick-iest part: Apply any effect to the layer (even Levels with the neutral defaults, which doesn't affect the look of the layer) and you force After Effects to render the collapsed layer, making blending modes operable. It is now what the Adobe developers call a *parenthesized* comp. Such a nested comp is both collapsed and not: You can apply a blending mode, but 3D data is passed through (**Figure 4.7**).

To collapse transformations but not 3D data, apply any effect—even one of the Expression Controls effects that don't by themselves do anything—to parenthesize the comp.

The 04_collapse_transformations folder and project on the disc con-tain relevant example comps.

Annoyed to find sequences import-ing at the wrong frame rate? Change the default Sequence Footage Frames per Second under Prefer-ences > Import.

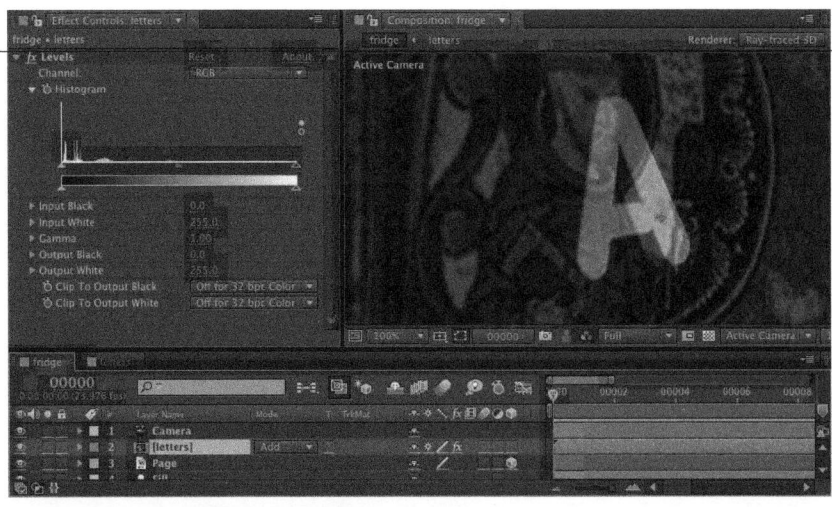

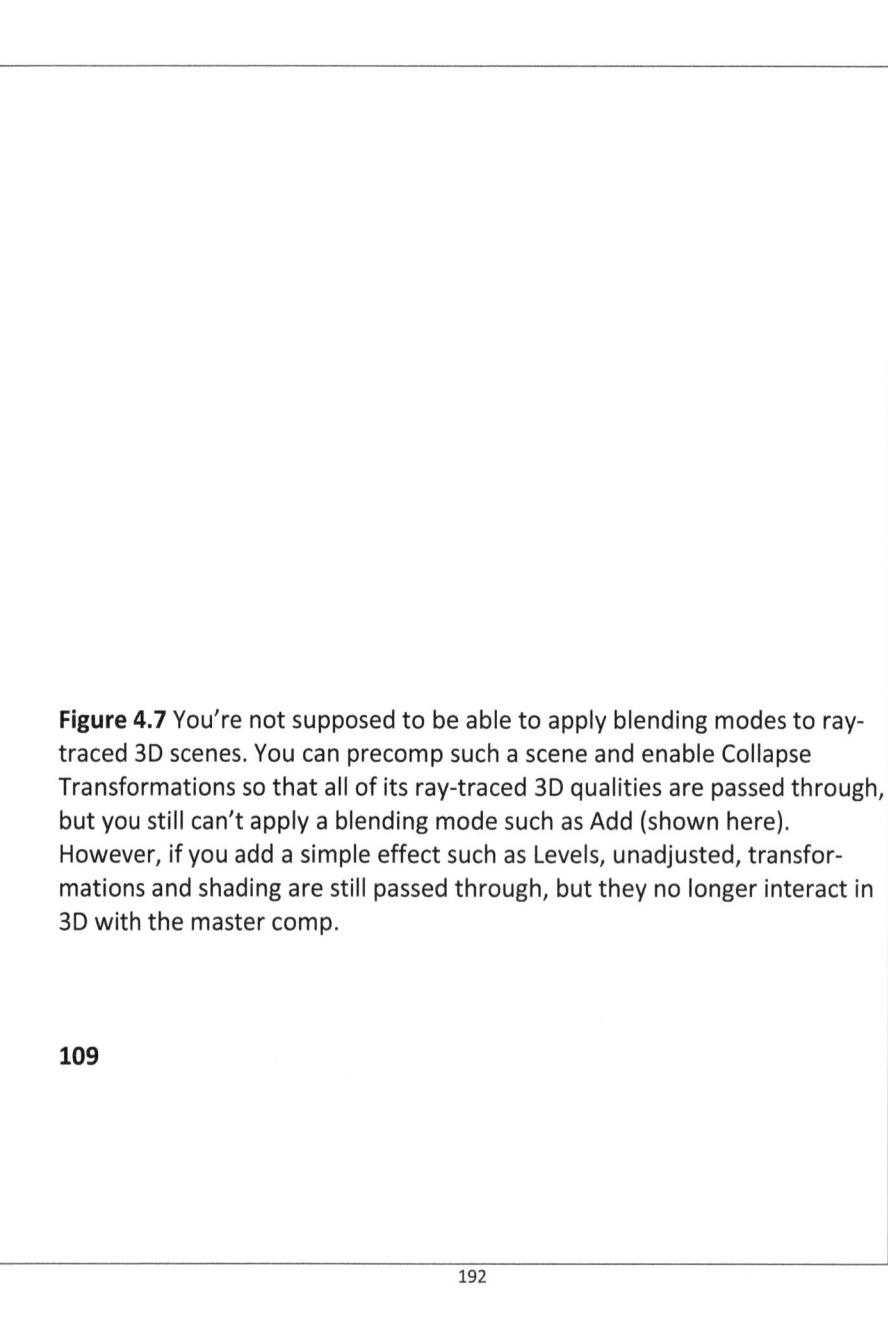

Figure 4.7 You're not supposed to be able to apply blending modes to ray-traced 3D scenes. You can precomp such a scene and enable Collapse Transformations so that all of its ray-traced 3D qualities are passed through, but you still can't apply a blending mode such as Add (shown here). However, if you add a simple effect such as Levels, unadjusted, transformations and shading are still passed through, but they no longer interact in 3D with the master comp.

109

Grow Bounds

Sometimes, enabling Collapse Transformations is not desirable—for example, if you set up 3D layers with a camera in a subcomp and don't want their position to be changed by a camera in the master comp. The Grow Bounds effect overcomes one specific (and fairly rare) problem (in which the embedded layer is too small for an applied effect), but it is also useful in cases where other effects create a comp boundary that leads visual data to appear cropped.

The Posterize Time effect will force any layer to the specified frame rate.

Alpha channel effects change the alphas of the layers below, not of the adjustment layer itself.

Nested time

After Effects is not rigid about time, but digital video itself is. You can freely mix and change frame rates among com- positions without changing the timing, as has been shown. However, because your source clips always have a very specific rate, pay close attention when you

import an image sequence

create a new composition

mix comps with different frame rates.

In the first two cases, you're just watching out for careless errors. But you might want to maintain specific frame rates in subcomps, in which case you must set them deliberately on the Advanced tab of the Composition Settings dialog.

Advanced Composition Settings

In addition to the Motion Blur settings covered in detail in Chapter 8, Composition Settings > Advanced contains two toggles that influence how time and space are handled when one composition is nested into another.

Preserve Frame Rate maintains the frame rate of the com-position wherever it goes— into another composition with a different frame rate, or into the render queue with different frame rate settings. So if a simple animation cycle looks right at 4 frames per second (fps), it won't be expanded across the higher frame rate, but will preserve the look of 4 fps.

Preserve Resolution When Nested controls what is called *concatenation*. Typically, if an element is scaled down in a precomp and the entire composition is nested into another comp and scaled up, the two operations are treated as one, so that no data loss occurs via quantization. This is concatenation, and it's usually a good thing. If the data in the subcomp is to appear pixilated, as if it were scaled up from a lower-resolution element, this toggle preserves the chunky pixel look.

Special Case: Adjustment and Guide Layers

Two special types of layers, adjustment and guide layers, offer extra benefits that might not be immediately appar-ent, and are often underused.

110

Adjustment Layers

From a nodal point of view, adjustment layers are a way of saying "at this point in the compositing process, I want these effects applied to everything that has already rendered." Because render order is not readily apparent in After Effects until you learn how it works, adjustment layers can seem trickier than they are.

The *adjustment layer* is itself invisible, but its effects are applied to all layers below it. It is a fundamentally simple feature with many uses. To create one, context-click in an empty area of the Timeline panel, and choose New > Adjustment Layer **(Ctrl+Alt+Y/Cmd+Opt+Y)** **(Figure 4.8)**.

Adjustment layers allow you to apply effects to an entire composition without precomping it. That by itself is pretty cool, but there's more:

Move the adjustment layer down the stack and any lay-ers above it are unaffected, because the render order in After Effects goes from the lowest layer upward.

Shorten the layer and the effects appear only on frames within the adjustment layer's In/Out points.

Use Opacity to attenuate any effect; most of them work naturally this way. Many effects do not themselves include such a direct control, even when it makes perfect sense to "dial it back 50%," which you can do by setting Opacity to 50%.

Apply a matte to an adjustment layer to hold out the effects to a specific area of the underlying image.

Add a blending mode and the adjustment layer is first applied and then blended back into the result **(Figure 4.9)**.

It's a good idea 99% of the time to make sure that an adjustment layer remains 2D, and you will most often also want it to be the size and length of the comp, as when applied. It's rare that you would ever want to move, rotate, or scale an adjustment layer in 2D or 3D, but it is possible to do so accidentally. If you enlarge the composition, resize the adjustment layers as well.

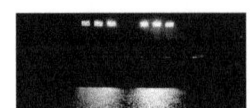

(b)

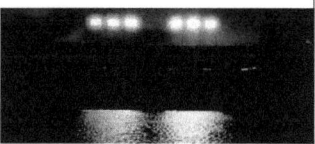

Figure 4.8 The highlighted column includes toggle switches, indicating an adjustment layer. Any layer can be tog-gled, but the typical way to set it is to create a unique layer. An adjustment layer created under Layer > New > Adjustment Layer (or via the shortcuts) is a white, comp-sized solid.

(c)

Figure 4.9 Here, the source plate image **(a)** is shown along with two alternates in which Camera Lens Blur has been applied via an adjustment layer, held out by a mask. With the adjustment layer blending mode set to Normal **(b)**, there is a subtle bloom of the background highlights, but changing it to Add **(c)** causes the effect to be applied as in **(b)** and then added over source image **(a)**.

(a)

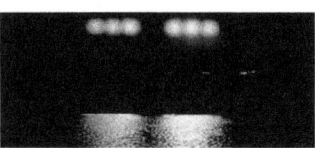

111

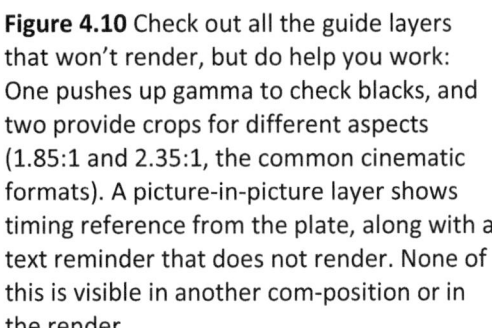

Figure 4.10 Check out all the guide layers that won't render, but do help you work: One pushes up gamma to check blacks, and two provide crops for different aspects (1.85:1 and 2.35:1, the common cinematic formats). A picture-in-picture layer shows timing reference from the plate, along with a text reminder that does not render. None of this is visible in another com-position or in the render.

Guide Layers

Like adjustment layers, *guide layers* are standard layers with special status. A guide layer appears in the current com-position but not in any subsequent compositions or the final render (unless it is specifically overridden in Render Settings). You can use this for

foreground reference clips (picture-in-picture timing reference, aspect ratio crop reference)

temporary backgrounds to check edges when creating a matte

text notes to yourself

adjustment layers that are used only to check images (described further in the next chapter); a layer can be both an adjustment and a guide layer.

Any image layer can be converted to a guide layer either by context-clicking it or by choosing Guide Layer from the Layer menu (**Figure 4.10**).

112

Image Pipeline, Global Performance Cache, and Render Speed

The *render pipeline* is the order in which operations happen; by controlling it, you can solve problems and overcome bottlenecks. For the most part, render order is plainly displayed in the timeline and follows consistent rules:

2D layers are calculated from the bottom to the top of the layer stack—the numbered layers in the timeline.

Layer properties (masks, effects, transforms, paint, and type) are calculated in strict top-to-bottom order (twirl down the layer to see it).

3D layers are instead calculated based on distance from the camera; coplanar 3D layers respect stacking order and should behave like 2D layers relative to one another.

So to review: In a 2D composition, After Effects starts at the bottom layer and calculates any adjustments to it in the order that properties are shown, top to bottom. Then, it calculates adjustments to the layer above it, composites the two of them together, and moves up the stack in this manner (**Figure 4.11**). Although effects within a given layer are generally calculated prior to transforms, an adjustment layer guarantees that its effects are rendered after the transforms of all layers below it.

Track mattes and blending modes are applied last, after all other layer properties (masks, effects, and transforms) have been calculated, *and* after their own mask, effect, and transform data are applied. Therefore, you don't generally need to pre-render a track matte simply because you've added masks and effects to it.

Global Performance Cache: Way Faster!

We're over 100 pages into the book and just now getting into the most revolutionary addition to the latest version of After Effects. You don't technically need a book to experi-ence what can be extraordinary benefits from how After Effects CS6 preserves your work in progress for instant playback; you probably already know and love this feature, but as a reader of a book like this you probably also want

3D calculations are precise well below the decimal level but do round at some point. To avoid render errors, precomp them in a nested 2D layer.

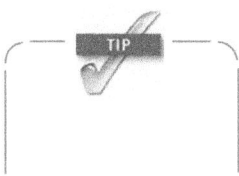

The Transform effect allows you to position, scale, or rotate a layer before other effects are applied, solely to avoid precomping.

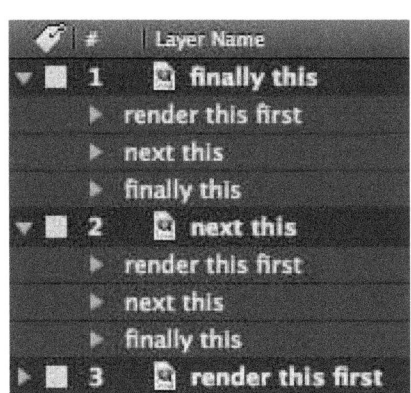

Figure 4.11 2D layers render starting with the bottom layer, rendering and compositing each layer above in order. Layer properties render in the order shown when twirled down; there is no direct way to change the order of these categories.

Although After Effects doesn't prohibit you from doing so, don't apply a track matte to another track matte and expect consistent results. Sometimes it works, but it's not really supposed to work, and most often it doesn't.

113

to know as much as you can about how it works so you can maximize what it does for you.

The feature name "Global Performance Cache" is a generic term for what is, in fact, a set of interrelated technologies:

a Global RAM cache that is smarter about dividing your work to save as many individual processes as possible

a persistent disk cache that saves those precalculated processes for continual reuse

an updated graphics pipeline that makes greater use of OpenGL to present and stream images onscreen, including the UI overlays that are a constant when working in After Effects

You have to hand it to the After Effects development team here. Engineers too easily assume they need to tear technology apart and rebuild it from scratch in order to modernize it. Global Performance Cache is the result of looking at what modern hardware can deliver that simply was not possible a few years ago, and figuring out how to make use of that hardware:

cheap and plentiful RAM, and the ability of a 64-bit operating system to access far more of it (up to 192 GB on Windows 7, and well in excess of the 2 GB per processor core recommended for After Effects)

fast attached storage, including SSD drives that rou-tinely double the access speed of even the fastest HDD drive or array

high-end graphics cards with GPUs that accelerate per-formance year after year at rates that way, way outstrip Moore's Law

In the past, After Effects has rather notoriously failed to take advantage of these advantages. Lots of RAM is no good if your RAM preview disappears each time you make an edit; fast storage doesn't mean spacebar play of a time-line in real-time; and until CS6, the high-end graphics card that you purchased to work in Maya or CINEMA 4D hardly made a dent in After Effects interactivity.

Each of these areas of performance is directly addressed in After Effects CS6. The result is completely subjective, but

114

can be quantified as a routine 10–20x acceleration of RAM previews. Depending on how often you review playback during your workday, this means either you can keep work-ing that much faster, or the whole way that you work with the application is changed.

Memory Acceleration: Global RAM Cache

After Effects has always loved plenty of RAM, but until CS6 it used it in a much more brute-force way. You have always needed lots of RAM to store and play back a given large-format clip using physical memory and perform opera-tions on that large frame. The brute-force part is that as soon as you made even a teeny change to all of that cached data, it all tended to be blown away, only to be recreated more or less from scratch the next time you previewed a frame or sequence.

By slicing a clip with its many selections and effects into discrete chunks and storing each of those render steps individually, After Effects CS6 greatly reduces the amount of re-rendering of cached footage. You can change a given effect setting or range of keyframes without disrupting other parts of the image and clip that are unrelated to that change.

Reusable frames are recognized anywhere on the timeline: when you use loop expressions (Chapters 8 and 10), remap time, or copy and paste keyframes. Duplicated layers or whole duplicated comps are also recognized.

The net result is that you can try something, preview the result without rendering from scratch, and undo the change without penalty. Since this, in essence, is how you spend your working day as an After Effects artist, the result-ing 5–15x speed increase ripples throughout the process, allowing you not only to get to a result more quickly but to try more options without worrying about the time cost.

This tends to work a lot better with 2D layers than with a ray-traced 3D comp. It is easy to consider an effect or setting in a 2D layer to be an island unto itself, but in 3D, light, reflection, shadows, refraction, and translucency are all considered to be influenced by the adjustment of a single element such as a light or the position of a layer.

115

Continuous Access: Persistent Disk Cache

Data in the RAM cache is now much less fragile because it is constantly backed up in a *persistent disk cache*. If you run out of RAM, increment and save to a new version of the project, or even quit the application and reopen the proj-ect. Its cache is available for instant playback and immedi-ate rendering (**Figure 4.12b**).

After Effects CS6 Persistent Disk Cache has been called "the closest thing After Effects will ever get to a cure for cancer."

Persistent disk cache is also the most tweakable of the Global Performance Cache options, and the one for which your choice of hardware may make the greatest difference. Here's a list of the most effective tweaks, followed by a breakdown:

dedicate **fast attached storage** to the After Effects cache

use the **Cache Work Area in Background** command as you work

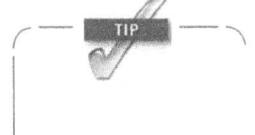

incorporate **Dynamic Link** with Premiere Pro

render locally

Want to see how caching behaves on individual layers? Under the Timeline panel menu, hold down Ctrl/Cmd and click Show Cache Indi-cators, even if it's already checked. Now each layer has its own blue or green bar if it's cached (**Figure 4.12a**). Turn it off when you have a good sense of how it works, because it will slow down your renders.

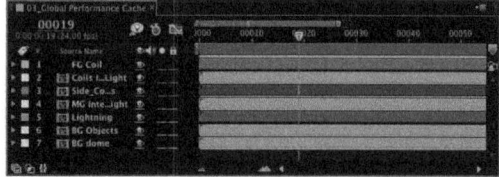

A

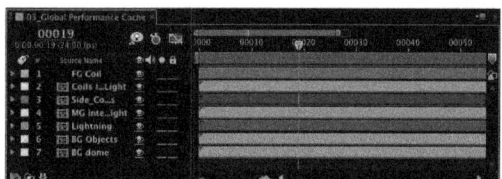

B

Figure 4.12 With Layer Cache Indicators on, you begin to see how After Effects breaks down the RAM cache into individual layers and even effects (**a**). With fast attached storage, you will see those green lines turn blue as they move from RAM to the disk (**b**).

Before drawing out the first three points in more detail, note that the persistent disk cache cannot be considered sharable or portable. Place the cache on a shared drive and point two systems to it and all you do is introduce the likeli-hood of instability; the two systems will not recognize those cached files in the same way and will simply continue to generate their own cache data. This data is designed to be accessed instantly and is cleverly designed to track a given comp and layers even as project versions change on a given system (**Figure 4.13**).

This is not to say that I haven't tried and succeeded at replacing the disk cache on a given system with one that's already preloaded with a bunch of rendered frames and effects, but I wouldn't make that standard practice. The disk cache is designed to be local to a given system. The benefit is that a cached comp may render faster locally than it will even on a large render network. The downside, if you want to think of it that way, is that the render net-work has essentially no opportunity to take advantage of a disk cache, at least not on the first pass.

Disk Cache Boost 1: Get Fast Attached Storage

The permanent disk cache can be a little like a huge RAM extension providing much longer memory and far greater capacity. As such, it's in your interest to maximize its per-formance and, if possible, capacity. Why? Not only because faster is better; After Effects actively evaluates whether it's in the application's best interests to commit a given process to disk. The greater the difference between processor and cache speed, the more likely a frame gets the blue cache indicator, ready to turn green at any time (and the faster it turns green, ready for real-time).

Let's start at the low end, with you laptop people. I know, I know, you are the cutting edge. But your single, slow hard disk drive will make you long for something better— something like a dedicated solid state drive, which at this writing is sparking a laptop evolution in which nearly useless DVD drives are replaced with a sled holding a high-capacity SSD. Yes, there is a cost involved. It will also set you free.

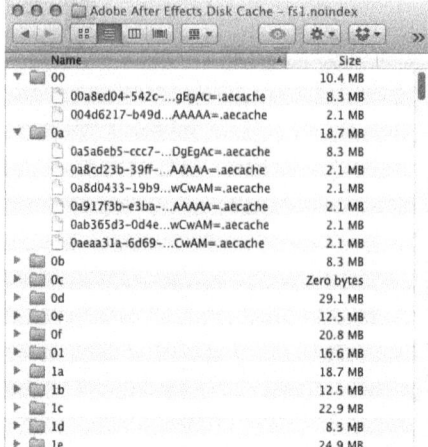

Figure 4.13 If you were thinking the disk cache is a bunch of easily recognized files you can share and edit, think again!

How do I get more stuff to cache?

You've followed the tip above to show layer cache indicators, and are dismayed to find a number of layers that don't cache, presumably because they don't pass the After Effects evaluation that it's not a faster option than re-rendering. You then have three options: load up, cheat, or get faster storage.

Add render-heavy effects to a given 2D layer, and at some point it will cache. Similarly, you can hack the preferences file (using instructions later in this chapter) and change the "proclivity" preference, the basic metric for caching.

The real, practical solution is to get more and faster attached storage. The faster the physical disk you have available for the hard-disk cache, the more likely that it will pass the test for providing better speed than simple re-rendering of elements.

Also, while a ray-traced 3D scene does cache nicely, ready to be replayed when you restart After Effects, changes to such a scene tend to wipe out the cache, because ray-tracing creates dependencies between all 3D elements in a scene.

117

Figure 4.14 The revolutionary power of fast attached storage.

At the other end—the high one—the release of After Effects CS6 coincided neatly with the debut of Fusion ioFX (**Figure 4.14**). It's not easy to quantify, but it's being regarded in After Effects circles as something like a half-terabyte extension to SDRAM, with the disk cache ready to fill it with your inspirations and missteps alike. It's all part of the process, and way less hard on your body than amphetamines, which never let you get out of the studio in time for a dinner date.

And in the middle, that striped RAID array you have attached to your system is still going to help you a bunch. Any drive other than the internal boot drive will work better, and if you edit footage professionally, you already have just such a dedicated drive available.

Bottom line? Everyone wins. Even on a laptop you can see 10–15x speed increases that will make you hungry to feed the disk cache more and faster storage space.

Disk Cache Boost 2: Commit a Comp

Disk caching in After Effects need not be a passive response, like Aslan, only appearing when not expected and most needed. It's true, you get all of the subcomps associated with the comp that you cache committed to disk as well (assuming After Effects judges them faster to render if committed to storage), so caching a master comp gets you a lot of free material to work with. But sometimes, for whatever reason, that master comp doesn't commit to disk when previewed, or more often, it needs way longer to render than you want to wait watching it draw frames.

I just realized as I typed the last sentence that the days of waiting and watching a RAM preview progress frame by frame could, in fact, be completely over if you want them to be. Composition > Cache Work Area in Background (**Ctrl/Cmd+Return**) renders a comp into the disk cache while you continue to work.

If you really hate waiting for a comp to preview, and have a half-decent system and something better to do with your time, you can select a whole set of comps in the Project panel and cache them. Yes, if you're on a non-CUDA-enabled Macbook Pro and those comps are all full of HD

118

ray-traced 3D animations, your system is going to sound like a jet preparing for takeoff and your laptop will scorch your lap. On the other hand, if you're on one of those systems that has more processor cores than you can count when you open up their little capacity meters in the system, well, you are finally going to get your money's worth.

Caveats? Downsides? You gotta pay to play. This is where gobs of low-latency storage is going to be your new best friend, other than the actual best friend that you get to spend time with when you are done for the day and not already burning the midnight oil. But there's always that CBB.

Disk Cache Boost 3: Rethink Dynamic Link

Odds are better than even that, alongside After Effects, sit a number of other apps (or *programs* as you Windows people and characters in Tron apparently call them) that also begin with the word "Adobe." Go ahead, take a look, I'll wait.

Oh, you're back! And you have just discovered that fully half the contents of the applications (programs) begin with A? Welcome to the world of video, in which company names start with A. While you wonder why you installed Flash Builder with no plans to build anything in Flash, go back, scroll down, and note the little nonlinear

editor that could. I'm talking about Premiere Pro.

No longer solely the favorite among wedding videogra-phers (and I say that with no disrespect, but let's face it, After Effects is not big with that group), Premiere Pro CS6 has become many people's favorite NLE, mine included. Like many others, I treated Premiere Pro as a utility, not a place I wanted to spend time working, and for me the CS6 version changes that. I find that I actually like working in it.

Premiere Pro has a unique ability to link directly to an After Effects comp. Dynamic Link is a feature that allows Adobe Premiere Pro to actually look inside an After Effects project for an existing comp that it can import (**Figure**

4.15), or designate a clip in a sequence as the basis for a new After Effects comp.

CBB stands either for Can't Be Bothered or Could Be Better. Both apply in visual effects circles, but unfortunately it's the latter that got the moniker.

119

Figure 4.15 If you've
never witnessed the
power of Dynamic Link to
peer inside an After
Effects Project from
Adobe Premiere Pro or
Adobe Media Encoder, it
may seem like magic.

Preferences > General > Dynamic Link with
After Effects Uses Project File Name with
Highest Number is unchecked by default, but
it could instead simply be called Make
Dynamic Link Usable in the Real World.

In the past, the difficulty with this approach has been that Premiere Pro has no real concept of render management, and the steps that you take for granted to make a preview render faster in After Effects, working at half or quarter resolution, aren't available. Imagine that every time you wanted to play something back, you had to render it at full resolution.

If you're thinking that Global Performance Cache helps in such a case, you are correct. Suppose you have a heavy comp that requires 10 seconds to render each frame at full resolution. If you cache the comp at full, Premiere Pro has access to those cached frames *even if After Effects isn't open.* Render the sequence and that clip is ready for real-time playback in seconds, not minutes or hours.

Note that you do, however, still have to render to get rid of the red line above that clip, even if it's completely cached at full resolution. And, when you do so, it doesn't add to the After Effects cache. The way to make this work is to generate a preview in After Effects. This still requires you

With either approach, there is an actual, live After Effects comp sitting in a Premiere Pro sequence. After Effects invis-ibly provides the ability to render it, headlessly, in the back-ground. As any change is made to the comp on the After Effects side, it remains up to date in the Premiere edit.

to perform an edit, but once you do so, it helps speed up the Premiere Pro timeline just as it does in After Effects.

Proxies, Previews, and Network Renders

Previous editions of this book advocated the use of proxies and previews as ways to accelerate the previewing and ren-dering process. This is exactly where Global Performance Cache changes the game, but only as long as you work on the "one artist, one project, one system" model, given that the cache is neither portable nor sharable.

For this reason, the old ways are still valid in any case where a project needs to be moved or shared, even if only for rendering purposes. The good news is that the cached data helps even this process to happen much more effi-ciently, because it is also used to render on the system that generated it.

Post-Render Options

Tucked away in the Render Queue panel, but easily visible if you twirl down the arrow next to Output Module, is a menu of three post-render actions to incorporate a render into a project. After the render is complete, you can use

Import simply to bring the result back into the project

Import & Replace Usage to replace the usage of the source comp in the project without blowing it away

Set Proxy to add a proxy to the source (the most elegant solution, but the most high-maintenance)

The latter two options even let you use the pick whip icon adjacent to the menu to connect whatever item in the Project panel needs replacement. If you've already created a pre-render or proxy, you can target that (**Figure 4.16**).

Proxies and Pre-Renders

Let's face it, dutifully rendering proxies is boring and will seem completely unnecessary with all of the new cache features—right up until the moment when you're in a rush and no longer have access to that cache, either when rendering remotely or handing off the project. Are you willing to buy some insurance on that cache? If so, this section is for you.

Preferences > Display > Show Rendering Progress in Info Panel and Flowchart shows what is happening on your system. It is disabled by default because it requires some extra processing power, but you may find you get that time back from the ability to spot and solve an obvious bottleneck.

121

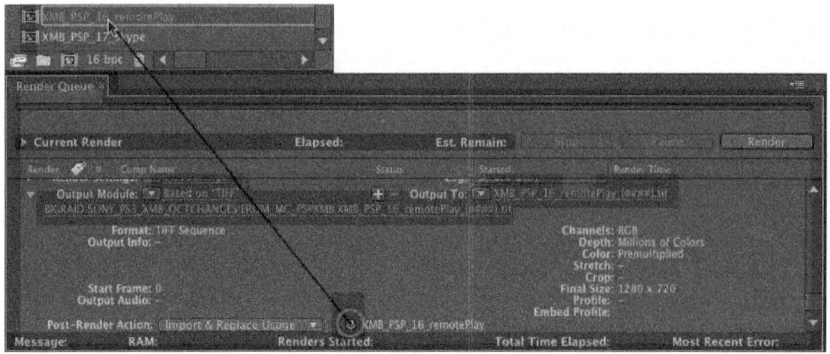

Figure 4.16 Virtually any project item can be the target for replacement or a proxy; click and drag the pick whip icon to choose the item to be replaced by the render.

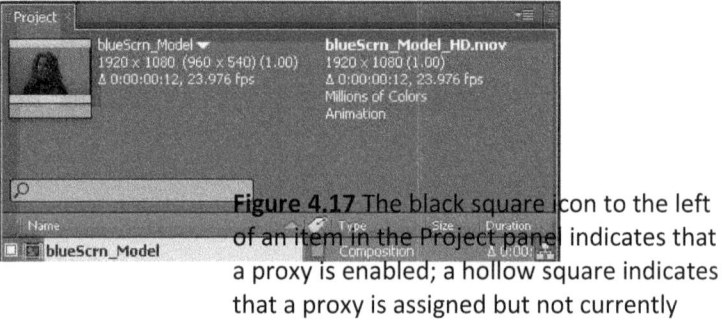

Figure 4.17 The black square icon to the left of an item in the Project panel indicates that a proxy is enabled; a hollow square indicates that a proxy is assigned but not currently

active. Both items are listed atop the Project panel, the active one in bold.

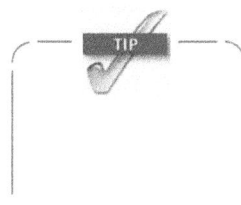

To remove a proxy from a project, select the item or items with proxies, context-click (or go to the File menu), and choose Set Proxy > None.

Any image or clip in your Project panel can be set with a proxy, which is an imported image or sequence that stands in for that item. Its pixel dimensions, color space, compres-sion, even its length and frame rate, can differ from the item it replaces. You can have a quick-and-dirty still or low-res, compressed, low-frame-rate clip stand in for a render-heavy comp.

To create a proxy, context-click an item in the Project panel and choose Create Proxy > Movie (or Still). A render queue item is created and, by default, renders at Draft quality and half-resolution; the Output Module settings create a video file with alpha, so that transparency is pre-served and Post-Render Action uses the Set Proxy setting.

Figure 4.17 shows how a proxy appears in the Project panel. Although the scale of the proxy differs from that of the source item, it is scaled automatically so that trans-form settings remain consistent. This is what proxies were designed to do: allow a low-resolution file to stand in, tem-porarily and nondestructively, for the high-resolution final.

There's another use for proxies. Instead of creating low-res temp versions, you can instead generate final quality pre-rendered elements. With a composition selected, choose Composition > Pre-render and change the settings to Best for Quality and Full for Resolution, making certain that Import and Replace Usage is set for Output Module.

122

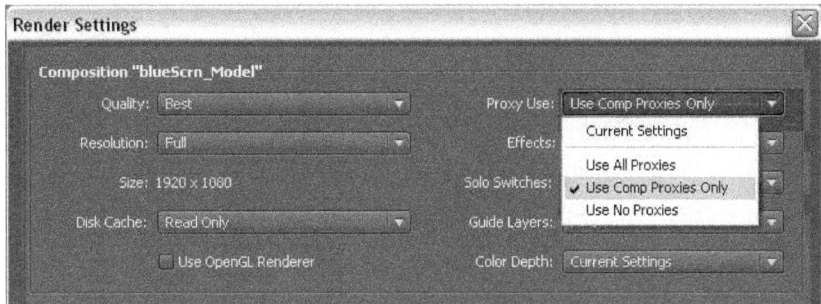

Figure 4.18 I typically set Proxy Use to Current Settings, but Use Comp Proxies Only lets you set low-res stand-ins for footage and full-resolution prerenders for comps, saving gobs of time.

Here's the key. By default, the source file or composition is used to render unless specifically set otherwise in Render Settings > Proxy Use. Choose Use Comp Proxies Only, Use All Proxies, or Current Settings (**Figure 4.18**) and proxies can be used in the final render.

Background Renders

Rendering from the render queue ties up the applica-tion and much of the machine's processing power, which used to mean that renders were left until lunchtime or off-hours. On a modern system with multiple processors, you can do much better than that (but take breaks anyway, they're good for you).

Adobe Media Encoder

It is easily overlooked that Adobe provides a background rendering application. Adobe Media Encoder (AME) has, for a couple of versions, been the best option to render certain video formats optimally—including Flash video (FLV and F4V), H.264, and MPEG-2—that don't work well with the frame-by-frame rendering model of After Effects. H.264, for example, is a "long GOP" format that relies on keyframes with lots of image data surrounded by in-between frames containing only shorthand for the changes for those keyframes, and it requires all of the frames to be rendered before it can work its magic. Only Adobe Media Encoder collects frames to compress them, and offers the option to render an After Effects comp on two passes.

Drag and drop an After Effects project into Adobe Media Encoder and you are able to look inside the project for renderable comps (**Figure 4.19**). You then choose render settings by either selecting them from the Preset Browser

123

Figure 4.19 Dynamic Link allows other Adobe applications to see your Project panel; Adobe Media Encoder uses this to let you render comps for heavily compressed video formats directly from the project.

variables you might miss that determine the priority and number of processors used to render (**Figure 4.20**).

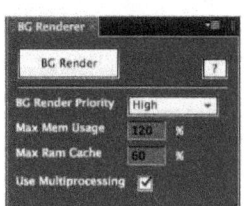

BG Renderer by Lloyd Alvarez (http://aescripts.com/bg-renderer/) may be the most universally used After Effects script. Not only does it automatically set up a background render by creating the command line for you, but it offers you a user interface for extra

Figure 4.20 BG Renderer uses ScriptUI, which means that it looks like it's part of the interface and can remain in an open panel as you work. When you're ready to render, you can specify priority and number of proces-sors; click the button and a terminal window opens that shows the render progress, line by line. You may miss the progress bar of the render queue, but if you can live without that, the benefit is that you can keep working while your machine renders.

and specifying your own (which you can then save as a preset).

The best thing about Adobe Media Encoder, in addition to multipass rendering, is that it provides the option to render in the background while you continue to work in After Effects, which a regular render doesn't permit. The challenge to AME is that it has a lot of presets without a lot of clues to which is the best for your situation. Worst of all, the layout for these settings is unfamiliar if you are accus-tomed to After Effects, and that alone stops a lot of people.

aerender

or customizing the settings by clicking on the Preset for the render item

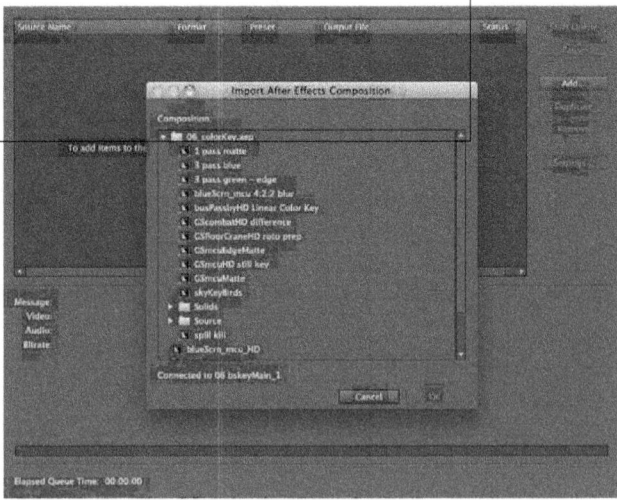

Background rendering allows a render to occur without the user interface, allowing you to continue working with it. The aerender application is found alongside the After Effects CS6 application on your system but runs via a command line (in Terminal Unix shell on Mac OS, or the command shell in Windows). You can drag it into the shell window to run it, or press **Enter** (**Return**) to reveal its Unix manual pages. This lists the arguments that can be added in quotes to the command aerender, and the location string of the project file.

But that's all such geeky gobbledygook when you have the BG Render script, which gives you access to all of these options via a panel in the After Effects UI, with no need to type any code.

Network Rendering

The aerender command is also used by third-party ren-dering solutions that work a lot like BG Renderer but are distributed across multiple machines on a network. These programs can manage renders on multiple machines and do tricky stuff like pause a render until an updated ele-ment from 3D is done, or automatically re-queue failed renders. Because these third-party rendering options— Rush Render Queue, Pipeline's Qube!, Überware's Smedge, or Muster by Virtual Vertex, to name a few— also support other terminal-friendly applications such as Maya and Nuke, it's an investment facilities that are large enough to have a render farm don't have to think twice about making.

These are not one-click installs and they're generally justi-fied only by dedicated machines and a dedicated nerd to manage it all. If that's beyond your facility at this point, you can still take advantage of all of this technology via the Cloud, or via a service such as Render Rocket. You upload your source files and get back rendered output. The downside for compositors is that we generally require a lot of source data to produce final shots, compared with 3D artists who can sometimes create a final cinematic image with virtually no source.

Watch Folder

The myopic and slightly dotty granddaddy of network rendering on After Effects is Watch Folder (File > Watch Folder). Watch Folder looks in a given folder for projects ready to be rendered; these are set up using the Collect Files option. The Adobe Help topic "Network rendering with watch folders and render engines" includes every-thing you need to know.

Watch Folder is kind of okay on small, intimate networks, but it requires much more hands-on effort than dedicated

Multiple After Effects Versions

When desperate, you can open more than one After Effects on Mac OS or Windows. This is memory intensive and not ideal for rendering (for which BG Renderer is much preferred), but it lets you work with two projects at once.

On Mac OS, locate Adobe After Effects CS6.app and duplicate it (**Cmd+D**); both will run after you clear the warning that the application has moved. On Windows, go to the Start menu, choose Run, type cmd, and click OK. In the DOS shell that opens, drag in AfterFX.exe from your Programs folder and then add −m (that's a space, a dash, and m as in "multiple"). Voilà, a second version initializes.

Suppose you just have one machine and a big render. You want it to keep running but shut down the system when it's done, and even notify you remotely that the render was a success. Render, Email, Save, and Shutdown by Lloyd Alvarez (http://aescripts.com/render-email-incremental-save-and-shutdown/) exists for this purpose; just queue up your render and fire one of them off.

slow you down on a network).

Preferences > Import: 29.97 for broadcast, 24 fps for film, 23.976 for both (film for broad-cast), and 25 fps for PAL-derived systems.

Preferences > Media & Disk Cache: Choose a folder on a fast, attached disk.

Setting Preferences and Project Settings Here are a few default preferences I always change.:

Preferences > Appearance: Cycle Mask Colors; on.

Preferences > General > Levels of Undo: Got RAM? Set this to 99.

. **Preferences > Auto-Save**: On.

Preferences > General: Check the options Allow Scripts to Write Files and Access Network.

Preferences > General: Toggle Default Spatial Interpolation to Linear.

Press **Alt+Ctrl+Shift**

Preferences > General: Dynamic Link with After Effects Uses Project File Name with High-est Number.

(**Opt+Cmd+Shift**) immediately after launching After Effects to reset Preferences. Hold **Alt** (**Opt**) while clicking OK to delete the shortcuts file as well.

Preferences > Display: Check all four boxes (unless you love those little thumbnails; they can

render management software, and it breaks easily, at which point it requires human intervention. Since individual systems have become so powerful, it's easy to become lazy about taking the trouble required to set up a Watch Folder render, but if you're up against a deadline, don't have the dedicated software, and want to maximize multiple machines, it will do the trick.

Optimize a Project

Here are a few more workflow tweaks to get the best per-formance out of After Effects.

Hack Shortcuts, Text Preferences, or Projects

Some people are comfortable sorting through lines of code gibberish to find editable tidbits. If you're one of those people, After Effects Shortcuts and Preferences are saved as text files that are fully editable and relatively easy to understand. Unless you're comfortable with basic hacking (learning how code works by looking at other bits of code), however, I don't recommend it. The files are located as follows:

Windows: [drive]:\Users\[user name]\AppData\ Roaming\Adobe\After Effects\11.0

Mac: [drive]:/Users/[user profile]/Library/ Preferences/Adobe/After Effects/11.0/

Mac OS X started hiding the User/Library folder with the release of 10.7 (Lion). The easiest way to reveal it from the Finder is to select Go > Go to Folder and then type Library. The names of the files are

Adobe After Effects 11.0-x64 Prefs.txt

Adobe After Effects 11.0 Shortcuts

These can be opened with any text editor that doesn't add its own formatting and works with Unicode. Make a backup copy before editing by simply duplicating the file (any variation in the filename causes it not to be recognized by After Effects). Revert to the backup by giving it the original filename should anything start to go haywire after the edit.

The Shortcuts file includes a bunch of comments at the top (each line begins with a # sign). The shortcuts themselves are arranged in a specific order that must be preserved, and if you add anything, it must be substituted in the exact right place.

Be extra careful when editing Preferences—a stray charac-ter in this file can make After Effects unstable. Most of the contents should not be touched, but here's one example of a simple and useful edit (for studios where a dot is preferred before the number prefix instead of the under-score): Change

"Sequence number prefix" = "_"

to

"Sequence number prefix" = "."

This is the format often preferred by Maya, for example.

In other cases, a simple and easily comprehensible numeri-cal value can be changed:

"Eye Dropper Sample Size No Modifier" = "1"
"Eye Dropper Sample Size With Modifier" = "5"

In many cases, the value after the = is a binary yes/no value, expressed as 0 for no and 1 for yes, so if you're nos-talgic for how the After Effects render chime sounded in its first several versions, find

"Play classic render chime" = "0"

and change the 0 to a 1. Save the file, restart After Effects, and invoke those 20th-century glory days of the beige Mac. Ask an After Effects veteran sometime what that chime evokes, and get ready to buy that warrior a beer.

XML

After Effects projects can be saved as .aepx files. These work the same way but are written in plain Unicode text; you can edit them with an ordinary text editor. Most of what is in these files is untouchable; the main use is to locate and change file paths to swap footage sources with-out having to do so manually in the UI. If that means noth-ing to you, you're probably not the shell scripting nerd for whom a feature like that was created.

A fantastic script for specifying your own modifier keys called KeyEd Up was developed specifically for After Effects by Jeff Almasol, author of other scripts included with

this book. Find it on Adobe After Effects Exchange at http://tinyurl.com/6cu6nq.

n-replace-paths/) may save you the need to dig around

in an .aepx file to change footage source locations; it also makes use of regular expressions to make the matching process more sophisti-cated than what is possible with an ordinary text editor.

Batch Search-n-Replace Paths by Lloyd Alvarez (http://aescripts.com/ batch-search-

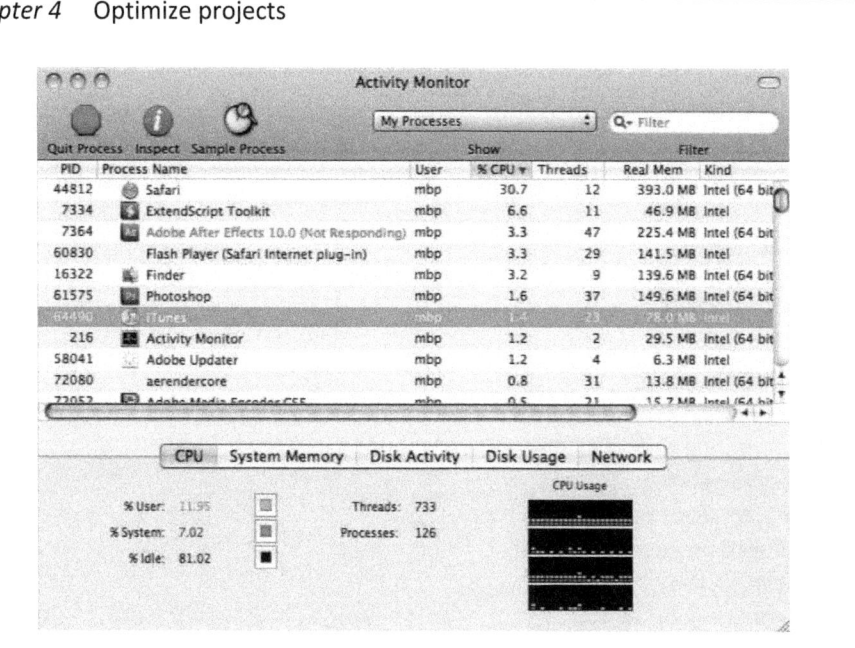

Figure 4.21 The Process ID for the nonresponding application is shown in the left column.

the application to crash and auto-save.

On the Mac: Force a Crash

When After Effects does crash, it attempts to do so gracefully, offering the option to save before it exits. The auto-save options, if used properly, further diminish the likelihood of losing project data. On Mac OS X, an extra feature may come in handy when the application becomes unresponsive without crashing.

Open Activity Monitor and look for After Effects to get its PID number (**Figure 4.21**). Now open Terminal, and enter kill –SEGV ### where "###" is replaced by the After Effects PID value. This should cause

Memory Management

Chapter 1 included advice about running After Effects with multiprocessing enabled on a system with multiple cores and a good deal of physical memory. If you see your system's wait icon come up—the hourglass in Windows, the spinning ball on a Mac—that means there is a fight going on somewhere for system resources. In addition to follow-ing the advice in Chapter 1 to leave memory available for outside applications, you may have to quit any application that is both resource-intensive and outside the memory pool managed by After Effects (in other words, any app besides Adobe Premiere Pro, Encore, Prelude, Adobe Media Encoder, or Photoshop).

The best idea is to provide the system with more physical memory. As a rule of thumb, 2 GB of RAM per proces-sor core is not a bad guide. You can go below this to, say, 1.5 GB per core, but much lower and your system will be less efficient unless you also limit the number

of cores After Effects uses (in Preferences > Memory & Multiprocessing).

These Are the Fundamentals

You've reached the end of Section I (if you're reading this book linearly, that is), and we've done everything we could think of to raise your game with the After Effects work-flow. Now it's time to focus more specifically on the art of visual effects. Section II, "Effects Compositing Essentials," will teach you the techniques, and Section III, "Creative Explorations," will show you how they work in specific effects situations.

So here comes the fun part.

Although the RAM cache is less likely to become full or fragmented with 64-bit processing, Throttle-n-Purge by Lloyd Alvarez (http://aescripts. com/throttle-n-purge/) provides a UI panel with a one-button solution to clear all caches and get maximum efficiency out of a preview render (**Figure 4.22**). It also lets you switch bit depths, more easily than the Project panel, and it lets you turn multiprocessing on and off without opening Preferences.

Figure 4.22 Throttle-n-Purge exposes controls to help you manage memory

usage as well as offering a one-button

option to purge all caches (undos and

image buffers) and start over.

Importing and interpreting footage items

About imported files and footage items

You import source files into a project as the basis for *footage items* and use them as sources for *layers*. The same file can be the source for multiple footage items, each with its own interpretation settings. Each footage item can be used as the source for one or more layers. You work with collections of layers in a *composition*.

You primarily work with footage items in the Project panel. You can use the Footage panel to evaluate footage and perform simple editing tasks, such as trimming the duration of a footage item.

You can import many different kinds of files, collections of files, or components of files as sources for individual footage items, including moving image files, still-image files, still-image sequences, and audio files. You can even create footage items yourself within After Effects, such as solids and precompositions. You can import footage items into a project at any time.

When you import files, After Effects does not copy the image data itself into your project but creates a reference link to the source of the footage item, which keeps project files relatively small.

If you delete, rename, or move an imported source file, you break the reference link to that file. When a link is broken, the name of the source file appears in italics in the Project panel, and the File Path column lists it as missing. If the footage item is available, you can reestablish the link—usually just by double-clicking the item and selecting the file again.

You can find footage items for which the source items are missing by typing missing in the search field in the Project ⌐ panel. See Search and filter in the Timeline, Project, and Effects & Presets panels.

To reduce rendering time and increase performance, it is often best to prepare footage before you import it into After Effects. For example, it is often better to scale or crop a still image in Photoshop before you bring it into After Effects, rather than scaling and cropping the image in After Effects. It is better to perform an operation once in Photoshop than to force After Effects to perform the same action many times per second—once for each frame in which the image appears.

To save time and minimize the size and complexity of a project, import a source item as a single footage item and then use it multiple times in a composition. It is occasionally useful, however, to duplicate a footage item and interpret each differently. For example, you can use the same footage at two different frame rates.

If you use another application to modify a footage item that is used in a project, the changes appear in After Effects the next time that you open the project or select the footage item and choose File > Reload Footage.

To replace the source footage item for a layer with another footage item, without affecting changes made to the layer ⌐ properties, select the layer and then Alt-drag (Windows) or Option-drag (Mac OS) the new footage item onto the layer in the Timeline panel.

To replace all uses of selected footage items with another footage item, select footage items in the Project panel, and then ⊙ Alt-drag (Windows) or Option-drag (Mac OS) the new footage item onto a selected footage item in the Project panel.

When After Effects imports video and audio in some formats, it processes and caches versions of these items that it can readily access when generating previews. This caching greatly improves performance for previews, because the video and audio items do not need to be reprocessed for each preview.

For more information about importing assets, see this video tutorial on the Creative COW website by Andrew Devis.

Native encoding and decoding of QuickTime files

After Effects can natively decode and encode QuickTime (.mov) files using the GoPro CineForm codecs on Mac OS and Windows. This means that you do not need to install additional codecs to use and create such files.

In MOV, After Effects has native import support for the following uncompressed formats:

DV, IMX, MPEG2, XDCAM, h264, JPEG, Avid DNxHD, Avid DNxHR, Apple ProRes, AVCI, and GoPro CineForm Native export support is available for the following uncompressed formats:

Avid DNxHD, Avid DNxHR, DV, and GoPro CineForm

Note: *Because After Effects can natively import and export many codecs (listed above), QuickTime is not required on Windows. For more details about compatibility issues, read the blog post QuickTime on Windows*

Supported import formats

Some filename extensions—such as MOV, AVI, MXF, FLV, and F4V—denote container file formats rather than denoting a specific audio, video, or image data format. Container files can contain data encoded using various compression and encoding schemes. After Effects can import these container files, but the ability to import the data that they contain is dependent on which codecs (specifically, decoders) are installed.

By installing additional codecs, you can extend the ability of After Effects to import additional file types. Many codecs must be installed into the operating system (Windows or Mac OS) and work as a component inside the QuickTime or Video for Windows formats. Contact the manufacturer of your hardware or software for more information about codecs that work with the files that your specific devices or applications create.

Importing and using some files requires the installation of additional Import plug-ins. (See Plug-ins.)

Adobe Premiere Pro can capture and import many formats that After Effects can't import natively. You can bring data from Adobe Premiere Pro into After Effects in many ways. (See Working with Adobe Premiere Pro and After Effects.)

For workflow guides and updates for P2, RED, XDCAM, AVCCAM, and DSLR cameras and footage, see the Adobe website.

Audio formats

Adobe Sound Document (ASND; multi-track files imported as merged single track)

Advanced Audio Coding (AAC, M4A)

Audio Interchange File Format (AIF, AIFF)

MP3 (MP3, MPEG, MPG, MPA, MPE)

Video for Windows (AVI; requires QuickTime on Mac OS)

Waveform (WAV)

Still-image formats

Adobe Illustrator (AI, AI4, AI5, EPS, PS; continuously rasterized)

Adobe PDF (PDF; first page only; continuously rasterized)

Adobe Photoshop (PSD)

Bitmap (BMP, RLE, DIB)

Camera Raw (TIF, CRW, NEF, RAF, ORF, MRW, DCR, MOS, RAW, PEF, SRF, DNG, X3F, CR2, ERF)

Cineon/DPX (CIN, DPX with 8-, 10-, 12-, and 16-bpc DPX files, including those with an alpha channel and timecode)

Discreet RLA/RPF (RLA, RPF; 16 bpc; imports camera data)

EPS

GIF

JPEG (JPG, JPE)

Maya camera data (MA)

Maya IFF (IFF, TDI; 16 bpc)

OpenEXR (EXR, SXR, MXR; 32 bpc)

PICT (PCT)

Portable Network Graphics (PNG; 16 bpc)

Radiance (HDR, RGBE, XYZE; 32 bpc)

SGI (SGI, BW, RGB; 16 bpc)

Softimage (PIC)

Note: *3D Channel effect plug-ins from fnord software are included with After Effects to provide access to multiple layers and channels of OpenEXR files. (See .)*

Note: After Effects can also read ZPIC files corresponding to imported PIC files. See Importing and using 3D files from other applications.)

Targa (TGA, VDA, ICB, VST)

TIFF (TIF)

You can import files of any still-image format as a sequence. See Preparing and importing still images .

Video and animation formats

Animated GIF (GIF)

Avid DNxHR

HEVC (H.265) MPEG-4

Support for ARRIRAW files from the ARRI ALEXA, or ARRIFLEX D-21 cameras For more information on ARRIRAW files, see the ARRIRAW FAQ on the ARRI Group website.

CinemaDNG

Note: CinemaDNG is a subset of Camera Raw. A subset of Camera Raw settings can be accessed via More Options in the Interpret Footage dialog box. Color management for CinemaDNG includes the same color spaces as After Effects existing Camera Raw: Adobe RGB, sRGB IEC619662.1, ColorMatch RGB, and ProPhoto RGB.

DV (in MOV or AVI container, or as containerless DV stream)

Last updated 3/8/2018

111

Importing footage

Electric Image (IMG, EI)

FLV, F4V

QuickTime (MOV; 16 bpc, only for codecs that do not have any native decoders)

Video for Windows (AVI, WAV; requires QuickTime on Mac OS)

Windows Media File (WMV, WMA, ASF; Windows only)

XDCAM HD and XDCAM EX

RED (R3D)

Media eXchange Format (MXF)

MXF is a container format. After Effects can only import some kinds of data contained within MXF files. After Effects can import the Op-Atom variety of MXF files used by Panasonic video cameras to record to Panasonic P2 media. After Effects can import video from these MXF files using the AVC-Intra 50, AVC-Intra 100, DV, DVCPRO, DVCPRO50, and DVCPRO HD codecs. After Effects can also import XDCAM HD files in MXF format, the MXF OP1format, which contains MPEG-2 video that complies with the XDCAM HD format.

MPEG-1, MPEG-2, and MPEG-4 formats: MPEG, MPE, MPG, M2V, MPA, MP2, M2A, MPV, M2P, M2T, M2TS (AVCHD), MP4, M4V, M4A

SWF (continuously rasterized)

Project formats

Adobe Premiere Pro 1.0, 1.5, 2.0, CS3, CS4, CS5, CS6, and CC (PRPROJ; 1.0, 1.5, and 2.0 Windows only), and later projects

Adobe After Effects 6.0 and later binary projects in After Effects CS5 (AEP, AET)

After Effects 7 can open projects from After Effects 3.0 through After Effects 7.

Adobe After Effects CS4 and later XML projects (AEPX)

The Automatic Duck Pro Import AE plug-in is now bundled with the application, and called Pro Import After Effects. With it, you can import AAF and OMF files from an Avid system, XML files from Final Cut Pro 7, or earlier, and project files from Motion 4, or earlier. For more information on using Pro Import After Effects, see its User Guide, accessible by choosing File > Import > Pro Import After Effects, then clicking the Help button.

You can also import Final Cut Pro projects into Premiere Pro and then bring that project's components into After Effects.

In this video by Todd Kopriva and video2brain, learn how to import projects using Pro Import After Effects. We demonstrate using a Final Cut Pro project, but the same procedure works for other formats, such as XML, AAF, and OMF.

Note:

After Effects can also read EIZ files corresponding to imported EI files. See Importing and using 3D files from other applications.)

Some MPEG data formats are stored in container formats with filename extensions that are not recognized by After Effects; examples include .vob and .mod. In some cases, you can import these files into After Effects after changing the filename extension to one of the recognized filename extensions. Because of variations in implementation in these container formats, compatibility is not guaranteed.

For information about MPEG formats, see the MPEG website and the MPEG page on the Wikipedia website.

Before working with QuickTime, read the alert issued by United States Computer Emergency Readiness Team in April 2016, which recommends Windows users uninstall Apple QuickTime from their computers.

Last updated 3/8/2018

112

Importing footage

R3D files are interpreted as containing 32-bpc colors in a non-linear HDTV (Rec. 709) color space. The RED R3D Source Settings color adjustments don't preserve overbright values. Color adjustments done within After Effects do preserve overbright colors when you work in 32-bpc (bits per channel) color. To avoid clipping, manipulate exposure in After Effects, rather than in the footage interpretation stage in the RED R3D Source Settings dialog box. (For more information on using R3D files, see the RED website and the Adobe website.)

After Effects can import Sony XDCAM HD assets if they were recorded to MXF files. After Effects cannot import XDCAM HD assets in IMX format. After Effects can import Sony XDCAM EX assets stored as essence files with the .mp4 filename extension in a BPAV directory. For information about the XDCAM format, see this PDF document on the Sony website.

SWF files are imported with an alpha channel. Audio is not retained. Interactive content and scripted animation are not retained. Animation defined by keyframes in the main, top-level movie is retained.

Import footage items

You can import media files into your project either by using the Import dialog box or by dragging. The imported footage items appear in the Project panel.

If the Interpret Footage dialog box appears after you import a footage item, it contains an unlabeled alpha channel, and you must select an alpha channel interpretation method or click Guess to let After Effects determine how to interpret the alpha channel. (See Alpha channel interpretation: premultiplied or straight.)

Import footage items using the Import dialog box

Choose File > Import > File, choose File > Import > Multiple Files, or double-click an empty area of the Project panel.

If you choose Import Multiple Files, then you can perform the next step more than once without needing to choose an Import command multiple times.

To display only supported footage files (excluding project files), choose All Footage Files from the Files Of Type ▾ (Windows) or Enable (Mac OS) menu.

Do one of the following:

Select a file, and then click Open.

Ctrl-click (Windows) or Command-click (Mac OS) multiple files to select them, and then click Open.

Click a file and then Shift-click another file to select a range of files, and then click Open.

(Windows only) Select an entire folder, and then click Import Folder.

Note: *If the Sequence option is selected, multiple files from the folder are imported as a sequence of still images.*

Import footage items by dragging

If you always want the layered still-image files that you drag into After Effects to be imported as a composition, choose ▾ Edit > Preferences > Import (Windows) or After Effects > Preferences > Import (Mac OS), and choose Composition or Composition - Retain Layer Sizes from the Drag Import Multiple Items As menu. (See Import a still-image sequence as a composition.)

To import a single file, drag it from Windows Explorer (Windows) or the Finder (Mac OS) into the Project panel.

To import the contents of a folder as a sequence of still images that appear in the Project panel as a single footage item, drag a folder from Windows Explorer (Windows) or the Finder (Mac OS) into the Project panel.

Last updated 3/8/2018

113

Importing footage

To import the contents of the folder as individual footage items that appear in the Project panel in a folder, Alt-drag a folder from Windows Explorer (Windows) or Option-drag a folder from the Finder (Mac OS) into the Project panel.

To import a rendered output file from the Render Queue panel, drag the corresponding output module from the Render Queue panel into the Project panel.

Note: *If you drag an output module from the Render Queue panel into the Project panel before rendering, After Effects creates a placeholder footage item. References to the placeholder footage item are automatically replaced when the output module is rendered; the placeholder footage item itself is not replaced.*

Interpret footage items

After Effects uses a set of internal rules to *interpret* each footage item that you import according to its best guess for the source file's pixel aspect ratio, frame rate, color profile, and alpha channel type. If After Effects guesses wrong, or if you want to use the footage differently, you can modify these rules for all footage items of a particular kind by editing the interpretation rules file (interpretation rules.txt), or you can modify the interpretation of a specific footage item using the Interpret Footage dialog box.

The interpretation settings tell After Effects the following about each footage item:

How to interpret the interaction of the alpha channel with other channels (See Alpha channel interpretation: premultiplied or straight.)

What frame rate to assume for the footage item (See Frame rate.)

Whether to separate fields and, if so, what field order to assume (See Interlaced video and separating fields.)

Whether to remove 3:2 or 24Pa pulldown (See Remove 3:2 or 24Pa pulldown from video.)

The pixel aspect ratio of the footage item (See Pixel aspect ratio and frame aspect ratio.)

The color profile of the footage item (See Interpret a footage item by assigning an input color profile.)

Note: In all of these cases, the information is used to make decisions about how to interpret data in the imported footage item—to tell After Effects about the input footage. The interpretation settings in the Interpret Footage dialog box should match the settings used to create the source footage file. Do not use the interpretation settings to try to specify settings for your final rendered output.

Generally, you don't need to change interpretation settings. However, if a footage item isn't of a common kind, After Effects may need additional information from you to interpret it correctly.

You can use the controls in the Color Management section of the Interpret Footage dialog box to tell After Effects how to interpret the color information in a footage item. This step is usually only necessary when the footage item does not contain an embedded color profile.

When you preview in the Footage panel, you see the results of the footage interpretation operations.

Jeff Almasol provides a script on his redefinery website that you can use to make guessing the 3:2 pulldown, 24Pa pulldown, or alpha channel interpretation more convenient.

Note: Select Preview in the Interpret Footage dialog box to preview the results of the settings made in this dialog box before you accept the changes.

Interpret a single footage item using the Interpret Footage dialog box

Select a footage item in the Project panel and do one of the following:

Click the Interpret Footage ⬛ button at the bottom of the Project panel.

Drag the footage item to the Interpret Footage button.

Last updated 3/8/2018

114

Importing footage

Choose File > Interpret Footage > Main.

Press Ctrl+Alt+G (Windows) or Command+Option+G (Mac OS).

Interpret a proxy using the Interpret Footage dialog box

Select the original footage item in the Project panel and do one of the following:

Alt-click (Windows) or Option-click (Mac OS) the Interpret Footage ✎ button at the bottom of the Project panel.

Alt-drag (Windows) or Option-drag (Mac OS) the footage item to the Interpret Footage button.

Choose File > Interpret Footage > Proxy.

Apply Interpret Footage settings to multiple footage items

You can ensure that different footage items use the same settings by copying interpretation settings from one item and applying them to others.

In the Project panel, select the item with the interpretation settings that you want to apply.

Choose File > Interpret Footage > Remember Interpretation.

Select one or more footage items in the Project panel.

Choose File > Interpret Footage > Apply Interpretation.

Edit interpretation rules for all items of a specific kind

The interpretation rules file contains the rules that specify how After Effects interprets footage items. In most cases, you don't need to customize the interpretation rules file. When you import a footage item, After Effects looks for a match in the interpretation rules file, and then determines interpretation settings for the footage item. You can override these settings after importing, using the Interpret Footage dialog box.

In most cases, the name of the interpretation rules file is interpretation rules.txt; however, some updates to After Effects install a new interpretation rules file with a name that indicates the updated version number, and the updated application uses this new file. If you've made changes to the old interpretation rules file, you may need to apply those changes to the new file, too.

Locations of the interpretation rules file in After Effects CC:

(Windows) <drive>\Users\<username>\AppData\Roaming\Adobe\After Effects <13.0>

(Mac OS) <drive>/Users/<username>/Library/Preferences/Adobe/After Effects <13.0> Locations of the interpretation rules file in previous versions of After Effects CC:

(Windows) <drive>\Users\<username>\AppData\Roaming\Adobe\After Effects <12.x>

(Mac OS) <drive>/Users/<username>/Library/Preferences/Adobe/After Effects <12.x>

Quit After Effects.

As a precaution, make a backup copy of the interpretation rules file. By default, this file is in the same location as the After Effects application.

Open the interpretation rules file in a text editor.

Modify the settings according to the instructions in the file.

Last updated 3/8/2018

115

Importing footage

Note: *You must supply a four-character file-type code for each footage type or codec. If you don't know the code for a file or codec in a project, press Alt (Windows) or Option (Mac OS) as you select the file in the Project panel. The file-type code and codec code (if the file is compressed) appear in the last line of the file description at the top of the Project panel.*

Save interpretation rules.txt.

Alpha channel interpretation: premultiplied or straight

Image files with alpha channels store transparency information in one of two ways: straight or premultiplied. Although the alpha channels are the same, the color channels differ.

With straight (or unmatted) channels, transparency information is stored only in the alpha channel, not in any of the visible color channels. With straight channels, the results of transparency aren't visible until the image is displayed in an application that supports straight channels.

With premultiplied (or matted) channels, transparency information is stored in the alpha channel and also in the visible RGB channels, which are multiplied with a background color. Premultiplied channels are sometimes said to be matted with color. The colors of semitransparent areas, such as feathered edges, are shifted toward the background color in proportion to their degree of transparency.

Some software lets you specify the background color with which the channels are premultiplied; otherwise, the background color is usually black or white.

Straight channels retain more accurate color information than premultiplied channels. Premultiplied channels are compatible with a wider range of programs, such as Apple QuickTime Player. Often, the choice of whether to use images with straight or premultiplied channels has been made before you receive the assets to edit and composite. Adobe Premiere Pro and After Effects recognize both straight and premultiplied channels, but only the first alpha channel they encounter in a file containing multiple alpha channels.

Setting the alpha channel interpretation correctly can prevent problems when you import a file, such as undesirable colors at the edge of an image or a loss of image quality at the edges of the alpha channel. For example, if channels are interpreted as straight when they are actually premultiplied, semitransparent areas retain some of the background color. If a color inaccuracy, such as a halo, appears along the semitransparent edges in a composition, try changing the interpretation method.

A footage item with premultiplied channels (top) appears with a black halo when interpreted as Straight-Unmatted (lower-left). When the footage item is interpreted as Premultiplied-Matted With Color and the background color is specified as black, the halo does not appear (lower-right).

You can use the Remove Color Matting effect to remove the fringes from the semi-transparent areas of a layer by unmultiplying it.

Last updated 3/8/2018

116

Importing footage

Set the alpha channel interpretation for a footage item

In the Project panel, select a footage item.

Choose File > Interpret Footage > Main.

If you want to switch the opaque and transparent areas of the image, select Invert Alpha.

In the Alpha section, select an interpretation method:

Guess Attempts to determine the type of channels used in the image. If After Effects cannot guess confidently, it beeps.

Ignore Disregards transparency information contained in the alpha channel. **Straight - Unmatted** Interprets the channels as straight.

Premultiplied - Matted With Color Interprets channels as premultiplied. Use the eyedropper or color picker to specify the color of the background with which the channels were premultiplied.

Set the default alpha channel preferences

Choose Edit > Preferences > Import (Windows) or After Effects > Preferences > Import (Mac OS).

Choose options from the Interpret Unlabeled Alpha As menu. The options in this menu are similar to the options in the Interpret Footage dialog box. Ask User specifies that the Interpret Footage dialog box opens each time a footage item with an unlabeled alpha channel is imported.

Frame rate

The composition frame rate determines the number of frames displayed per second, and how time is divided into frames in the time ruler and time display. In other words, the composition frame rate specifies how many times per second images are sampled from the source footage items, and it specifies the time divisions at which keyframes can be set.

Note: *After Effects contains a menu for drop-frame or non-drop-frame timecode in the Composition Settings dialog box.*

In previous releases, this option was a global setting per project.

Composition frame rate is usually determined by the type of output that you are targeting. NTSC video has a frame rate of 29.97 frames per second (fps), PAL video has a frame rate of 25 fps, and motion picture film typically has a frame rate of 24 fps. Depending on the broadcast system, DVD video can have the same frame rate as NTSC video or PAL video, or a frame rate of 23.976. Cartoons and video intended for CD-ROM or the web are often 10–15 fps.

Setting the composition frame rate to twice the rate of the output format causes After Effects to display each field of interlaced source footage as its own, separate frame in the Composition panel. This process lets you set keyframes on individual fields and gain precision when animating masks.

When you render a movie for final output, you can choose to use the composition frame rate or another frame rate. The ability to set the frame rate for each output module is useful when you are using the same composition to create output for multiple media.

Support for high-frame-rate footage

You can set any frame rate field up to a maximum of 999 fps in the April 2017 release of After Effects CC. The update lets you use higher frame rates for rendering, unlike the earlier versions where the maximum frame rate you could set for a composition was 99 fps.

117

Importing footage

Each motion-footage item in a composition can also have its own frame rate. The relationship between the footage-item frame rate and the composition frame rate determines how smoothly the layer plays. For example, if the footage-item frame rate is 30 fps and the composition frame rate is 30 fps, then whenever the composition advances one frame, the next frame from the footage item is displayed. If the footage-item frame rate is 15 fps and the composition frame rate is 30 fps, then each frame of the footage item appears in two successive frames of the composition. (This assumes, of course, the simple case in which no time stretching or frame blending has been applied to the layer.)

Ideally, use source footage that matches the final output frame rate. This way, After Effects renders each frame, and the final output does not omit, duplicate, or interpolate frames. If, however, the source footage has a frame rate slightly different from what you want to output to (for example, 30-fps footage and 29.97-fps final output), you can make the footage frame rate match the composition frame rate by conforming it.

Conforming the frame rate of a footage item does not alter the original file, only the reference that After Effects uses. When conforming, After Effects changes the internal duration of frames but not the frame content. Afterward, the footage plays back at a different speed. For example, if you conform the frame rate from 15 fps to 30 fps, the footage plays back twice as fast. In most cases, conform the frame rate only when the difference between the footage frame rate and the output frame rate is small.

Note: Conforming can change the synchronization of visual footage that has an audio track, because changing the frame rate changes the duration of the video but leaves the audio unchanged. If you want to stretch both audio and video, use the Time Stretch command. (See Time-stretch a layer.) Keyframes applied to the source footage remain at their original locations (which retains their synchronization within the composition but not the visual content of the layer). You may need to adjust keyframe locations after conforming a footage item.

You can change the frame rate for any movie or sequence of still images. For example, you can import a sequence of ten still images and specify a frame rate for that footage item of 5 frames per second (fps); this sequence would then have a duration of two seconds when used in a composition.

Note: When you import a sequence of still images, it assumes the frame rate specified by the Sequence Footage preference in the Import category. The default rate is 30 frames per second (fps). You can change the frame rate after importing by reinterpreting the footage item. (See Interpret footage items.)

Lower frame rates tend to give the impression of unreality, so many people prefer to work at a lower frame rate such as 24 frames per second for creative work instead of working at the 29.97 frames per second that is standard for NTSC video.

Note: If you remove 3:2 pulldown from interlaced video footage, After Effects automatically sets the frame rate of the resulting footage item to four-fifths of the original frame rate. When removing 3:2 pulldown from NTSC video, the resulting frame rate is 24 fps.

The frame rate of the composition should match the frame rate of the final output format. In most cases, you can simply choose a composition settings preset. In contrast, set the frame rate for each footage item to the frame rate of the original source footage.

Trish and Chris Meyer provide tips and tricks regarding conforming footage items to a specific frame rate in an article (PDF) on Artbeats website.

Change frame rate for a footage item

Select the footage item in the Project panel.

Choose File > Interpret Footage > Main.

Select Conform To Frame Rate, enter a new frame rate for Frames Per Second, and then click OK.

Last updated 3/8/2018

118

Importing footage

Instead of using Interpret Footage to change a footage item's frame rate, you can time-stretch a layer based on the footage *item. For example, time-stretch a layer by 100.1% to convert between 30fps and 29.97fps. Time-stretching modifies the speed of audio as well as video. (See Time-stretch a layer.)*

Change frame rate for a composition

Choose Composition > Composition Settings.

Do one of the following:

Choose a composition settings preset from the Preset menu.

Set the Frame Rate value.

Note: *Jeff Almasol provides a script on is redefinery website to set the frame rate and duration of the current composition and all compositions nested within it.*

Pixel aspect ratio and frame aspect ratio

Pixel aspect ratio (PAR) is the ratio of width to height of one pixel in an image. *Frame aspect ratio* (sometimes called *image aspect ratio* or *IAR*) is the ratio of width to height of the image frame.

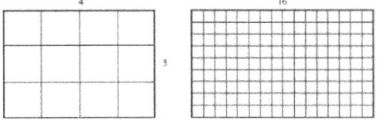

A 4:3 frame aspect ratio (left), and a wider 16:9 frame aspect ratio (right)

Most computer monitors use square pixels, but many video formats—including ITU-R 601 (D1) and DV—use non-square rectangular pixels.

Some video formats output the same frame aspect ratio but use a different pixel aspect ratio. For example, some NTSC digitizers produce a 4:3 frame aspect ratio, with square pixels (1.0 pixel aspect ratio), and a frame with pixel dimensions of 640x480. D1 NTSC produces the same 4:3 frame aspect ratio but uses nonsquare pixels (0.91 pixel aspect ratio) and a frame with pixel dimensions of 720x486. D1 pixels, which are always nonsquare, are vertically oriented in systems producing NTSC video and horizontally oriented in systems producing PAL video.

If you display nonsquare pixels on a square-pixel monitor without alteration, images and motion appear distorted; for example, circles distort into ellipses. However, when displayed on a video monitor, the images are correct. When you import D1 NTSC or DV source footage into After Effects, the image looks slightly wider than it does on a D1 or DV system. (D1 PAL footage looks slightly narrower.) The opposite occurs when you import anamorphic footage using D1/DV NTSC Widescreen or D1/DV PAL Widescreen. Widescreen video formats have a frame aspect ratio of 16:9.

Note: *To preview non-square pixels on a computer monitor, click the Toggle Pixel Aspect Ratio Correction button ▦ at the bottom of the Composition panel. The quality of the pixel aspect ratio correction for previews is affected by the Zoom Quality preference in the Previews category. (See Viewer Quality preferences.)*

Last updated 3/8/2018

119

Importing footage

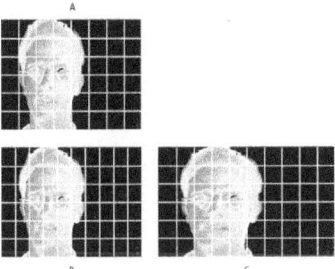

Square and nonsquare pixels

*A Square pixels and 4:3 frame aspect ratio **B** Nonsquare pixels and 4:3 frame aspect ratio **C** Nonsquare pixels displayed on a square-pixel monitor*

If a footage item uses nonsquare pixels, After Effects displays the pixel aspect ratio next to the thumbnail image for the footage item in the Project panel. You can change the pixel aspect ratio interpretation for individual footage items in the Interpret Footage dialog box. By ensuring that all footage items are interpreted correctly, you can combine footage items with different pixel aspect ratios in the same composition.

After Effects reads and writes pixel aspect ratios directly from QuickTime movies. For example, if you import a movie captured as widescreen (16:9 DV), After Effects automatically tags it correctly. Similarly, AVI and PSD files contain information that explicitly indicates the pixel aspect ratio of the images.

If a footage item does not contain information that explicitly indicates the pixel aspect ratio of the image, After Effects uses the pixel dimensions of the footage item frame to make a guess. When you import a footage item with either the D1 pixel dimensions of 720x486 or the DV pixel dimensions of 720x480, After Effects automatically interprets that footage item as D1/DV NTSC. When you import a footage item with the D1 or DV pixel dimensions of 720x576, After Effects automatically interprets that footage item as D1/DV PAL. However, you can make sure that all files are interpreted correctly by looking in the Project panel or the Interpret Footage dialog box.

Note: Make sure to reset the pixel aspect ratio to Square Pixels when you import a square-pixel file that happens to have a D1 or DV pixel dimensions—for example, a non-DV image that happens to have pixel dimensions of 720x480.
The pixel aspect ratio setting of the composition should match the pixel aspect ratio of the final output format. In most cases, you can simply choose a composition settings preset. In contrast, set the pixel aspect ratio for each footage item to the pixel aspect ratio of the original source footage.

Trish and Chris Meyer provide tips and tricks regarding pixel aspect ratio in two PDF documents on the Artbeats website:

Pixel aspect ratio, part 1

Pixel aspect ratio, part 2

Chris Pirazzi provides technical details about aspect ratios on his Lurker's Guide to Video website.

Upgrade pixel aspect ratios to correct values

After Effects CS3 and earlier used pixel aspect ratios for standard-definition video formats that ignore the concept of *clean aperture*. By not accounting for the fact that clean aperture differs from *production aperture* in standard-definition video, the pixel aspect ratios used by After Effects CS3 and earlier were slightly inaccurate. The incorrect pixel aspect ratios cause some images to appear subtly distorted.

Last updated 3/8/2018

120

Importing footage

Note: The clean aperture is the portion of the image that is free from artifacts and distortions that appear at the edges of an image. The production aperture is the entire image.

Todd Kopriva summarizes information about the corrected pixel aspect ratios in a post on the Adobe website.

The following table provides details about pixel aspect ratio values in After Effects:

format	value in After Effects CS4 and later	previous value
D1/DV NTSC	0.91	0.9
D1/DV NTSC Widescreen	1.21	1.2
D1/DV PAL	1.09	1.07
D1/DV PAL Widescreen	1.46	1.42

This discrepancy is limited to these older, standard-definition formats for which clean aperture differs from production aperture. This discrepancy doesn't exist in newer formats.

New projects and compositions created in After Effects CS4 and later use the correct pixel aspect ratio values by default.

Projects and compositions created in After Effects CS3 or earlier are upgraded to use the correct pixel aspect ratios when these projects are opened in After Effects CS4 and later.

Note: If you have a custom interpretation rules file, then you should update it with the correct pixel aspect ratio values.

If you use square-pixel footage items that are designed to fill the frame in a composition with non-square pixels, you may find that the change in pixel aspect ratios causes a difference in behavior. For example, if you previously created 768x576 square-pixel footage items to use in a PAL D1/DV composition, you should now create those items with square-pixel dimensions of 788x576.

Composition settings presets for square-pixel equivalents of standard definition formats have changed as follows:

format	pixel dimensions in After Effects CS4 and later	previous pixel dimensions
NTSC D1 square-pixel equivalent	720x534	720x540
NTSC D1 Widescreen square-pixel equivalent	872x486	864x486
PAL D1/DV square-pixel equivalent	788x576	768x576
PAL D1/DV Widescreen square-pixel equivalent	1050x576	1024x576

Change pixel aspect ratio interpretation for a footage item

Select a footage item in the Project panel.

Choose File > Interpret Footage > Main.

Choose a ratio from the Pixel Aspect Ratio menu and click OK.

Change pixel aspect ratio for a composition

Choose Composition > Composition Settings.

Do one of the following:

Choose a composition settings preset from the Preset menu.

Choose a value from the Pixel Aspect Ratio menu.

Last updated 3/8/2018

121

Importing footage

Common pixel aspect ratios

	Pixel aspect ratio	When to use
Square pixels	1.0	Footage has a 640x480 or 648x486 frame size, is 1920x1080 HD (not HDV or DVCPRO HD), is 1280x720 HD or HDV, or was exported from an application that doesn't support nonsquare pixels. This setting can also be appropriate for footage that was transferred from film or for customized projects.
D1/DV NTSC	0.91	Footage has a 720x486 or 720x480 frame size, and the desired result is a 4:3 frame aspect ratio. This setting can also be appropriate for footage that was exported from an application that works with nonsquare pixels, such as a 3D animation application.
D1/DV NTSC Widescreen	1.21	Footage has a 720x486 or 720x480 frame size, and the desired result is a

		16:9 frame aspect ratio.
D1/DV PAL	1.09	Footage has a 720x576 frame size, and the desired result is a 4:3 frame aspect ratio.
D1/DV PAL Widescreen	1.46	Footage has a 720x576 frame size, and the desired result is a 16:9 frame aspect ratio.
Anamorphic 2:1	2.0	Footage was shot using an anamorphic film lens, or it was anamorphically transferred from a film frame with a 2:1 aspect ratio.
HDV 1080/DVCPRO HD 720, HD Anamorphic 1080	1.33	Footage has a 1440x1080 or 960x720 frame size, and the desired result is a 16:9 frame aspect ratio.
DVCPRO HD 1080	1.5	Footage has a 1280x1080 frame size, and the desired result is a 16:9 frame aspect ratio.

Importing and interpreting video and audio

Interlaced video and separating fields

Interlacing is a technique developed for transmitting television signals using limited bandwidth. In an interlaced system, only half the number of horizontal lines for each frame of video are transmitted at a time. Because of the speed of transmission, the afterglow of displays, and the persistence of vision, the viewer perceives each frame in full resolution. All of the analog television standards use interlacing. Digital television standards include both *interlaced* and *noninterlaced* varieties. Typically, interlaced signals are generated from interlaced scanning, whereas noninterlaced signals are generated from *progressive scanning*.

Each interlaced video frame consists of two *fields*. Each field contains half the number of horizontal lines in the frame; the *upper field* (or *Field 1*) contains the odd-numbered lines, and the *lower field* (or *Field 2*) contains the even-numbered lines. An interlaced video monitor displays each frame by first drawing all of the lines in one field and then drawing all of the lines in the other field. *Field order* specifies which field is drawn first. In NTSC video, new fields are drawn to the screen approximately 60 times per second, corresponding to a frame rate of approximately 30 frames per second.

Last updated 3/8/2018

Importing footage

Noninterlaced video frames aren't separated into fields. A *progressive-scan* monitor displays a noninterlaced video frame by drawing all the horizontal lines, from top to bottom, in one pass. Computer monitors are almost all progressive-scan monitors, and most video displayed on computer monitors is noninterlaced.

The terms *progressive* and *noninterlaced* are thus closely related and are often used interchangeably, but *progressive scanning* refers to the recording or drawing of the scan lines by a camera or monitor, whereas *noninterlaced* refers to the fact that the video data itself isn't separated into fields.

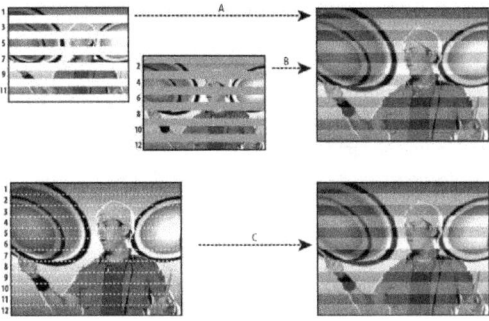

Interlaced scanning of interlaced video fields compared with progressive scanning of noninterlaced video frame.

A For interlaced video, entire upper field (odd-numbered lines) is drawn to screen first, from top to bottom, in one pass. B Next, entire lower field (even-numbered lines) *is drawn to screen, from top to bottom, in one pass. **C** For noninterlaced video, entire frame (all lines in counting order) is drawn to screen, from top to bottom, in one pass.*

Separate video fields

If you want to use interlaced or field-rendered footage (such as NTSC video) in an After Effects project, you get the best results if you separate the video fields when you import the footage. After Effects separates video fields by creating a full frame from each field, preserving all of the image data from the original footage.

Separating fields is critical if you plan to make significant changes to the image. When you scale, rotate, or apply effects to interlaced video, unwanted artifacts, such as crossed fields, are often introduced. By separating fields, After Effects accurately converts the two interlaced frames in the video to noninterlaced frames, while preserving the maximum amount of image quality. Using noninterlaced frames allows After Effects to apply edits and effects consistently and at the highest quality.

After Effects creates field-separated footage from a single formerly interlaced frame by splitting it into two independent frames. Each new frame has only half the information of the original frame, so some frames may appear to have a lower resolution than others when viewed at Draft quality. When you render the final composition, After Effects reproduces high-quality interlaced frames for output. When you render a movie at Best quality, After Effects interpolates between the scan lines of a field to produce maximum image quality.

If your output will not be interlaced, it's best to use noninterlaced source footage, to avoid the need to separate fields.

However, if a noninterlaced version of your source footage is not available, interlaced footage will work fine.

Always separate fields for interlaced footage. Never separate fields for noninterlaced footage items.

You can only remove pull-down after you have separated fields.

Last updated 3/8/2018

123

Importing footage

When you render a composition containing field-separated footage, set the Field Rendering option to the same field order as your video equipment. If you don't field-render the composition, or if you field-render with the incorrect settings, the final movie may appear too soft, jerky, or distorted.

To quickly give video footage a more film-like appearance, import the footage twice, and interpret each footage item ▪ with a different field order. Then add them both to the same composition and blend them together. The misinterpreted layer adds some film-like blur.

After Effects automatically separates fields for D1 and DV video footage items. You can manually separate fields for all other types of video footage in the Interpret Footage dialog box.

Select the footage item in the Project panel.

Choose File > Interpret Footage > Main.

Choose an option from the Separate Fields menu.

Click Preserve Edges (Best Quality Only) to increase image quality in nonmoving areas when the image is rendered at Best quality. Then click OK.

Note: *If the field settings in the Interpret Footage dialog box are correct for the input footage and the field settings in the Render Settings dialog box are correct for the output device, you can mix footage items of different field orders in a composition. If either of these settings is incorrect, however, the frames will be in the correct order, but the field order may be reversed, resulting in jerky, unacceptable images.*

Determine the original field order

The *field order* for an interlaced video footage item determines the order in which the two video fields (upper and lower) are displayed. A system that draws the upper lines before the lower lines is called *upper-field first*; one that draws the lower lines before the upper lines is called *lower-field first*. Many standard-definition formats (such as DV NTSC) are lower-field first, whereas many high-definition formats (such as 1080i DVCPRO HD) are upper-field first.

The order in which the fields are displayed is important, especially when the fields contain motion. If you separate video fields using the wrong field order, motion does not appear smooth.

Some programs, including After Effects, label the field order when rendering interlaced video files. When you import a labeled video file, After Effects honors the field order label automatically. You can override this field order by applying different footage interpretation settings.

If a file does not contain a field order label, you can match the original field order of your footage. If you are not sure which field order was used to interlace a footage item, use this procedure to find out.

Select the item in the Project panel.

Choose File > Interpret Footage > Main.

In the Interpret Footage dialog box, select Upper Field First from the Separate Fields menu, and then click OK.

In the Project panel, press Alt (Windows) or Option (Mac OS) as you double-click the footage to open it in the Footage panel.

If the Preview panel is not visible, choose Window > Preview.

In the Footage panel, find a segment that contains one or more moving areas.

Using the Next Frame button ▪► in the Preview panel, step forward at least five frames in the Footage panel. Moving areas should move consistently in one direction. If the moving areas move backward every other frame, the wrong field-separation option has been applied to the footage.

Last updated 3/8/2018

124

Importing footage

Online resources about fields and interlaced video

Chris Pirazzi provides technical details of fields and interlacing on his Lurker's Guide to Video website.

Trish and Chris Meyer provide a variety of materials about interlacing, field order, field dominance, field rendering, and separating fields:

article introducing interlacing and field order on the ProVideo Coalition website

Remove 3:2 or 24Pa pulldown from video

When you transfer 24-fps film to 29.97-fps video, you use a process called *3:2 pulldown*, in which the film frames are distributed across video fields in a repeating 3:2 pattern. The first frame of film is copied to fields 1 and 2 of the first frame of video, and also to field 1 of the second video frame. The second frame of film is then spread across the next two fields of video—field 2 of the second video frame and field 1 of the third frame of video. This 3:2 pattern is repeated until four frames of film are spread over five frames of video, and then the pattern is repeated.

The 3:2 pulldown process results in *whole frames* (represented by a W) and *split-field* frames (represented by an S). The three whole video frames contain two fields from the same film frame. The remaining two split-field frames contain a video frame from two different film frames. The two split-field frames are always adjacent to each other. The *phase* of 3:2 pulldown refers to the point at which the two split-field frames fall within the first five frames of the footage.

Phase occurs as a result of two conversions that happen during 3:2 pulldown: 24-fps film is redistributed through 30-fps video, so each of four frames of 24-fps film is spread out over five frames of 30(29.97)-fps video. First, the film is slowed down 0.1% to match the speed difference between 29.97 fps and 30 fps. Next, each film frame is repeated in a special pattern and mated to fields of video.

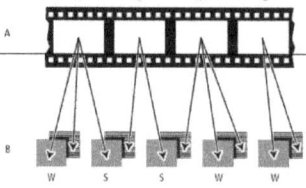

When you apply 3:2 pulldown to footage, one frame of the film (A) is separated into two or three interlaced video fields (B) which are grouped into video frames containing two fields each.

When importing interlaced video that was originally transferred from film, you can remove the 3:2 pulldown that was applied during the transfer from film to video as you separate fields so that effects you apply in After Effects don't appear distorted.

It's important to remove 3:2 pulldown from video footage that was originally film so that effects you add in After Effects synchronize perfectly with the original frame rate of film. Removing 3:2 pulldown reduces the frame rate by 1/5—from 30 to 24 fps or from 29.97 to 23.976 fps, which also reduces the number of frames you have to change. To remove 3:2 pulldown, you must also indicate the phase of the 3:2 pulldown.

After Effects also supports Panasonic DVX100 24p DV camera pulldown, called *24P Advance (24Pa)*. Some cameras use this format to capture 23.976 progressive-scan imagery using standard DV tapes.

Last updated 3/8/2018

125

Importing footage

Before you remove 3:2 pulldown, separate the fields as either upper-field first or lower-field first. Once the fields are separated, After Effects can analyze the footage and determine the correct 3:2 pulldown phase and field order. If you already know the phase and field order, choose them from the Separate Fields and the Remove menus in the Interpret Footage dialog box.

In the Project panel, select the footage item from which to remove 3:2 pulldown.

Choose File > Interpret Footage > Main.

In the Fields and Pulldown section, select Upper Field First or Lower Field First from the Separate Fields menu.

Do one of the following and click OK:

If you know the phase of the 3:2 or 24Pa pulldown, choose it from the Remove menu.

To have After Effects determine the correct settings, click Guess 3:2 Pulldown or Guess 24Pa Pulldown.

Note: *If your footage file contains frames from different sources, the phase may not be consistent. If the phase is inconsistent, import the footage multiple times, once for each phase, and interpret each footage item with a different setting. Then, add each footage item to your composition and trim each layer to use only the appropriate frames. In other words, if you have an asset that has multiple pulldown phases, then you need to cut that asset into pieces and remove pulldown separately for each of the pieces. This can come up if the asset is a movie that has been edited together from several sources in an NLE.*

Import assets in Panasonic P2 format

A P2 card is a solid-state memory device that plugs into the PCMCIA slot of a Panasonic P2 video camera. The digital video and audio data from the video camera is recorded onto the card in a structured, codec-independent format known as *MXF*

(Media eXchange Format). Specifically, Adobe Premiere Pro and After Effects support the Panasonic Op-Atom variant of MXF, with video in AVC-Intra 50, AVC-Intra 100, DV, DVCPRO, DVCPRO50, and DVCPRO HD formats. A clip is said to be in the *P2 format* if its audio and video are contained in Panasonic Op-Atom MXF files, and these files are located in a specific folder structure.

The root of the P2 folder structure is a CONTENTS folder. Each *essence* item (an item of video or audio) is contained in a separate MXF wrapper file; the video MXF files are in the VIDEO subfolder, and the audio MXF files are in the AUDIO subfolder. The relationships between essence files and the metadata associated with them are tracked by XML files in the CLIP subfolder.

Note: *Adobe Premiere Pro and After Effects do not support proxies recorded by Panasonic P2 camcorders in P2 card PROXY folders.*

The video and audio on a P2 card are already in a digital form, as if the P2 card were a hard disk, so no capture step is involved in importing media from a P2 card. The process of reading the data from the card and converting it to a format that can be used in a project is sometimes referred to as ingest.

For your computer to read P2 cards, you must install the appropriate driver, which you can download from the Panasonic website. Panasonic also provides the P2 Viewer application, with which you can browse and play media stored on a P2 card.

Because Panasonic P2 cards use the FAT32 file system, each file is limited to a size of 4 GB. When a shot is recorded that requires more than the 4 GB, a P2 camera creates another file and continues recording the shot to the new file without interruption. This is referred to as clip spanning, because the shot spans more than one file or clip. Similarly, a camera may span a shot across files on different P2 cards: if the camera has more than one P2 card loaded, it will record the shot until it runs out of room on the first P2 card, create a new file on the next P2 card with available space, and

Last updated 3/8/2018

126

Importing footage

continue recording the shot to it. Although a single shot can be recorded to a group of multiple spanned clips, the multiple-file shot is designed to be treated as a single clip or footage item in a video editing application. For After Effects to automatically import a group of spanned clips simultaneously and assemble them into a single footage item, they must all have been recorded to the same P2 card and none of the files can be missing, including the associated XML metadata file.

(Optional) Copy the entire contents of the P2 card to a hard disk.

Though it is possible to import assets into Adobe Premiere Pro or After Effects directly from a P2 card, it is usually more efficient to copy the contents of the P2 card to a hard disk before importing.

Choose File > Import.

Navigate to the CONTENTS folder.

Select one or more MXF files:

To import a video essence item and its associated audio essence items, select the MXF files from the VIDEO folder.

To import only the audio essence items, select the MXF files from the AUDIO folder.

To import a group of spanned clips for a shot that were recorded onto the same P2 card, select only one of the MXF files in the group from the VIDEO folder. The group is imported as a single footage item with a duration equal to the total duration of all the spanned clips it includes. If you select more than one of these spanned clips, you import duplicates of the whole group of spanned clips, as duplicate footage items in the Project panel.

You cannot import spanned clips from a shot that spans two different cards as a single footage item. Rather, you must select a single MXF file belonging to the shot from each card to create a separate footage item for the part of the shot recorded on each card. For example, if a group of spanned clips for a single shot itself spans two cards, you must select a spanned clip from the group on card 1 and another from the group on card 2. This imports the contents of the shot into two footage items in the Project panel.

The Date column in the Project panel shows when each source clip was acquired. After you import spanned clips, you can use the Date value to determine their correct chronological order within the shot.

Note: *After Effects can't directly export to the P2 format. To render and export to the P2 format, use Adobe Media Encoder or Premiere Pro.*

For additional information on the Panasonic P2 format and workflows with Adobe digital video software, see the

Adobe website:

Adobe workflow guides for P2, RED, XDCAM, AVCCAM, and DSLR cameras and footage

P2 workflow guide for Adobe digital video products

Dave Helmly's video introduction to the P2 workflow in After Effects

Preparing and importing 3D image files

Importing 3D images from Photoshop and Illustrator

3D object layers in PSD files

Adobe Photoshop can import and manipulate 3D models (3D objects) in several popular formats. Photoshop can also create 3D objects in basic, primitive shapes.

Last updated 3/8/2018

127

Importing footage

After Effects cannot import 3D objects from PSD files.

See working with 3d layers video on the learn tutorials page.

Vanishing Point exchange

When you use the Vanishing Point feature in Photoshop Extended, you can then use the File > Export For After Effects (.vpe) command to save the results as a collection of PNG files—one for each plane—and a .vpe file that describes the geometry of the scene. You can then import the .vpe file into After Effects. After Effects uses the information in the .vpe file to re-create the scene as a composition containing a camera layer and one perspective-corrected 3D layer for each PNG file.

The camera is on the negative z axis, at $(x,y)=(0,0)$. The point of interest for the camera is in the center of the composition. The camera zoom is set according to the field of view in the Vanishing Point scene.

The 3D layers for the planes in the scene have a parent layer with its anchor point at the center of the composition, so the whole scene can be transformed together.

Vanishing Point exchange only works well for images that have square pixels in Photoshop.

Bob Donlon provides a tutorial on his blog that shows how to use Vanishing Point Exchange.

Lester Banks provides a video tutorial on his website that demonstrates how to use Vanishing Point in Photoshop Extended and then either bring the 3D scene into After Effects as a .vpe file or bring the 3D scene in as a 3D object layer in a PSD file.

Andrew Kramer provides a video tutorial on his Video Copilot website that shows how to use Vanishing Point Exchange.

Importing PSD files as 3D scenes

Paul Tuersley provides a script on the AE Enhancers website that turns a layered PSD file into a 3D scene in After Effects. The script creates a composition and adds expressions to the layers from the PSD file. When you move the layers along the z axis, the scene looks exactly like the original artwork through the Active Camera view. You can animate the camera around the scene to see that the layers are at different depths in 3D space.

Illustrator 3D effects

The effects in the 3D category in Illustrator—Extrude & Bevel, Revolve, and Rotate—give a three-dimensional appearance to any vector graphics object, including text and drawings. If you want to add depth to your vector art and text, consider creating it in Illustrator, using the 3D effects, and then importing the results into After Effects.

Importing and using 3D files from other applications

After Effects can import 3D-image files saved in Softimage PIC, RLA, RPF, OpenEXR, and Electric Image EI format. These 3D-image files contain red, green, blue, and alpha (RGBA) channels, as well as auxiliary channels with optional information, such as z depth, object IDs, texture coordinates, and more.

Though you can import composited files with 3D information into After Effects, you cannot modify or create 3D models directly with After Effects.

After Effects treats each composited 3D file from another application as a single 2D layer. That layer, as a whole, can be given 3D attributes and treated like any After Effects 3D layer, but the objects contained within that 3D file cannot be manipulated individually in 3D space. To access the 3D depth information and other auxiliary channel information in 3D image files, use the 3D Channel effects. (See .)

3D Channel effect plug-ins from fnord software are included with After Effects to provide access to multiple layers and channels of OpenEXR files. (See .)

Last updated 3/8/2018

128

Importing footage

After Effects can also import baked camera data, including focal length, film size, and transformation data, from Maya project files as a single composition or two compositions. (See Baking and importing Maya data.)

After Effects imports camera data saved with RLA or RPF sequence files. (See Import RLA or RPF data into a camera layer.)

Softimage PIC files have a corresponding ZPIC file that contains the z-depth channel information. Although you can't import a ZPIC file, you can access the additional channel information as long as the ZPIC file is stored in the same folder as the imported PIC file.

Similarly, Electric Image (EI) files can have associated EIZ files with z-depth channel data. As with ZPIC files, you cannot import EIZ files into After Effects; instead, you simply store them in the same folder as the EI files. For information about creating EIZ files, see your Electric Image documentation.

A common technique when working in a 3D modeling application is to insert null objects, such as null lights or null locator nodes in the locations where you want to composite in an image in After Effects. Then, after you have imported the 3D file into After Effects, you can use these null objects as a reference for the placements of other visual elements.

Online resources about importing and using 3D files from other applications

Lutz Albrecht provides a two-part document on the Adobe website about integrating 3D applications with After Effects. These articles cover the creation of UV maps, mattes, and channels from various 3D applications, including Maxon Cinema 4D, NewTek Lightwave, and Luxology modo. The articles then show you how to use RE:Vision Effects RE:Map and fnord ProEXR plug-ins to use that data in After Effects.

Tyson Ibele provides tutorials on his website that show how to use output from 3ds Max (3D Studio MAX) in After Effects.

Dave Scotland provides a pair of tutorials on the CG Swot website in which he demonstrates how to create RPF files in a 3D application and how to use RPF files in After Effects. The first part explains the RPF format and how to create RPF files in 3DS Max. The second part shows how to use the Object ID and Z depth information in an RPF file within After Effects, using the ID Matte, Depth of Field, Depth Matte, and Fog 3D effects.

Using 3D tracking completes camera movements so that additional elements can be composited into the scene to make it appear to honor the same camera movement. The 3D camera tracker effect analyzes video sequences to extract camera motion and 3D scene data. The 3D camera motion allows you to correctly composite 3D elements over your 2D footage. For details about using the 3D camera tracker effect, see this video tutorial by Angie Taylor from Learn by Video. To know more about 3D camera tracker feature, see Tracking 3D camera movement.

Bartek Skorupa provides a tutorial on his website about using Blender and exporting the animation to After Effects.

You can also watch the camera tracking in Blender tutorial that shows focuses on lens distortion issues.

Harrison Ambs provides a two-part video tutorial on the CGTUTS+ website that demonstrates how to import data from Cinema 4D into After Effects:

Video Part 1

Video Part 2

The tutorial Use Cinema 4D Lite with After Effects cameras and lights explains how to create an After Effects comp with cameras, lights, and solid layers, and then open it in Cinema 4D Lite to add 3D objects.

Last updated 3/8/2018

129

Importing footage

Import RLA or RPF data into a camera layer

After Effects imports camera data saved with RLA or RPF sequence files. That data is incorporated into camera layers— one for each camera in the sequence—that After Effects creates in the Timeline panel. You can access the camera data of an imported RLA or RPF sequence and create a camera layer containing that data.

Add the sequence to a composition, and select its layer in the Timeline panel.

Choose Animation > Keyframe Assistant > RPF Camera Import.

Note: *To create an RLA or RPF file with the camera data in 3D Studio Max, save your rendering in RPF format with Coverage, Z Depth, and Alpha Channels enabled.*

Baking and importing Maya data

After Effects imports camera data from Maya project files. Before importing Maya camera information, you need to bake it. Baking camera data makes it easier to animate with keyframes later in your project. Baking places a keyframe at each frame of the animation. You can have 0, 1, or a fixed number of keyframes for each camera or transform property. For example, if a property is not animated in Maya, either no keyframes are set for this property or one keyframe is set at the start of the animation. If a property has more than one keyframe, it must have the same number as all of the other animation properties with more than one keyframe.

Reduce import time by creating or saving the simplest Maya file possible. In Maya, reduce keyframes by deleting static channels before baking, and save a version of the Maya project that contains the camera animation only.

Note: *The following transformation flags are not supported: query, relative, euler, objectSpace, worldSpace, worldSpaceDistance, preserve, shear, scaleTranslation, rotatePivot, rotateOrder, rotateTranslation, matrix, boundingBox, boundingBoxInvisible, pivots, CenterPivots, and zeroTransformPivots. After Effects skips these unsupported flags, and no warnings or error messages appear.*

By default, After Effects treats linear units specified in the Maya file as pixels.

You can import camera data from Maya project files (.ma) and work with the data as a single composition or two compositions.

For each Maya file you import, After Effects creates either one or two compositions:

If the Maya project has a square pixel aspect ratio, After Effects creates a single, square-pixel composition containing the camera data and transformations.

If the Maya project has a nonsquare pixel aspect ratio, After Effects creates two compositions. The first composition, which has a filename prefixed by *Square*, is a square-pixel composition containing the camera data. The second, or *parent*, composition is a nonsquare-pixel composition that retains the dimensions of the original file and contains the square-pixel composition. When working with imported camera data, use 3D layers and square-pixel footage in the square-pixel composition, and use all nonsquare-pixel footage in the containing composition.

When you import a Maya file with a 1-node camera, After Effects creates a camera in the square-pixel composition that carries the camera's focal length, film size, and transformation data.

When you import a Maya file with a 2-node or targeted camera, After Effects creates a camera and an additional parent node in the square-pixel composition. The parent node contains only the camera's transformation data. After Effects imports 2-node cameras automatically with the locator node as the point of interest, with the Auto-Orientation option of the camera set to Orient Towards Point Of Interest.

After Effects doesn't read 3-node cameras.

Last updated 3/8/2018

130

Importing footage

Note: After Effects reads only the rendering cameras in Maya files and ignores the orthographic and perspective cameras. Therefore, always generate a rendering camera from Maya, even if it's the same as the perspective camera. If you apply the FilmFit camera setting, make sure to use either horizontal or vertical FilmFit, not fill.

After Effects can read Maya locator nodes, which enable you to track objects from the Maya scene as it is translated into After Effects. After Effects creates a null layer and applies the relevant transformations to it if the name of a Maya locator node contains the word *Null*, *NULL*, or *null*. Avoid parenting locator nodes to each other in Maya; instead, parent the locator nodes to geometry.

Note: After Effects doesn't read World or Underworld coordinates in the LocatorShape. Use a transform node to place them.

Working with Cinema 4D and Cineware

For detailed information on working with MAXON Cinema 4D files and Cineware (a full-featured workflow integration between Adobe After Effects CC and Cinema 4D), see CINEMA 4D and Cineware.

Working with footage items

Organize, view, manage, and trim footage items

Compositions and footage items are listed in the Project panel. Unlike items in the Timeline panel and Effect Controls panel, the order of items in the Project panel has no influence on the appearance of the movies that you create. You can organize footage items and compositions however you like, including organizing them using folders. Solid-color footage items are automatically placed in the Solids folder.

Folders that you create in the Project panel exist only in the Project panel. You can expand a folder to reveal its contents, and put folders inside other folders. To move a file or folder to the top level of the Project panel, drag it to the gray information area at the top of the panel.

You can use the search field in the Project panel to find footage items that meet various criteria, such as those with missing source files. See Search and filter in the Timeline, Project, and Effects & Presets panels.

For a helpful video tutorial about organizing assets in the Project panel, see this video tutorial by Jeff Sengstack and Infinite Skills.

Scripts for managing footage items

Jeff Almasol provides a script on his redefinery website that automatically writes specified information about footage items or layers to the Comment fields for the respective items in the Project panel or Timeline panel.

Christopher Green provides a script (Project_Items_Renamer.jsx) on his website with which you can rename compositions and footage items selected in the Project panel. You can search and replace text in the names, append characters to the beginning or end of the names, or trim a specified number of characters from the beginning or end of the names.

Lloyd Alvarez provides a script on the After Effects Scripts website with which you can search an After Effects project and replace the file paths for the sources of footage items. This is convenient for swapping out source files, updating a project after moving sources, or updating a project after moving it to a different computer system.

Last updated 3/8/2018

131

Importing footage

Show information for items

To show information about a footage item or composition, select it in the Project panel. Information is displayed at the top of the Project panel next to the thumbnail image.

To show the file creator ID for a footage item, Alt-click (Windows) or Option-click (Mac OS) it in the Project panel.

Create a folder

Choose File > New > New Folder, or click the Create A New Folder icon ▪ at the bottom of the Project panel.

Rename and sort items

To rename a composition, footage item, or folder, do one of the following:

Select the item in the Project panel, press Enter (Windows) or Return (Mac OS), and enter the new name.

Right-click (Windows) or Control-click (Mac OS) the item, choose Rename, and enter the new name.

To rename the Comment column, right-click (Windows) or Control-click (Mac OS) the column heading and choose Rename This.

You can use the Comment column to create a custom sorting option. Rename the column, enter corresponding information for each item (for example, camera number), and then sort by that column.

To sort items by entries in any column, click the column name in the Project panel.

Copy items

To duplicate or copy an item in the Project panel, select it and choose Edit > Duplicate or Edit > Copy.

To copy a footage item to Windows Explorer (Windows) or the Finder (Mac OS), drag the footage item from the Project panel to the desktop.

Reveal footage items

To reveal where a footage item is used in a composition, right-click (Windows) or Control-click (Mac OS) the footage item in the Project panel and choose Reveal In Composition; then select the specific instance you want to reveal (*composition name*, *layer name*).

To reveal the source footage item for a layer in the Project panel, right-click (Windows) or Control-click (Mac OS) the layer in the Timeline panel, and then choose Reveal Layer Source In Project.

To reveal the location of a footage item in Adobe Bridge, Windows Explorer, or the Finder, right-click (Windows) or Control-click (Mac OS) the footage item in the Project panel and choose Reveal In Bridge, Reveal In Windows Explorer, or Reveal In Finder.

Refresh footage items

To refresh footage items selected in the Project panel to use the current versions of the source footage files, choose File > Reload Footage.

View footage item in the Footage panel or media player assigned by operating system

When items are previewed in the Footage panel, they show the results of the footage interpretation operations. (See Interpret footage items.)

To open a footage item in a Footage panel, double-click the footage item in the Project panel.

To open selected footage items in the Footage panel, press Enter on the numeric keypad when the Project panel is active.

Last updated 3/8/2018

132

Importing footage

Note: *To open the source for a footage item using the player application associated with that file type, Alt-double-click (Windows) or Option-double-click (Mac OS) the footage item in the Project panel. See the documentation for your operating system for instructions for changing the associations between applications and file types.*

Trim footage items in the Footage panel

You can use the Set In Point ⥾ , Set Out Point ⥿ , Ripple Insert Edit ⬛ , and Overlay Edit ⬛ controls in the Footage panel to trim a footage item and insert it into a composition. Trimming in the Footage panel can be more convenient than adding the footage item to a composition and then trimming its layer in the Timeline panel.

Enhanced solids folder organization

You can organize your solids, adjustments layers, and nulls better with enhanced solids folder organization. You can perform the following tasks:

Rename the solids folder: You can rename the existing solids folder and every new solid is created in the renamed folder instead of a separate folder named 'Solids.' To rename the folder, do any of the following options:

Option 1:

Select the folder and press Enter (Win) or Return (Mac).

Type a new name in the name field. Option 2:

Right-click and choose Rename. For example, rename the folder to Color Squares.

After renaming the folder, a warning message is displayed when you try to create a solid.

Click Yes, and use "Color Squares" to continue using the renamed folder.

If you want to create the solid in a new solids folder, click No, use "Solids".

Set a default name for the solids folder: You can change the default name for solids folder you create in your new projects. To change the name, follow these steps:

To open Preferences window, select Preferences > New Project.

In the Preferences window, enter the new name in New Projects Solids Folder text box and click OK.

Note: These settings are applied to the new folders you create. Your current projects are not affected.

Nest the solids folder in other folders: You can nest the Solids folder within other folders. Drag the solids folder inside another folder in your current project to nest. Once the folders are nested, new solids continue to be created in the nested folder.

Note: You can not nest folders in Team Porjects.

Set any folder as the solids folder: You can set a folder as a solids folder. To set a folder as a solids folder, follow the steps:

Right-click the preferred folder in the Project panel.

Choose solids folder from the menu to set it as the solids folder.

Note: You can only set one folder at a time as the solids folder.

For more information, see Creating layers.

Last updated 3/8/2018

133

Importing footage

Edit footage in its original application

You can open and edit a footage item in the application in which it was created, directly from an After Effects project. The original application must be installed on the computer that you are using, which must have enough available RAM for it to run. When you edit and save changes to the footage in the original application, the changes are applied to all instances of the footage when After Effects becomes the active application.

Note: *If you're editing footage that has an alpha channel, make sure that you're viewing and editing all of the channels, including the alpha channel, in the other application. Otherwise, changes you make may not be applied to the alpha channel, and it may become misaligned with the color channels.*

When you edit a still-image sequence selected in the Timeline or Composition panel, the individual image that is currently displayed opens. When you edit a still-image sequence selected in the Project panel, the first image in the sequence opens.

In the Project panel, Composition panel, or Timeline panel, select the footage item or a layer that uses the footage item as its source. If you selected a still-image sequence from the Composition or Timeline panel, move the current-time indicator to the frame displaying the still image you want to edit.

Choose Edit > Edit Original.

Edit the footage in its original application, and save the changes.

Remove items from a project

Before reducing your project, removing unused footage, or consolidating footage, consider making a backup by incrementing and saving your project first. (See Save and back up projects in After Effects .)

Carl Larsen demonstrates the use of the Collect Files command and the Consolidate All Footage command in a video tutorial on the Creative COW website that shows how to organize, consolidate, and archive project files and footage.

To remove an item from a project, select the item in the Project panel and press Delete.

To remove all unused footage items from a project, choose File > Remove Unused Footage.

To remove all duplicate footage items from a project, Choose File > Consolidate All Footage. After Effects considers footage items to be duplicates only if they use the same Interpret Footage settings.

When a duplicate item is removed, layers that refer to the duplicate item are updated to refer to the remaining copy.

To remove unselected compositions and unused footage items from selected compositions in the Project panel, choose File > Reduce Project. This command is available only when the Project panel is active.

This command removes both unused footage items and all other compositions that are not included within a selected composition as nested (subordinate) compositions.

If the selected composition includes items that are turned off (that is, the Video or Audio switch is deselected in the Timeline panel), the Reduce Project command does not remove those items.

If an expression in a selected composition refers to an element in a nonsubordinate composition, Reduce Project removes the nonsubordinate composition and the applied expression. A message appears after you choose Reduce Project to remind you of this possibility, so you can undo the command if needed. To avoid removing the expressions from a nonsubordinate composition, drag the nonsubordinate composition into the composition that refers to it. Then deselect the Audio and Video switches for the composition that you added.

The SaveCompAsProject script from Sebastian Perier on the AEScripts website saves selected compositions as individual projects.

Last updated 3/8/2018

134

Importing footage

Placeholders and proxies

When you want to temporarily use a substitute for a footage item, use either a *placeholder* or a *proxy*.

Placeholder A still image of color bars used to temporarily take the place of a missing footage item. Use a placeholder when you are building a composition and want to try out ideas for a footage item that is not yet available. After Effects generates placeholders automatically, so you do not have to provide a placeholder footage item.

Proxy Any file used to temporarily replace a footage item, but most often a lower-resolution or still version of an existing footage item used to replace the original. Often, storyboard images are used as proxies. You can use a proxy either before you have the final footage or when you have the actual footage item but you want to speed up previewing or rendering of test movies. You must have a file available to use as a proxy.

Any masks, attributes, expressions, effects, and keyframes that you apply to the layer are retained when you replace its placeholder or proxy with the final footage item.

In the Project panel, After Effects marks the footage name to indicate whether the actual footage item or its proxy is currently in use:

A filled box indicates that a proxy item is currently in use throughout the project. The name of the proxy appears in bold type at the top of the Project panel when the footage item is selected.

An empty box indicates that the footage item is in use throughout the project, though a proxy has been assigned.

No box indicates that no proxy is assigned to the footage item.

Work with placeholders and missing footage items

For best results, set the placeholder to the same size, duration, and frame rate as the actual footage.

If After Effects cannot find source footage when you open a project, the footage item appears in the Project panel labeled Missing, and the name of the missing footage appears in italics. Any composition using that item replaces it with a placeholder. You can still work with the missing item in the project, and any effects you applied to the original footage remain intact. When you replace the placeholder with the source footage, After Effects places the footage in its correct location in all the compositions that use it.

You can find footage items for which the source items are missing by typing missing in the search field in the Project ▪ *panel. See Search and filter in the Timeline, Project, and Effects & Presets panels.*

To use a placeholder, choose File > Import > Placeholder.

To replace the selected footage item with a placeholder, choose File > Replace Footage > Placeholder.

To replace a placeholder with the actual footage item, select the placeholder you want to replace in the Project panel, choose File > Replace Footage > File, and locate the actual footage.

Work with proxies for footage items

When you use a proxy, After Effects replaces the actual footage with the proxy in all compositions that use the actual footage item. When you finish working, you can switch back to the actual footage item in the project list. After Effects then replaces the proxy with the actual footage item in any composition.

When you render your composition as a movie, you may choose to use either all the actual high-resolution footage items or their proxies. You may want to use the proxies for a rendered movie if, for example, you simply want to test motion using a rough movie that renders quickly.

135

Importing footage

For best results, set a proxy so that it has the same frame aspect ratio as the actual footage item. For example, if the actual footage item is a 640x480-pixel movie, create and use a 160x120-pixel proxy. When a proxy item is imported, After Effects scales the item to the same size and duration as the actual footage. If you create a proxy with a frame aspect ratio that is different from the frame aspect ratio of the actual footage item, scaling takes longer.

In the Project panel, do any of the following:

To locate and use a proxy, select a footage item, choose File > Set Proxy > File, locate, and select the file you want to use as a proxy, and click Open.

To toggle between using the original footage and its proxy, click the proxy indicator to the left of the footage name.

To stop using a proxy, select the original footage item, and choose File > Set Proxy > None.

Create a proxy

Use the Create Proxy command to create a proxy from footage or compositions selected in the Project panel or the Timeline panel. This command adds the selected footage to the Render Queue panel and sets the Post-Render Action option to Set Proxy.

Open a footage item or composition in the Project or Timeline panel.

Move the current-time indicator in the Footage panel to the frame that you want to use as the proxy still item, or for the poster frame for the movie footage item.

Choose one of the following commands:

File > Create Proxy > Still to create a still image proxy.

File > Create Proxy > Movie to create a moving image proxy.

Specify a name and output destination for the proxy.

In the Render Queue panel, specify render settings, and click Render.

Create placeholders for output

You can create placeholder files that can be used in different compositions. For example, you can create a placeholder for an item in the render queue that will create a 24-fps movie and then drag that placeholder into a 30-fps composition. Then, when you render the 30-fps composition, After Effects first renders the placeholder at 24 fps and uses this rendered version as it renders the 30-fps composition.

Drag the Output Module heading for a queued item from the Render Queue panel to the Project panel. After Effects creates a placeholder for output in the Project panel and sets the Post-Render Action option for the item to Import & Replace Usage.

Additional resources for working with placeholders and proxies

Andrew Kramer provides a video tutorial with tips for working with proxies, output modules, and output module templates on the Video Copilot website.

Jeff Almasol provides a script on his redefinery website that creates, sets, and unsets proxies and placeholders.

Charles Bordenave (nab) provides a script on the After Effects Scripts website with which you can create proxies for multiple selected items.

See this video tutorial on the Video2Brain website by Todd Kopriva for information about saving time by pre-rendering and using proxies in After Effects.

Loop a footage item

If you intend to loop a visual footage item continuously in your project, you only need to create one cycle of the footage item in After Effects.

In the Project panel, select the footage item to loop.

Choose File > Interpret Footage > Main.

Type an integer value for Loop and click OK.

Lloyd Alvarez provides a script on the After Effects Scripts website that automatically loops a footage item, composition, or layer.

Freeze on last frame

You can now freeze the last frame of a layer until the end of the composition. After Effects sets time remapping keyframes in the layer and extends the layer duration until the end of the composition.

To freeze the composition on the last frame of your footage, choose Layer > Time > Freeze on Last Frame.

CINEMA 4D and Cineware

CINEMA 4D is a popular 3D modeling and animation tool from Maxon (www.maxon.net).

Closer integration with CINEMA 4D allows you to use Adobe After Effects and Maxon CINEMA 4D together. You can create a CINEMA 4D file (.c4d) from within After Effects and you can work with complex 3D elements, scenes, and animations.

To enable interoperability, CineRender, the Maxon CINEMA 4D rendering engine, is integrated with Adobe After Effects. After Effects can render CINEMA 4D files, and you can control some aspects of rendering, camera, and scene content on a per-layer basis. This streamlined workflow does not require you to create intermediate pass or image sequence files.

Maxon CINEMA 4D Lite R19

Maxon CINEMA 4D Lite R19 application gets installed along with After Effects. You can create, import, and edit CINEMA 4D files. However, if you have another edition of CINEMA 4D, such as CINEMA 4D Prime, you can use it instead. The CINEMA 4D Lite R19 application gives you the ability to edit, create, and work with native CINEMA 4D files. The features in the Lite version are similar to CINEMA 4D Prime.

The default behavior uses the higher version of the installed CINEMA 4D application.

See this tutorial to learn to use CINEMA 4D Lite with After effects cameras and lights.

Watch this video Overview of CINEMA 4D Lite by Chris Meyer.

Importing footage

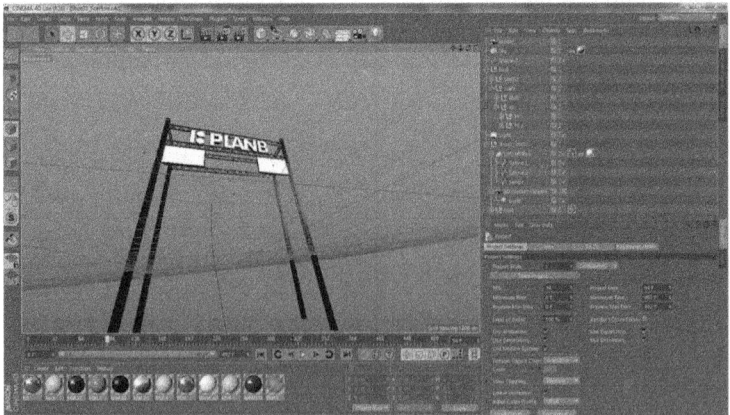

Working with CINEMA 4D files

There are several options available to create, import, and edit CINEMA 4D files from within After Effects.

Import CINEMA 4D files

To import CINEMA 4D files into After Effects, do the following:

Choose File > Import > File.

Select the CINEMA 4D file and click Import. The file is placed in the Project panel as a footage item. You can place the footage item on an existing composition, or create a matching composition.

Note: When you place the footage on a new composition using the new composition icon in the project panel, a composition is created that matches the CINEMA 4D file settings and then a CINEMA 4D layer is created and the 3D scene is placed on it. If you drop the footage in an existing composition, the footage picks up the composition size/aspect instead.

Note: Before importing, enable Save Polygons For Melange and Save Animation For Melange preferences in CINEMA 4D application preferences. These settings are especially useful in cases where CINEMA 4D frames depend on previous frames.

Edit CINEMA 4D files

You can edit CINEMA 4D files placed in compositions or CINEMA 4D source items in the Project. The files open in the CINEMA 4D Lite R19 application. If you have a different version of CINEMA 4D installed, that is used to edit the file instead. See Edit footage in its original application.

You can choose the version of CINEMA 4D you want to use with Edit Original. See Working with different instances of CINEMA 4D in Cineware Effect

For more information, see the video by Jeff Sengstack on Importing and editing CINEMA 4D files.

Create CINEMA 4D files

You can create a CINEMA 4D file within After Effects. To do so, select File > New > Maxon CINEMA 4D File or Layer > New > Maxon CINEMA 4D File.

Specify a name and location of the file.

The CINEMA 4D application opens.

Create a C4D scene and select **File > Save** to save the file.

For more information, see this video by Jeff Sengstack on Creating CINEMA 4D files.

Export to Maxon CINEMA 4D and roundtrip your edits using Live 3D Pipeline

You can export your compositions with 3D animated text and shape layers to Maxon CINEMA 4D using the After Effects' Live 3D pipeline for round-tripped 3D workflow.

3D Shape layers are exported as extruded spline objects, and includes animation of shape layer properties.

The Extrude Text as Shapes option exports 3D text layers as extruded spline objects in the .c4d file. This option retains the fidelity of the layer: character and paragraph formatting, and animation of text layer properties. You cannot modify the font and text content in CINEMA 4D.

The Preserve Editable Text option exports 3D text layers as extruded text objects in the .c4d file. In this option, you can modify the font and text in CINEMA 4D. However, this option has limited support for character and paragraph formatting, and animation of text layer properties. Text animation features that are not supported include: text animators, kerning, tracking, vertical text, paragraph text, and text on path.

Strokes are exported for 3D text and shape layers into the .c4d file. While the Ray-traced 3D renderer in After Effects does not render strokes for 3D text layers, strokes are still exported when enabled. To view 3D text layer strokes before exporting, make sure that the composition renderer is set to Classic 3D.

Export to Maxon CINEMA 4D

To export to Maxon CINEMA 4D:

Select File > Export > Maxon CINEMA 4D Exporter and save the C4D file.

In the Export to Maxon CINEMA 4D dialog box, select one of the following:

Extrude Text as Shapes: Creates a .c4d file with basic extrusion.

Preserve Editable Text: Exports 3D text layers as extruded text objects in the .c4d file, allowing you to modify the font and text in CINEMA 4D.

If your text is unlikely to change after export, it is recommended to choose CINEMA 4D: Extrude Text as Shapes option in the Text Exporting dialog box.

When you export, the scene coordinates for the parent null object is shifted so that the center of an After Effects composition matches CINEMA 4D's center at 0,0,0.

The exported .c4d files are saved in CINEMA 4D version 17.0.

Import the .c4d file and edit it in Maxon CINEMA 4D

You can import the .c4d file that you have created in to your After Effects composition for editing. Choose Edit > Edit Original to edit the .c4d file in CINEMA 4D.

When you import and add a .c4d file that was created by the Cineware 3.1 version of the Exporter to your composition, you can view the scene through an After Effects camera by first adding a camera and then setting the Camera setting in the Cineware effect to Centered Comp Camera.

Any After Effects 3D layers that you add to the composition line up with the CINEMA 4D scene layer after export. The extracted 3D Scene data from the .c4d file such as nulls, cameras, and lights also line up, provided that any new objects added to the .c4d file are grouped under the same parent null object as created in the exported .c4d file.

To open the exported CINEMA 4D file in After Effects and CINEMA 4D for advanced 3D edits:

Select File > Import and select the .c4d file to import it to your composition.

To customize the 3D elements using CINEMA 4D, select the Cineware layer and select Edit > Edit Original (or press the keyboard shortcut Command + E on Mac OS or Control + E on Windows). The C4D file opens in CINEMA 4D, which is included in After Effects CC.

Make changes and save the file. Your After Effects composition is automatically updated with all the changes.

Cineware effect

The integration of CineRender, which is based on the CINEMA 4D render engine, enables rendering of layers based on CINEMA 4D files directly in After Effects. The Cineware effect lets you control the render settings, and provides some control over the render quality-speed tradeoff. You can also specify cameras, passes, or C4D layers used for a render. The Cineware effect is automatically applied when you create a layer based on C4D footage on the composition. Each CINEMA 4D layer has its own render and display settings.

For more information, see Understanding the Cineware effect and render engine.

Synchronize Layer

When adding multiple instances of a CINEMA 4D scene layer in a composition, including adding Multi-Pass layers, you can select the CINEMA 4D layers that are to be synchronized with the rest of the layers in the composition.

When you check the Synchronize AE Layer option at the top of the Effect Controls panel, the Render Settings and Camera options on all instances of the layer automatically synchronize, but CINEMA 4D layers can be set independently. If the check box is disabled for a specific CINEMA 4D scene layer, none of that layer's settings synchronize with the rest of the layers in the composition.

Live Link

Live Link synchronizes the timelines of CINEMA 4D and After Effects.

To work with Live Link, click the Enable button for Live Link. The specified CINEMA 4D version opens the current file. To enable Live Link in CINEMA 4D, choose Edit > Preferences > Communication > Live Link, and then select Live Link Enabled At Startup. The timelines are synchronized when switching between After Effects and CINEMA 4D. When you select a different C4D layer in After Effects, press Enable to synchronize that layer.

Render settings

The Cineware render settings determine how to render the scene inside After Effects. These settings can help you speed up the rendering process while you're working.

Renderer Determines which renderer to use. The following options are available:

Standard (Final): Uses the Standard renderer as specified in the C4D file. Use the CINEMA 4D application to edit these settings.

Standard (Draft): Uses the Standard renderer but turns off slower settings like anti-aliasing for better interactivity.

Software: Uses the settings to provide the fastest rendering, by letting you choose Display settings. Shaders and multi-passes are not displayed. Use the Software renderer to preview while you continue to work on the composition.

OpenGL: Hardware-accelerated rendering for better quality and higher speed as compared to the software render option. The OpenGL renderer in CINEWARE supports the same level of enhanced OpenGL quality as CINEMA 4D for the Transparency, Shadows, Post effects, and Noises properties.

Note: When you save your .c4d file in a full retail version of CINEMA 4D (not CINEMA 4D Lite R19, which is bundled with After Effects) with Render Settings set to the Physical or Hardware renderer, your file is rendered with those settings when the CINEWARE renderer is set to Standard (Final) or Standard (Draft).

Display This option is only enabled when you choose the Software renderer. The available options are Current Shading, Wireframe, and Box. The wireframe and box modes provide a simplified representation of the scene.

No Textures/Shader Check this option to speed up your render by not rendering textures and shaders.

No pre-calculation Check this option to speed up your render by disabling pre-calculations for computing motion dynamics or particle simulations. Do not check this option for final rendering.

Keep Textures in RAM Check this option to cache textures in the RAM so that they are not reloaded from disk and can be accessed more quickly. On the other hand, if you cache large textures, it may lead to reduction in available RAM.

Render Server Purge Memory: Clears the memory of the render server. Over a period, the response of the render server might degrade as it continues to store the scenes being processed. Clearing the up memory that the render server uses for internal caches can help After Effects extend the length of previews of complex scenes.

Project Settings

The following project settings are available in the Cineware effect:

Camera

CINEMA 4D Layers

Multi-Pass (Linear Workflow)

Commands

Camera Choose the camera to use for rendering.

CINEMA 4D Camera: Uses the camera that is defined as the render view camera in CINEMA 4D, or the default camera if none is defined.

Select CINEMA 4D camera: Use this option to choose a camera. When this option is enabled, click Set Camera.

Centered Comp Camera: Use this option to use the After Effects camera, and recalculate the CINEMA 4D co-ordinates to adapt to the After Effect co-ordinates. When you import an existing C4D file (typically modeled around 0,0,0) to be rendered with a new After Effects camera (which is centered on the composition), use this option to render the C4D model in the After Effects center. Otherwise the model may be unexpectedly shifted due to origin difference.

Comp Camera: Use this option to use the active After Effects camera. For this option to work, you must have added an After Effects camera. For example, use this option for a camera that has been added by extracting it from a Cinema 4D project (since those cameras reference CINEMA 4D's coordinate system with 0,0,0 at the center of the CINEMA 4D viewport). This option is suited for cameras that are added to After Effects by using the Layer > New > Camera command.

Set Camera: If a CINEMA 4D scene contains cameras other than the default camera, click this button and select the camera.

Set Take: This option is enabled if your c4d file contains takes. You can create multiple takes of your scene and modify any parameter in a take. If the current renderer does not support take selections, the main take is used.

CINEMA 4D Layers Enable and select the CINEMA 4D layers to render.

Set Layers Click to choose layers. Click the Set Layers button to choose one or more layers. In CINEMA 4D, layers let you organize multiple elements. You can use CINEMA 4D layers to composite between elements in the After Effects comp.

Multi-Pass (Linear Workflow) Use the Cinema 4D Multi-Pass option to specify which pass to render. The multi-pass features are only available when using the Standard renderer.

Multi-passes give you the ability to quickly make fine adjustments to a C4D scene by compositing different kinds of passes together in After Effects, such as adjusting just the shadows or reflections in the scene. For the results to match CINEMA 4D's default Linear Workflow project setting, you must work in a project in which colors are blended in linear light (either in a color-managed linear working space or with Blend Colors Using 1.0 Gamma set in the Project Settings dialog box).

Set Multi-Pass Click to select which pass to render on this layer. This option is only available if CINEMA 4D Multi-Pass option is enabled.

Defined Multi-Passes When enabled, adds the passes explicitly added in the .c4d file. This can include passes other than Image Layers.

Add Image Layers Use this option to create multiple pass layers with proper blending modes depending on the setting of Defined Multi-Passes. When the Defined Multi-Passes option is enabled, Add Image Layers restricts you to just adding the passes defined in the CINEMA 4D render settings rather than adding all supported types.

Note: When adding image layers, the layer that was originally selected are placed at the bottom of the Timeline stack, and renamed with RGBA Image appended to the layer name to reflect its multi-pass type.

Commands Use the following commands.

Comp Camera into CINEMA 4D Click Merge to add the current After Effects camera as a C4D camera in the C4D file. This modifies the C4D file. Use File > Revert to Saved in C4D to see the newly added After Effects camera. This command is especially useful to transfer camera data created by the 3D Camera Tracker effect. AE is prefixed to the camera name.

Note: If you merge again, the previous camera is not updated. A new copy is created instead.

CINEMA 4D Scene Data Click Extract to create 3D data such as cameras, lights, solids, or nulls for objects that have an External Compositing tag applied in the CINEMA 4D project.

Always enable Save Polygons for Melange option and Save Animation for Melange option in the CINEMA 4D preferences to avoid problems extracting scene data in After Effects.

Note: *Depending on your computer's security settings, you may see some warnings about TCP communication. This is because After Effects and the background CINEMA 4D renderer communicate using TCP which some security software may interpret as dangerous malware communication. For example, Mac OS may require you to confirm if you want to run this software "downloaded from the Internet". Confirm that you want to run this software.If you are able to import a .c4d file, but it fails to render, check if your Mac OS Gatekeeper or your firewall has blocked the background CINEMA 4D renderer from functioning and communicating with After Effects. For Mac users, set Allow Applications Downloaded From (under the General tab of Security and Privacy system preferences) to Anywhere.The TCP port used is defined in the Options in the Cineware effect, and this value is stored in the After Effects preferences file.*

Working with different instances of CINEMA 4D in Cineware Effect

You can specify the instance of CINEMA 4D that you want to use in the Cineware effect.

Cineware settings

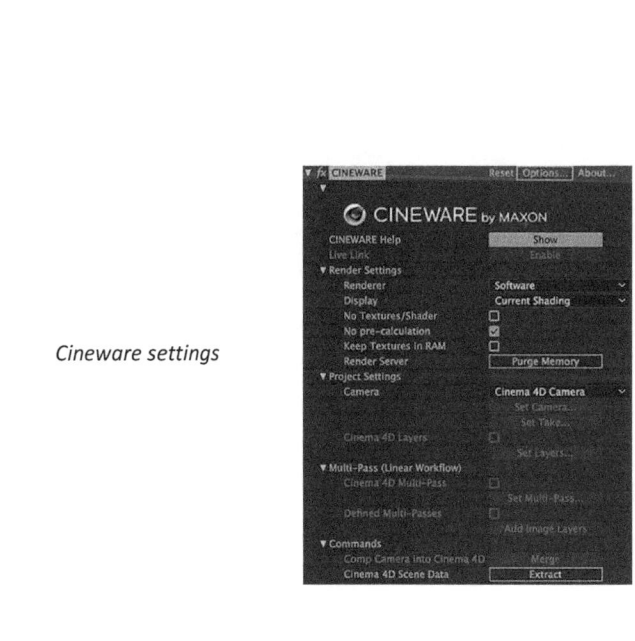

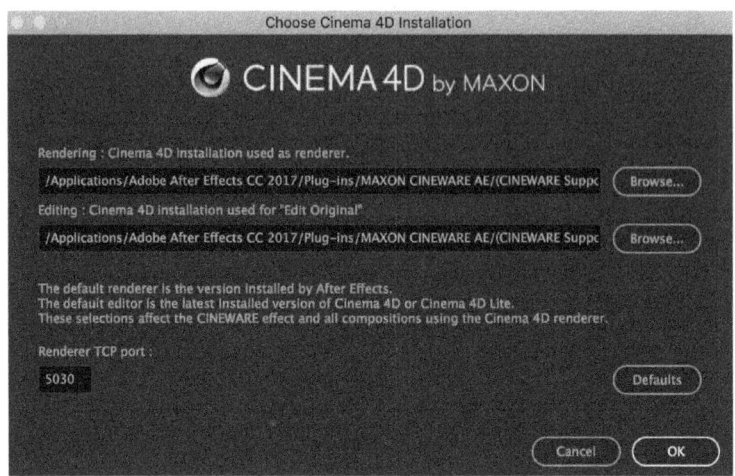

CINEMA 4D Render path and Editor path

Select Cineware Effect > Options and choose from the following settings:

CINEMA 4D Render Path - Choose CINEMA 4D for rendering in After Effects if you have the full retail version of CINEMA 4D installed.

CINEMA 4D Editor Path - Choose the version of CINEMA 4D to use when opening a .c4d file with Edit Original or when creating a CINEMA 4D file from After Effects. The default Editor is the latest installed version of CINEMA 4D or CINEMA 4D Lite R19.

The default CINEMA 4D application is located at :

C:\Program Files\Adobe\Adobe After Effects CC\Support Files\Plug-Ins\MAXON CINEWARE AE\(CINEWARE Support)\lite\CINEMA 4D Lite.exe (Windows)

/Applications/Adobe After Effects CC/Plug-ins/MAXON CINEWARE AE/(CINEWARE Support)/Lite/CINEMA 4D Lite.app (Mac OS).

After using a full retail version of CINEMA 4D as renderer, if you want to switch back to the default Cineware renderer, click the Defaults button in the Choose CINEMA 4D Installation dialog box.

Switch render paths

Follow the steps below to switch render paths (such as changing CINEMA 4D rendering application):

Options > Browse To Set Render Path

Select the new application.

Exit After Effects.

Launch After Effects.

Select Edit > Purge > All Memory & Disk Cache for the new settings to take effect.

If you experience a connection failure after switching the renderer, exit After Effects, wait for 20-30 seconds, and then ● relaunch the application again.

Rendering capabilities

When you choose CINEMA 4D versions R14 and above as the renderer, you can use various rendering capabilities within the After Effects Cineware plug-in other than the default renderer, such as Physical renderer and Sketch and Toon.

To use the Physical renderer, do the following:

Choose the Physical renderer in the CINEMA 4D Render Settings dialog. **a** From the Render menu, Select Render > Edit Render Settings.
b In the Render Settings dialog, set the pop-up to Renderer: Physical.

Click Physical and set other settings such Depth of Field or Motion Blur options.

Save the .c4d file with the renderer settings.

The renderer specified in CINEMA 4D is the one that is used by the Cineware effect when the Renderer Settings option in the effect is set to Standard (Final) and Standard (Draft).

Note: *You can control Sketch and Toon for individual objects in the Object manager by adding Tags > Sketch Tags > Sketch Style (see the Maxon CINEMA 4D Help documentation for more information about Sketch and Toon).*

To render Sketch and Toon, do the following:

From the Create menu in the CINEMA 4D application, select Create > Material > Sketch Material.

In the Render Settings dialog, set the pop-up to Renderer: Standard.

In the Render Settings dialog, ensure that Sketch and Toon post effects are added and checked.

Save the .c4d file with Sketch and Toon enabled.

Sketch and Toon is rendered by the Cineware effect when the renderer settings in the effect is set to Standard (Final).

Note: *The following versions of CINEMA 4D are compatible with Cineware:*

R14.042 or above. Use the CINEMA 4D online updater to install the current version.

R15.037 or above

R16

R17

R19

See CINEMA 4D Composition Renderer to learn about the new 3D Renderer used for extruding texts and shapes.

Import an After Effects project

You can import one After Effects project into another. Everything from the imported project—including footage items, compositions, and folders—appears inside a new folder in the current Project panel.

You can import an After Effects project from a different operating system, as long as you maintain the filenames, folder names, and either full or relative paths (folder locations) for all files in the project. To maintain relative paths, the source footage files must reside on the same volume as the project file. Use the File > Collect Files command to gather copies of all files in a project or composition into a single location. (See Cross-platform project considerations.)

Choose File > Import > File.

Select the After Effects project to import, and click Open.

If the operating system that you are using does not support a file format, if the file is missing, or if the reference link is broken, After Effects substitutes a placeholder item containing color bars. You can reconnect the placeholder to the appropriate file by double-clicking the entry in the Project panel and navigating to the source file. In most cases, you need to relink only one footage file. After Effects locates other missing items if they're in the same location.

Note: When you render a movie and export it to the QuickTime (MOV), Video for Windows (AVI) format, you can embed a link to the project in the container file. To import the project, import the MOV or AVI file, and choose Project from the Import As menu in the Import File dialog box. If the file contains a link to a project that has been moved, you can browse to locate the project..

Import an Adobe Premiere Pro project

Note: Importing an Adobe Premiere Pro project into After Effects does not use Dynamic Link. After Effects can't import a Premiere Pro project if one or more sequences in it are already dynamically linked to After Effects. (See Working with Adobe Premiere Pro and After Effects.)

When you import an Adobe Premiere Pro project, After Effects imports it into the Project panel as both a new composition containing each Adobe Premiere Pro clip as a layer, and as a folder containing each clip as an individual footage item. If your Adobe Premiere Pro project contains bins, After Effects converts them to folders within the Adobe Premiere Pro project folder. After Effects converts nested sequences to nested compositions.

Not all features of an Adobe Premiere Pro project are preserved when the project is imported into After Effects. The same features are preserved when you import a Premiere Pro project into After Effects as when you copy and paste between Premiere Pro and After Effects. (See Importing from After Effects and Adobe Premiere Pro .)

After Effects preserves the order of clips in the timeline, the footage duration (including all trimmed In and Out points), and marker and transition locations. After Effects bases the arrangement of layers in the Timeline panel on the arrangement of clips in the Adobe Premiere Pro Timeline panel. After Effects adds Adobe Premiere Pro clips to the Timeline panel as layers in the order in which they appeared—from the bottom up and from left to right—in the Adobe Premiere Pro Timeline panel. After Effects preserves changes made to the speed of a clip, for example, with the Clip > Speed command, and these changes appear as a value in the Stretch column in the After Effects Timeline panel.

After Effects imports effects common to Adobe Premiere Pro and After Effects, and preserves keyframes for these effects.

Transitions and titles (except for dissolves) included in your Adobe Premiere Pro project appear in the After Effects composition as solid layers with their original location and duration.

Audio Level keyframes are preserved.

Choose File > Import > File or File > Import > Adobe Premiere Pro Project.

If you choose Import > Adobe Premiere Pro Project, then only Adobe Premiere Pro projects are shown.

Select a project, and click OK.

Do any of the following:

To import only one sequence, choose a sequence from the menu.

To import audio, select Import Audio.

To add a single item from a track in an Adobe Premiere Pro project, copy the item in Adobe Premiere Pro, and choose Edit> Paste in After Effects.

Copy between After Effects and Adobe Premiere Pro

From the After Effects Timeline panel, you can copy layers based on audio or video footage items (including solids) and paste them into the Adobe Premiere Pro Timeline panel.

From the Adobe Premiere Pro Timeline panel, you can copy assets (any items in a track) and paste them into the After Effects Timeline panel.

From either After Effects or Adobe Premiere Pro, you can copy and paste footage items to the other's Project panel.

Note: *You can't, however, paste footage items from the After Effects Project panel into the Adobe Premiere Pro Timeline panel.*

If you want to work with all clips or a single sequence from an Adobe Premiere Pro project, use the Import command instead to import the project into After Effects.

Use Adobe Dynamic Link to create dynamic links, without rendering, between new or existing compositions in After Effects and Adobe Premiere Pro. (See About Dynamic Link)

Copy from After Effects to Adobe Premiere Pro

You can copy a layer based on a footage item from an After Effects composition and paste it into an Adobe Premiere Pro sequence. Adobe Premiere Pro converts these layers to clips in the sequence and copies the source footage item to its Project panel. If the layer contains an effect that is also used by Adobe Premiere Pro, Adobe Premiere Pro converts the effect and all of its settings and keyframes.

You can also copy nested compositions, Photoshop layers, solid-color layers, and audio layers. Adobe Premiere Pro converts nested compositions to nested sequences, and solid-color layers to color mattes. You cannot copy shape, text, camera, light, or adjustment layers to Adobe Premiere Pro.

Start Adobe Premiere Pro (you must start Adobe Premiere Pro before you copy the layer in After Effects).

Select a layer (or layers) from the After Effects Timeline panel.

Note: *If you select multiple layers and the layers don't overlap in After Effects, they're placed on the same track in Adobe Premiere Pro. On the other hand, if the layers overlap in After Effects, the order in which you select them determines the order of their track placement in Adobe Premiere Pro. Each layer is placed on a separate track, and the last selected layer appears on Track 1. For example, if you select layers from top to bottom, the layers appear in the reverse order in Adobe Premiere Pro, with the bottom-most layer on Track 1.*

Choose Edit > Copy.

In Adobe Premiere Pro, open a sequence in the Timeline panel.

Move the current-time indicator to the desired location, and choose either Edit > Paste or Edit > Paste Insert.

Results of pasting into Adobe Premiere Pro

When you paste a layer into an Adobe Premiere Pro sequence, keyframes, effects, and other properties in the copied layer are converted as follows:

After Effects item	Converted to in Adobe Premiere Pro	Notes
Audio volume property	Channel Volume filter	
Blending modes	Blending modes supported by Adobe Premiere Pro are converted	
Effect properties and keyframes	Effect properties and keyframes, if the effect also exists in Adobe Premiere Pro	Adobe Premiere Pro lists unsupported effects as offline in the Effect Controls panel. Some After Effects effects have the same names as those in Adobe Premiere Pro, but since they're actually different effects, they aren't converted.
Expressions	Not converted	
Layer markers	Clip markers	
Masks and mattes	Not converted	
Stereo Mixer effect	Channel Volume filter	
Time Remap property	Time Remapping effect	
Time Stretch property	Speed property	Speed and time stretch have an inverse relationship. For example, 200% stretch in After Effects converts to 50% speed in Adobe

		Premiere Pro.
Transform property values and keyframes	Motion or Opacity values and keyframes	The keyframe type—Bezier, Auto Bezier, Continuous Bezier, or Hold—is retained.
Source settings for R3D source files	Source settings for R3D source files	

Copy from Adobe Premiere Pro to After Effects

You can copy a video or audio asset from an Adobe Premiere Pro sequence and paste it into an After Effects composition. After Effects converts assets to layers and copies the source footage items into its Project panel. If the asset contains an effect that is also used by After Effects, After Effects converts the effect and all of its settings and keyframes.

You can copy color mattes, stills, nested sequences, and offline files, too. After Effects converts color mattes into solid-color layers and converts nested sequences into nested compositions. When you copy a Photoshop still image into After Effects, After Effects retains the Photoshop layer information. You cannot paste Adobe Premiere Pro titles into After Effects, but you can paste text with attributes from the Adobe Premiere Titler into After Effects.

Select an asset from the Adobe Premiere Pro Timeline panel.

Choose Edit > Copy.

In After Effects, open a composition in the Timeline panel.

With the Timeline panel active, choose Edit > Paste. The asset appears as the topmost layer in the Timeline panel.

Note: *To paste the asset at the current-time indicator, place the current-time indicator and press Ctrl+Alt+V (Windows) or Command+Option+V (Mac OS).*

Results of pasting into After Effects

When you paste an asset into an After Effects composition, keyframes, effects, and other properties in a copied asset are converted as follows:

Adobe Premiere Pro asset	Converted to in After Effects	Notes
Audio track	Audio layers	Audio tracks that are either 5.1 surround or greater than 16-bit aren't supported. Mono and stereo audio tracks are imported as one or two layers.
Bars and tone	Not converted	
Blending modes	Converted	
Clip marker	Layer marker	
Color mattes	Solid-color layers	
Crop filter	Mask layer	
Frame Hold	Time Remap property	
Mask	Converted	All mask properties in Premiere Pro, for example, feather, opacity, expansion, and so on, get copied in After Effects when you copy the mask into an After Effects composition.
Motion or Opacity values and keyframes	Transform property values and keyframes	Keyframe type—Bezier, Auto Bezier, Continuous Bezier, or Hold—is retained.
Sequence marker	Markers on a new solid-	To copy sequence

	color layer	markers, you must either copy the sequence itself or import the entire Adobe Premiere Pro project as a composition.
Speed property	Time Stretch property	Speed and time stretch have an inverse relationship. For example, 50% speed in Adobe Premiere Pro is converted to 200% stretch in After Effects.
Time Remapping effect	Time Remap property	
Titles	Not converted	
Universal counting leaders	Not converted	
Video and audio transitions	Opacity keyframes (Cross dissolve only) or solid-color layers	
Video effect properties and keyframes	Effect properties and keyframes, if the effect also exists in After Effects	After Effects doesn't display unsupported effects in the Effect Controls panel.
Volume and Channel Volume audio filters	Stereo mixer effect	Other audio filters are not converted.
Source settings for R3D source files	Source settings for R3D source files	

Note: When you import a Premiere Pro project into After Effects, features are converted in the same manner as they are converted when copying from Premiere Pro to After Effects.

Preparing and importing still images

Importing footage

Preparing still-image files for importing

You can import individual still images into After Effects or import a series of still images as a sequence. For information about the still-image formats that After Effects imports, see Supported import formats.

After Effects works internally in an RGB color space, but it can import and convert CMYK images. However, when possible, you should work in an RGB color space in applications such as Illustrator and Photoshop when creating images for video, film, and other non-print media. Working in RGB provides a larger gamut and more accurately reflects your final output.

Before you import a still image into After Effects, prepare it as completely as possible to reduce rendering time. It is usually easier and faster to prepare a still image in its original application than to modify it in After Effects. Consider doing the following to an image before importing it into After Effects:

Make sure that the file format is supported by the operating system you plan to use.

Crop the parts of the image that you do not want to be visible in After Effects.

Note: Illustrator files can have fractional dimensions (for example, 216.5x275.5 pixels). When importing these files, After Effects compensates for the fractional dimensions by rounding up to the next whole number of pixels (for example, 217x278 pixels). This rounding results in a black line at the right (width) or bottom (height) edge of the imported image. When cropping in Illustrator, make sure that the dimensions of the cropped area are whole numbers of pixels.

If you want to designate areas as transparent, create an alpha channel or use the transparency tools in applications such as Photoshop or Illustrator.

If final output will be broadcast video, avoid using thin horizontal lines (such as 1-pixel lines) for images or text because they may flicker as a result of interlacing. If you must use thin lines, add a slight blur so that the image or text appears in both video fields instead of flickering between them. (See Interlaced video and separating fieldsand Best practices for creating text and vector graphics for video.)

If final output will be broadcast video, make sure that important parts of the image fall within the action-safe and title-safe zones. When you create a document in Illustrator or Photoshop using a preset for film and video, the safe zones are shown as guide lines. (See Safe zones, grids, guides, and rulers.)

If the final output will be broadcast video, keep colors within the broadcast-safe ranges. (See Broadcast-safe colors.)

Save the file using the correct naming convention. For example, if you plan to import the file into After Effects on Windows, use a three-character filename extension.

Set the pixel dimensions to the resolution and frame aspect ratio that you will use in After Effects. If you plan to scale the image over time, set image dimensions that provide enough detail at the largest size the image has in the project. After Effects supports a maximum image size of 30,000x30,000 pixels for importing and rendering files. The size of image that you can import or export is influenced by the amount of physical RAM available to After Effects. The maximum composition dimensions are also 30,000x30,000 pixels.

Note: The image size or pixel dimensions setting in Photoshop (or other image-editing application) is relevant for the preparation of image data for import into After Effects—not dpi (dots per inch) or ppi (pixels per inch) settings. The image size determines how many pixels wide and tall an image is, whether those pixels are the tiny ones on a mobile device or the big ones on a motion billboard. The dpi or ppi settings are relevant to printing an image and to the scale of copied and pasted paths.

Import a single still image or a still-image sequence

You can import still image files as individual footage items, or you can import a series of still image files as a still-image sequence, which is a single footage item in which each still image is used as a single frame.

Importing footage

To import multiple image files as a single still-image sequence, the files must be in the same folder and use the same numeric or alphabetic filename pattern (such as Seq1, Seq2, Seq3).

When you import a file that appears to After Effects to be one file in a still-image sequence, After Effects by default imports all other files in the same folder that appear to be in the same sequence. Similarly, when you select multiple files that appear to be in a sequence, After Effects by default imports them as a sequence. You can see what After Effects is about to import by looking at the bottom of the Import dialog box. You can also import images and sequences by dragging files and folders into the Project panel.

To prevent After Effects from importing unwanted files when you want to import only a single file, or to prevent After Effects from interpreting multiple files as a sequence, deselect the Sequence option in the Import dialog box. After Effects remembers this setting and thereafter uses it as the default.

You can import multiple sequences from the same folder simultaneously by selecting files from different sequences and selecting Multiple Sequences at the bottom of the Import dialog box.

When importing a sequence of still images, you can use the Force Alphabetical Order option in the Import dialog box to import a sequence with gaps in its numbering (for example, Seq1, Seq2, Seq3, Seq5). If you import a sequence with gaps in its numbering without selecting this option, After Effects warns you of missing frames and replaces them with placeholders (if the Report Missing Frames option is checked in Edit > Preferences > Import).

After Effects uses settings of the first image in the sequence to determine how to interpret the images in the sequence.

If the image files in a sequence are of a layered file type—such as Adobe Photoshop or Adobe Illustrator documents— then you can choose to import the sequence as a standard footage item, or as a composition in which each layer in each file is imported as a separate sequence and appears as a separate layer in the Timeline panel.

Note: When you render a composition that contains a numbered sequence, the output module uses the start frame number as the first frame number. For example, if you start to render on frame 25, the name of the file is 00025.

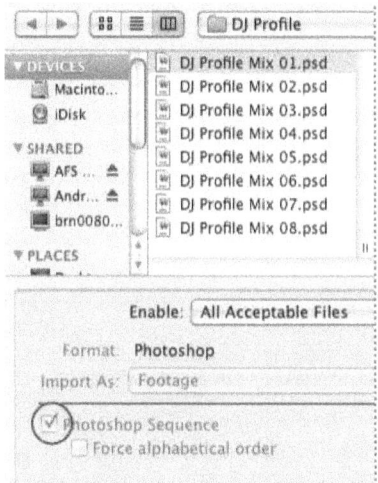

A sequence of still-image files (left) becomes one image sequence when imported into After Effects (right).

Verify individual image sequence files

When you import image sequence files in After Effects CC 2015.3 and later versions, it does not individually verify every file in the sequence. This accelerates the image sequence import process, especially when you import from network storage. However, if the sequence includes files that are aliases or shortcuts that do not resolve, for example if the drive is offline, After Effects does not report those files as missing.

Importing footage

If you encounter unexpected missing frames while importing an image sequence, you can enable the Verify Individual Files option, which is comparatively slower, but verifies all files in the sequence (Edit > Preferences > Import and enable the Sequence Footage: Verify Individual Files).

Import a still-image sequence as a single footage item

Choose File > Import > File.

Select any file in the sequence. To import a subset of files in a sequence, select the first file, hold down Shift, and then select the last file to import.

Choose Footage from the Import As menu.

Click Open (Windows) or Import (Mac OS).

Click OK.

If at any time you decide that you want access to the individual components of the footage item, you can convert it to a composition. See Convert a merged footage item into a composition.

Import a still-image sequence as a composition

When you import a Photoshop or Illustrator file as a composition, you have access to the individual layers, blending modes, adjustment layers, layer styles, masks, guides, and other features created in Photoshop or Illustrator. The imported composition and a folder containing each of its layers as footage items appears in the Project panel.

Choose File > Import > File.

Select any file in the sequence. To import a subset of files in a sequence, select the first file, hold down Shift, and then select the last file to import.

Choose one of the following from the Import As menu:

Composition - Retain Layer Sizes Import the layers, each with its original dimensions.

One reason to import as a composition with layers at their original dimensions (rather than importing each layer at the composition frame size) is so that each layer has its anchor point set at the center of the cropped graphics object, rather than at the center of the composition frame. This more often makes transformations work more as you'd expect and prefer when animating individual layers of an imported graphic item. For example,

if you have a car with a separate layer for each wheel, importing as a composition with layers at their original sizes puts the anchor point of each wheel in the center of the wheel, which makes rotating the wheels work as you'd expect.

Composition Import layers and have the dimensions of each match the dimensions of the composition frame.

Click Open (Windows) or Import (Mac OS).

Convert a merged footage item into a composition

When you import a layered file, such as a Photoshop or Illustrator file, as footage, all of its layers are merged together. If at any time you decide that you want access to the individual components of the footage item, you can convert it to a composition.

To convert all instances of a footage item, select it in the Project panel and choose File > Replace Footage > With Layered Comp.

To convert only one instance of the footage item, select the layer in the Timeline panel, and choose Layer > Convert To Layered Comp.

Note: It may take a few moments to convert a merged footage item to a layered composition.

Importing footage

Change the frame rate of a sequence

When you import a sequence of still images, it assumes the frame rate specified by the Sequence Footage preference in the Import category. The default rate is 30 frames per second (fps). You can change the frame rate after importing by reinterpreting the footage item:

Select the sequence in the Project panel, choose File > Interpret Footage > Main, and then enter a new value for Assume This Frame Rate.

For more information, see Frame rate.

Preparing and importing Photoshop files

Note: *For information and instructions that apply to all kinds of still image files, see Preparing still-image files for importingand Import a single still image or a still-image sequence.*

Note: *In After Effects CS6 and later, video layers in Photoshop .psd documents are not supported.*

Because After Effects includes the Photoshop rendering engine, After Effects imports all attributes of Photoshop files, including position, blending modes, opacity, visibility, transparency (alpha channel), layer masks, layer groups (imported as nested compositions), adjustment layers, layer styles, layer clipping paths, vector masks, image guides, and clipping groups.

Before you import a layered Photoshop file into After Effects, prepare it thoroughly to reduce preview and rendering time. Avoid problems importing and updating Photoshop layers by doing the following:

Organize and name layers. If you change a layer name in a Photoshop file after you have imported it into After Effects, After Effects retains the link to the original layer. However, if you delete a layer, After Effects is unable to find the original layer and lists it as Missing in the Project panel.

Make sure that each layer has a unique name. This is not a requirement of the software, but helps to keep you from becoming confused.

If you think that you might add layers to the Photoshop file in Photoshop after you have imported it into After Effects, go ahead and add a small number of placeholder layers before you import the file into After Effects. When you refresh the file in After Effects, it will not pick up any layers that have been added since the file was imported.

Unlock layers in Photoshop before importing into After Effects. This is not necessary for most kinds of layers, but it is required for some kinds of layers. For example, background layers that must be converted to RGB may not be imported correctly if they are locked.

A convenient command within After Effects is Layer > New > Adobe Photoshop File, which adds a layer to a composition and then opens the source of that layer in Photoshop for you to begin creating a visual element, such as a background layer for your movie. The layer in Photoshop is created with the correct settings for your After Effects composition. As with many of the Creative Suite applications, you can use the Edit Original command in After Effects to open a PSD file in Photoshop, make and save changes, and have those changes appear immediately in the movie that refers to the PSD source file. Even if you don't use Edit Original, you can use the Reload Footage command to have After Effects refresh its layers to use the current version of the PSD file. (See Create a layer and new Photoshop footage itemand Edit footage in its original application.)

Note: *One good way to prevent interlace flicker from thin horizontal lines in still images is to run the Interlace Flicker Removal action in Photoshop before you bring the still images into After Effects. Photoshop includes several video actions for utility purposes such as this.*

Online resources about preparing and importing Photoshop files

Importing footage

Richard Harrington and Ian Robinson provide a free sample chapter from their "Motion Graphics with Adobe Creative Suite 5 Studio Techniques" book on the Peachpit Press website. This chapter shows how to prepare Illustrator and Photoshop files.

See this video tutorial by Andrew Devis on the Creative Cow website about importing and using Photoshop PSD files in After Effects.

Color modes

Layered Photoshop (PSD) files need to be saved in RGB or Grayscale color mode for After Effects to import them as a composition and to separate the layers. CMYK, LAB, Duotone, Monotone, and Tritone color modes are not supported for layered files; After Effects will import a file that uses one of these color modes as a single, flattened image.

(Regarding the other color modes available in Photoshop such as Bitmap and Indexed: Photoshop does not support layers in these color modes.)

To determine or change the color mode of a document in Photoshop, choose Image > Mode. (The color mode is also displayed in the title bar of the document window.)

Masks and alpha channels

Adobe Photoshop supports a transparent area and one optional layer mask (alpha channel) for each layer in a file. You can use these layer masks to specify how different areas within a layer are hidden or revealed. If you import one layer, After Effects combines the layer mask (if present) with the transparent area and imports the layer mask as a straight alpha channel.

If you import a layered Photoshop file as a merged file, After Effects merges the transparent areas and layer masks of all the layers into one alpha channel that is premultiplied with white.

When you import a Photoshop file as a composition, vector masks are converted to After Effects masks. You can then modify and animate these masks within After Effects.

Photoshop clipping groups, layer groups, and Smart Objects

If the layered Photoshop file contains clipping groups, After Effects imports each clipping group as a precomposition nested within the main composition. After Effects automatically applies the Preserve Underlying Transparency option to each layer in the clipping-group composition, maintaining transparency settings. These nested precompositions have the same dimensions as the main composition.

Paul Tuersley provides a script on the AE Enhancers forum that crops the precompositions to the size of their contents, while retaining their correct position in the main composition.

Photoshop layer groups are imported as individual compositions.

It is often valuable to group layers into Smart Objects in Photoshop so that you can import meaningful collections of Photoshop layers as individual layers in After Effects. For example, if you used 20 layers to create your foreground object and 30 layers to create your background object in Photoshop, you probably don't need to import all of those individual layers into After Effects if all that you want to do is animate your foreground object flying in front of your background object; consider grouping them into a single foreground Smart Object and a single background Smart Object before importing the PSD file into After Effects.

Photoshop layer styles and blending modes

After Effects also supports blending modes and layer styles applied to the file. When you import a Photoshop file with layer styles, you can choose the Editable Layer Styles option or the Merge Layer Styles Into Footage option:

Editable Layer Styles Matches appearance in Photoshop and preserves supported layer style properties as editable.

Importing footage

Note: *A layer with a layer style interferes with intersection of 3D layers and the casting of shadows.*

Merge Layer Styles Into Footage Layer styles are merged into the layer for faster rendering, but the appearance may not match the appearance of the image in Photoshop. This option doesn't interfere with intersection of 3D layers or casting of shadows.

Preparing and importing Illustrator files

Note: *For information and instructions that apply to all kinds of still image files, see Preparing still-image files for importingand Import a single still image or a still-image sequence.*

Before you save an Illustrator file for importing into After Effects, consider doing the following:

Create your document in Illustrator using one of the Video And Film document profiles. In addition to creating a document at the appropriate size for video or film work, this creates a document with two artboards: one at the appropriate frame size, and one much larger. When you bring such a document into After Effects, the area outside the smaller artboard isn't cropped and lost; it's retained outside of the composition frame. This only works for an Illustrator document with multiple layers imported as a composition.

To ensure that Illustrator files appear correctly in After Effects, select Create PDF Compatible File in the Illustrator Options dialog box.

To copy paths between Illustrator and After Effects, make sure that the Preserve Paths option is selected in the Files & Clipboard section of the Illustrator Preferences dialog box.

To ensure that files rasterize most faithfully in After Effects, save your file in AI format instead of Illustrator 8.x or 9.x EPS format.

To separate objects in an Illustrator file into separate layers, use the Release To Layers command in Illustrator. Then, you can import the layered file into After Effects and animate the layers separately.

If you are working with Edit Original to move objects and layers in Illustrator, import the Illustrator document into After Effects as a composition with document-sized layers (not using the Retain Layer Size option).

When you import an Illustrator file, After Effects makes all empty areas transparent by converting them into an alpha channel.

Note: When you've imported an Illustrator file, you can specify whether anti-aliasing is to be performed at higher quality or at higher speed. Select the footage item in the Project panel and choose File > Interpret Footage > Main, and click the More Options button at the bottom of the dialog box.

After Effects does not read embedded color profiles from Illustrator files. To ensure color fidelity, assign an input color profile to the Illustrator footage item that matches the color profile with which the Illustrator file was created.

After Effects can't read blending modes from AI documents saved as a version later than Illustrator CS2. If you need to ■ retain blending mode information when importing a file into After Effects from Illustrator, save the document as an Illustrator CS2 document.

For information on preserving sharpness of vector graphics (avoiding pixelation), see Continuously rasterize a layer containing vector graphics.

Online resources for preparing and importing Illustrator files

Dave Nagel provides instructions on the DMN website for importing an Illustrator document into After Effects with the Illustrator objects on separate layers in After Effects.

In a thread on the After Effects user-to-user forum, JETalmage provides a script that converts sub-layers in Illustrator into top-level layers. This is a necessary step in preparing an Illustrator file for importing into After Effects if you intend to animate these items independently.

Importing footage

Steve Holmes provides a tutorial on the Layers Magazine website that shows how to create and prepare vines, swirls, and flourishes in Illustrator and then import, reveal, and animate them in After Effects using the Stroke effect.

Richard Harrington and Ian Robinson provide a free sample chapter from their "Motion Graphics with Adobe Creative Suite 5 Studio Techniques" book on the Peachpit Press website. This chapter shows how to prepare Illustrator and Photoshop files.

Importing camera raw files with Camera Raw

You can import sequences of camera raw files much as you import sequences of other kinds of still image files.

After Effects applies the settings for the first camera raw image in the sequence to all of the images in the sequence that do not have their own XMP sidecar files. After Effects does not check the Camera Raw database for image settings.

Note: *Camera raw files are uncompressed. Their large size may increase rendering time.*

Choose File > Import > File.

Select the camera raw file, and click Open.

Make any necessary adjustments in the Camera Raw dialog box, and click OK.

You can adjust a camera raw image after importing it. To open the image in the Camera Raw dialog box, select the footage item in the Project panel, choose File > Interpret Footage > Main, and click More Options.

Note: *You can't assign an input color profile to a camera raw image for use in a color-managed project. For information on how colors are automatically interpreted, see Interpret a footage item by assigning an input color profile.*
See this blog post for links to free excerpts from books about Camera Raw by Conrad Chavez, Bruce Fraser, Jeff Schewe, ▪ Ben Willmore, and Dan Ablan.

Cineon and DPX footage items

A common part of the motion-picture film production workflow is scanning the film and encoding the frames into the Cineon or DPX file format. The DPX (Digital Picture Exchange) format is a standard format closely related to the Cineon format.

You can import Cineon 4.5 or Digital Picture Exchange (DPX) files directly into an After Effects project as individual frames or as a sequence of numbered stills. Once you have imported a Cineon or DPX file, you can use it in a composition and then render the composition as an image sequence.

To preserve the full dynamic range of motion-picture film, Cineon files are stored using logarithmic 10-bpc color. However, After Effects internally uses 8-bpc, 16-bpc, or 32-bpc color, depending on the color bit depth of the project. Work with Cineon files in a 16- or 32-bpc project—by default, After Effects stretches the logarithmic values to the full range of values available.

Cineon data has a 10-bit white point of 685 and a 10-bit black point of 95. Values above 685 are retained, but are treated as highlights. Rather than abruptly clipping highlights to white, After Effects interprets highlights using a gradual ramp defined by the Highlight Rolloff value. You can modify the 10-bit white point and 10-bit black point input levels and the output (converted) white point and black point levels to match your specific footage items or creative needs.

Use a project color depth of 32 bpc when working with Cineon footage items so that highlights are preserved, in which case you don't need to roll off the highlights.

When you choose DPX/Cineon Sequence from the Format menu in the Output Module Settings dialog box, you can then open the Cineon Settings dialog box to set output options. Choose whether to output DPX (.dpx) files or FIDO/Cineon 4.5 (.cin) files in the File Format section of the Cineon Settings dialog box.

After Effects provides three basic ways of working with the colors in Cineon footage items:

The easiest—and recommended—way is to enable color management and assign an input color profile to a Cineon footage item in the Color Management tab of the Interpret Footage dialog box, corresponding to the film stock on which the footage was recorded. If creating output for film, use the same profile as the output color profile so that the output file matches the film stock. One advantage of using color management features to work with Cineon footage items is that compositing with images from other footage types is made easier. See Interpret a footage item by assigning an input color profile.

If you need the settings for the interpretation of the Cineon footage item to change over time, then you can apply the Cineon Converter effect to a layer that uses the Cineon footage item as its source. See .

If you need to manually modify the settings for a Cineon footage item, or if you don't want to use color management, then you can use the Cineon Settings dialog box. To open this dialog box, click the Cineon Settings button in the Color Management tab of the Interpret Footage dialog box.

Manual settings in the Cineon Settings dialog box:

Converted Black Point Specifies the black point used for the layer in After Effects.

Converted White Point Specifies the white point used for the layer in After Effects.

10 Bit Black Point
10 Bit White Point
Current Gamma

Highlight Rolloff Specifies the rolloff value used to correct bright highlights. To get over range values when working in 32 bpc, set the value to 0.

Logarithmic Conversion Converts the Cineon sequence from log color space to the target gamma specified by the Current Gamma setting. When you're ready to produce output from the Cineon file, it is important that you reverse the conversion. (To convert from logarithmic to linear, set Current Gamma to 1.)

Units Specifies the units After Effects uses to display dialog values.

Using 3D Features

Create a 3D environment in After Effects.

Look at a 3D scene from multiple views.

Create 3D text.

Rotate and position layers along x, y, and z axes.

Animate a camera layer.

Add lights to create shadows and depth.

Export an After Effects composition to use in Maxon Cinema 4D.

Import a Cinema 4D scene into After Effects.

PROJECT: TITLE CARD FOR A PRODUCTION COMPANY

By clicking a single switch in the Timeline panel in After Effects, you can turn a 2D layer into a 3D layer, opening up a whole new world of creative possibilities. Maxon Cinema 4D Lite, included with After Effects, gives you even greater flexibility.

Getting started

Adobe After Effects can work with layers in two dimensions (x, y) or in three dimensions (x, y, z). So far in this book, you've worked primarily in two dimensions. When you specify a layer as three-dimensional (3D), After Effects adds the z axis, which provides control over the layer's depth. By combining this depth with a variety of lights and camera angles, you can create animated 3D projects that take advantage of the full range of natural motion, lighting and shadows, perspective, and focusing effects. In this lesson, you'll explore how to create and animate 3D layers. Then you'll use Maxon Cinema 4D Lite (installed with After Effects) to create high-end 3D text for a title card for a fictional production company.

First, you'll preview the final movie and then set up the project.

Make sure the following files are in the Lessons/Lesson11 folder on your hard disk, or download them from your Account page at www.peachpit.com now:

In the Assets folder: Lunar.mp3, Space_Landscape.jpg

In the Sample_Movie folder: Lesson11.mov

Open and play the Lesson11.mov file to see what you will create in this lesson. When you are done, quit QuickTime Player. You may delete this sample movie from your hard disk if you have limited storage space.

When you begin this lesson, restore the default application settings for After Effects. See

"Restoring default preferences" on page 2.

Start After Effects, and then immediately hold down Ctrl+Alt+Shift (Windows) or Command+Option+Shift (Mac OS). When prompted, click OK to delete your preferences. Close the Start window.

After Effects opens to display an empty, untitled project.

Choose File > Save As > Save As.

In the Save Project As dialog box, navigate to the Lessons/Lesson11/Finished_Project folder. Name the project **Lesson11_Finished.aep**, and click Save.

Click the Create A New Composition button (▣) at the bottom of the Project panel.

In the Composition Settings dialog box, do the following, and then click OK:

Name the composition **Lunar Landing Media**.

Choose HDTV 1080 24 from the Preset menu.

Enter **3:00** for the Duration.

Make sure the Background Color is black.

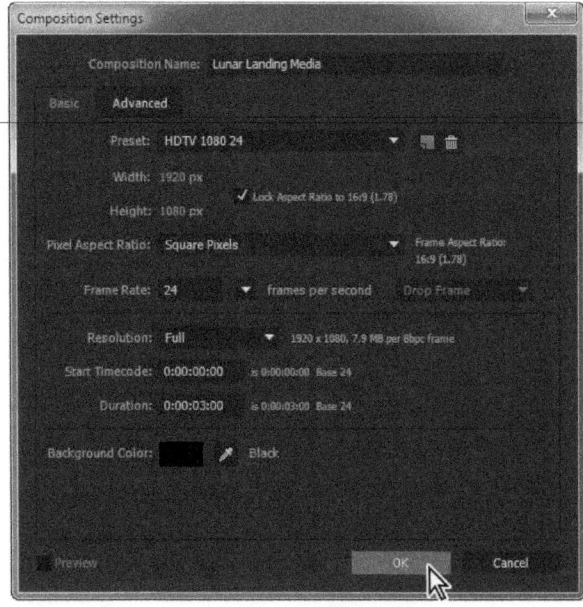

Choose File > Save.

Creating 3D text

In order to move something in 3D space, you need to make it a 3D object. Initially, any layer is flat, with only x (width) and y (height) dimensions, and can be moved only along those axes. But all you have to do to move a layer in three dimensions in After Effects is to turn on its 3D layer switch, which lets you manipulate the object along its z axis (depth). You'll create text, and then make it 3D. This layer will serve as a placeholder for text you'll create later in Cinema 4D.

Click in the Timeline panel to make it active.

Select the Horizontal Type tool (T) in the Tools panel.

After Effects adds the Character and Paragraph panels to the stack and opens the Character panel.

● Note

If Blackoak Std is not available, install it using Typekit. Choose File > Add Fonts From Typekit, search for Blackoak Std, and sync it using Creative Cloud. Once you've synced the font, it will be available in all applications on your system.

Make the Character panel wider, if necessary, and then select the following settings:

Font: Blackoak Std

Fill Color: Black

Stroke Color: White

Font Size: **70** px

Leading: **70** px

Tracking: **20%**

Stroke Width: **5** px

Vertical Scale: **65%**

Select All Caps, and then make sure Stroke Over Fill is chosen from the pop-up menu in the Character panel. (You may need to drag the bottom of the Character panel to extend it in order to see all settings.)

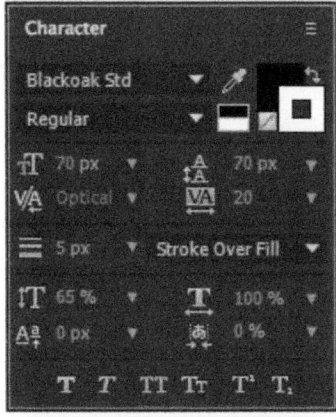

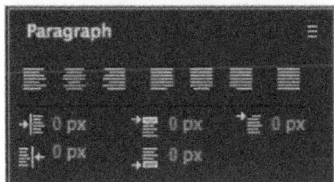

Open the Paragraph panel, and select the Center Text alignment option.

Click anywhere in the Composition panel and type **Lunar Landing Media**, with each word on its own line, as in the image below.

Select the Selection tool (▶).

In the Timeline panel, expand the Transform properties for the Lunar Landing Media layer, and change the Position property to **960, 540**.

⬤ **Note**

After Effects uses a different coordinate numbering convention than other 3D applications. In After Effects, the upper left corner of the composition is considered 0, 0. In many 3D applications, including Maxon Cinema 4D, the center of the world (often the screen) is the origin, or 0, 0, 0 point.

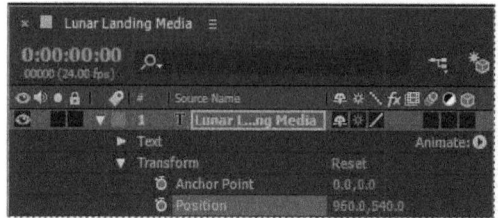 

The text is centered in the composition.

In the Timeline panel, select the 3D Layer switch (◉) for the Lunar Landing Media layer to give it three dimensions.

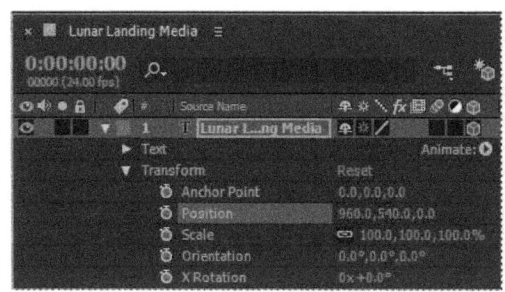

Three 3D Rotation properties appear in the Transform group for the layer, and properties that previously supported only two dimensions now display a third value for the z axis. In addition, a new property group named Material Options appears.

When the layer is selected, a color-coded 3D axis appears over the layer's anchor point in the Composition panel. The red arrow controls the x axis, the green arrow controls the y axis, and the blue arrow controls the z axis. At the moment, the z axis appears at the intersection of the x and y axes; it may be difficult to see against the black background. The letter x, y, or z appears when you position the Selection tool over the corresponding axis. When you move or rotate the layer while the pointer is over a particular axis, the layer's movement is restricted to that axis.

Hide the properties for the Lunar Landing Media layer.

Using 3D views

Sometimes the appearance of 3D layers can be deceptive. For example, a layer might appear to be scaling smaller along its x and y axes when it's actually moving along the z axis. You can't always tell from the default view in the Composition panel. The Select View Layout pop-up menu at the bottom of the Composition panel lets you divide the panel into different views of a single frame, so you can see your work from multiple angles. You specify different views using the 3D View pop-up menu.

At the bottom of the Composition panel, click the Select View Layout pop-up menu, and choose 4 Views, if your screen is large enough to display them. Otherwise, choose 2 Views - Horizontal.

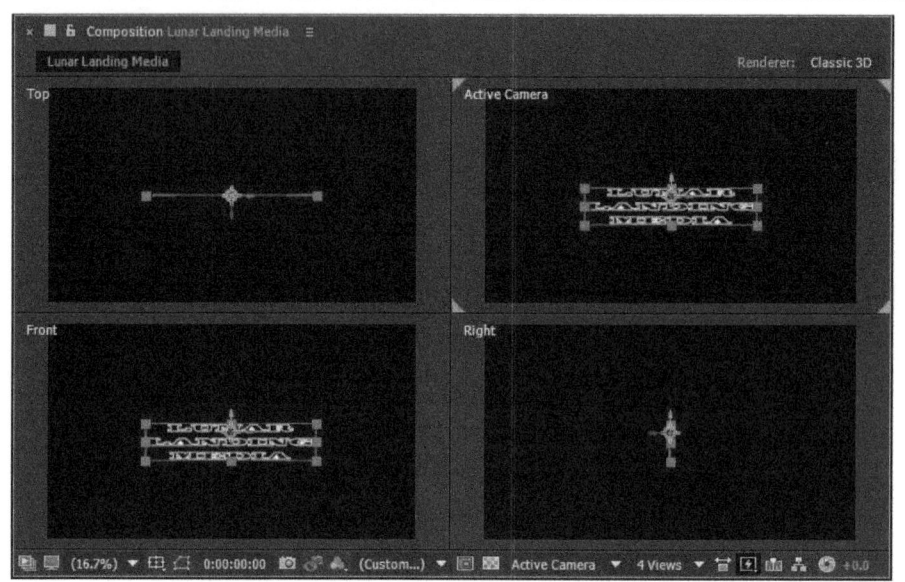

With 4 Views selected, the upper left quadrant displays the scene from the top (along the y axis). There, you can see the z axis, and it's clear that the text layer has no depth. The lower left quadrant shows the view from the front. The upper right quadrant displays what the camera sees, but because there is no camera in the scene, it's the same as the front view. The lower right quadrant shows the view from the right, as if you were observing it along the x axis.

With 2 Views - Horizontal selected, the left view shows the scene from the top, and the right shows the camera's view (currently the front view).

Click the Front view to make it active. (Blue corner tabs appear around the active view.) Then, from the 3D View pop-up menu, choose Custom View 1 to see the scene from a different perspective. (If your Composition window displays only two views, click the Top view, and choose Custom View 1 from the 3D View pop-up menu.)

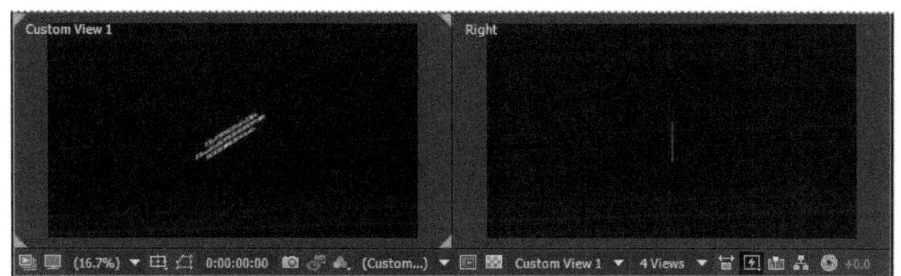

Viewing your 3D scene from different perspectives can help you align elements more accurately, view how layers are interacting with each other, and understand how objects, lights, and cameras are positioned in 3D space.

Importing a background

The text in your title card should appear to be moving in outer space. You'll import an image to use as a background.

Double-click an empty area of the Project panel to open the Import File dialog box.

Navigate to the Lesson11/Assets folder, and double-click the Space_Landscape.jpg file.

Drag the Space_Landscape.jpg item into the Timeline panel, placing it at the bottom of the layer stack.

Rename the Space_Landscape.jpg layer **Background**.

In the Timeline panel, select the Background layer, and then click the 3D Layer switch (⊚) to convert it to a 3D layer.

Make sure the Background layer is selected. Then, in the Right view in the Composition panel, drag the z-axis arrow (the blue arrow) to the right to move the Background layer further behind the text. Watch the other layers as you drag to see how the layer interacts with 3D space.

⊚ **Note**

If you're displaying only two views, select the Active Camera view, and choose Right from the 3D View pop-up menu. Then complete step 6.

In the Timeline panel, press the P key to display the Position property for the Background layer. Change the Position to **960**, **300**, **150**.

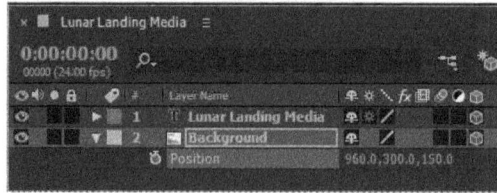 

Choose File > Save to save your work so far.

Adding 3D lights

You've created a 3D scene, but it doesn't yet look three-dimensional from the front. Adding light to a composition creates shadows that give depth to the scene. You'll create two new lights for your composition.

Creating a light layer

In After Effects, a *light* is a type of layer that shines light on other layers. You can choose from among four different types of lights—Parallel, Spot, Point, and Ambient—and modify them with various settings. Lights, by default, are directed toward a point of interest, which is the focus area of the scene.

Deselect all layers so that the new layer you create will appear at the top of the layer stack.

Press the Home key, or move the current-time indicator to the beginning of the time ruler.

Choose Layer > New > Light.

In the Light Settings dialog box, do the following:

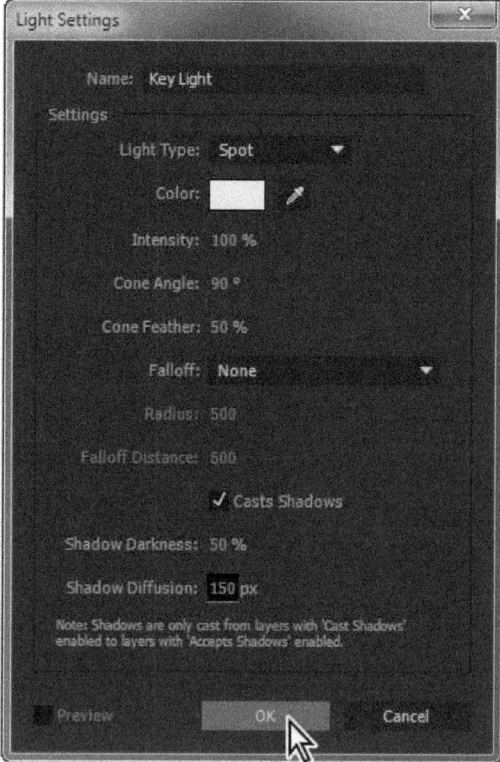

Name the layer **Key Light**.

Choose Spot from the Light Type menu.

Set Color to a light orange (R=**255**, G=**235**, B=**195**).

Make sure Intensity is set to **100%** and Cone Angle to **90** degrees.

Make sure Cone Feather is set to **50%**.

Select the Casts Shadows option.

Set Shadow Darkness to **50%** and Shadow Diffusion to **150** pixels.

Click OK to create the light layer.

In the Timeline panel, the light layer is represented by a light bulb icon (💡). In the Composition panel, a wireframe illustrates the light's position, with a cross-hairs icon (⊕) representing the point of interest.

Positioning the spotlight

The point of interest for this light is currently pointed at the center of the scene. Because that's where the text layer is located, you don't need to adjust it. However, you'll change the light position so the scene looks less bleak.

Select the Key Light layer in the Timeline panel, and press the P key to reveal the Position property for the light layer.

In the Timeline panel, type **955, −102, −2000** in the Position property. The light is now in front of and above the object, aiming down.

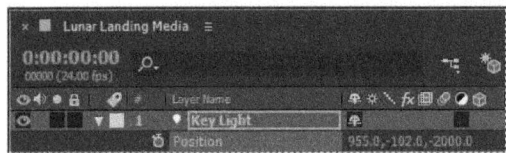

Creating and positioning the fill light

The key light gives the scene a moody look, but it's still very dark. You'll add a fill light to lighten the darker areas.

Choose Layer > New > Light.

In the Light Settings dialog box, do the following:

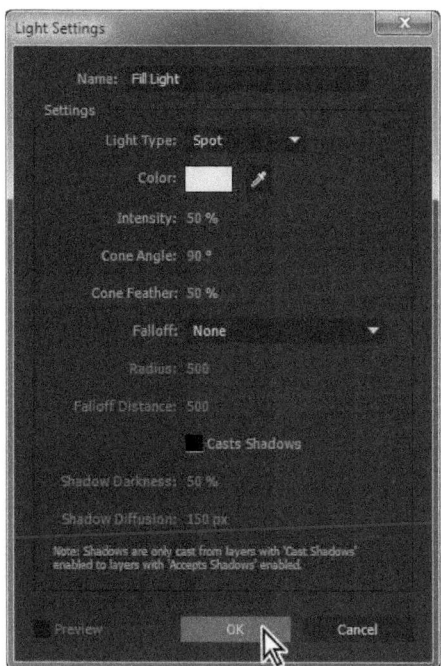

Name the layer **Fill Light**.

Choose Spot from the Light Type menu.

Set the Color to a light blue (R=**205**, G=**238**, B=**251**).

Set Intensity to **50%** and Cone Angle to **90** degrees.

Make sure Cone Feather is set to **50%**.

Deselect Casts Shadows.

Click OK to create the light layer.

In the Timeline panel, select the Fill Light layer, and press the P key to reveal its Position property.

Change the position to **2624**, **370**, **−1125**.

The text stroke, stars, and moon highlight are all much brighter now.

Hide the open properties for all layers, and choose File > Save.

Casting shadows and setting material properties

The scene is looking better, with a mix of warm and cool colors. However, it still doesn't look three-dimensional. You'll change the Material Options properties to determine how the 3D layers interact with the lights and shadows.

Select the Lunar Landing Media layer in the Timeline panel, and press the A key twice (AA) to reveal the Material Options properties for the layer.

The Material Options property group defines the surface properties of the 3D layer. You can also set shadow and light transmission values.

For Casts Shadows, click the word *Off* to toggle the setting on. (Make sure it says *On*, not *Only*.)

The text layer now casts shadows based on the lights in the scene.

Change the Diffuse value to **60%** and the Specular Intensity to **60%** so that the text layer reflects more of the light in the scene.

Increase the Specular Shininess to **15%** to give the surface a more metallic shine.

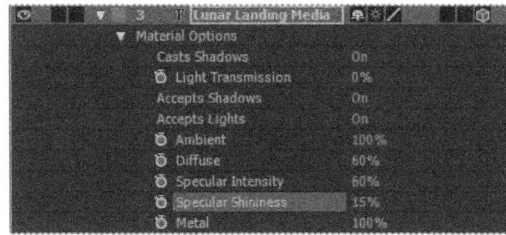 

Hide the properties for the Lunar Landing Media layer.

Adding a camera

You've already seen that you can view a 3D scene from different perspectives. You can also view 3D layers from various angles and distances using layers called *cameras*. When you set a camera view for your composition, you look at the layers as though you were looking through that camera. You can view a composition through the active camera or through a named, custom camera. If you have not created a custom camera, then the active camera is the same as the default composition view.

So far, you have been viewing this composition primarily from the Front, Right, and Custom View 1 angles. Currently, the Active Camera view doesn't let you see your composition from any specific angle. To see everything you want to see, you'll create a custom camera.

Deselect all layers, and then choose Layer > New > Camera.

In the Camera Settings dialog box, choose 20mm from the Preset menu, and click

OK.

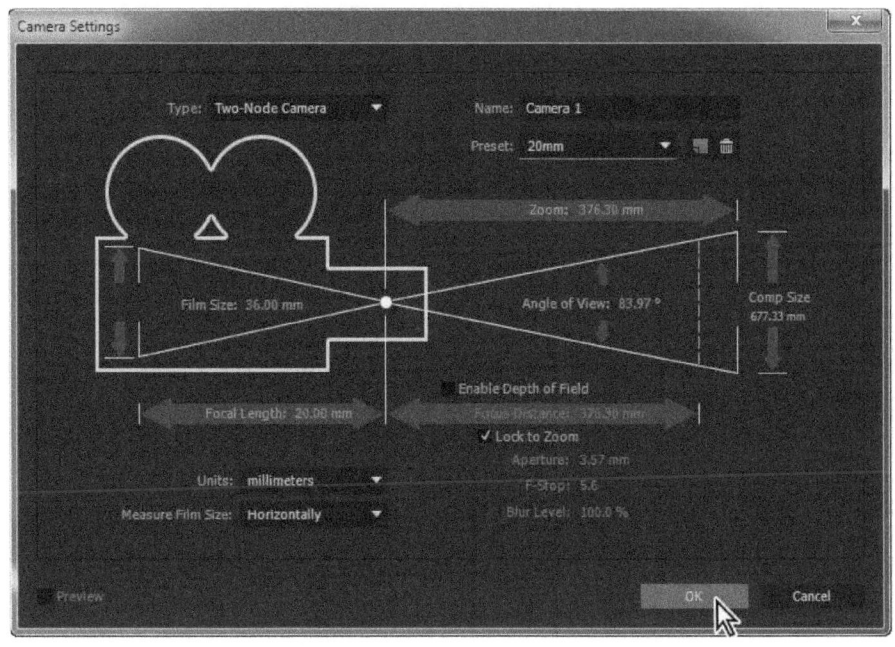

The Camera 1 layer appears at the top of the layer stack in the Timeline panel (with a camera icon next to the layer name), and the Composition panel updates to reflect the new camera layer's perspective. The view should change slightly, because the 20mm preset shows a wider field of view than the default. If you didn't notice the scene change, toggle the visibility of the Camera 1 layer to see it, and then make sure it's visible.

> **Tip**

After Effects displays the wireframes for cameras by default. You can instruct After Effects to display wireframes only when cameras (or spotlights) are selected, or not at all. Choose View Options from the Composition panel menu, and then choose the options you want from the Camera Wireframes and Spotlight Wireframes menus. Then click OK.

Choose 2 Views - Horizontal from the Select View Layout pop-up menu at the bottom of the Composition panel. Change the view on the left to Right, and make sure the view on the right is set to Active Camera.

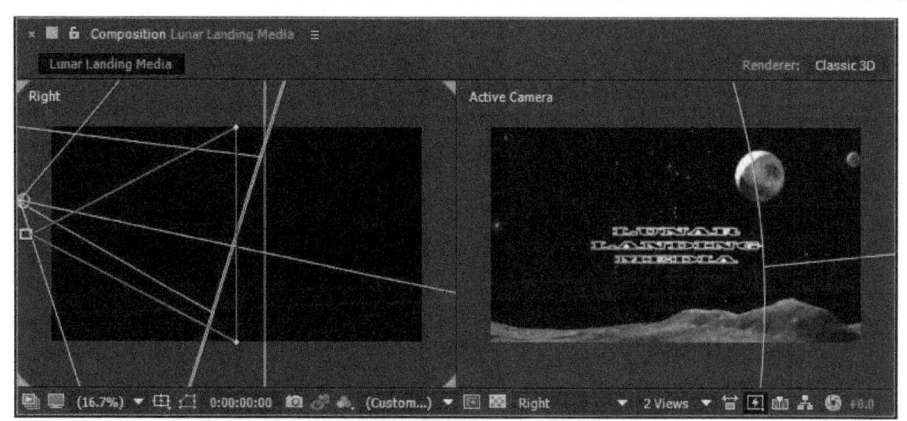

Like light layers, camera layers have a *point of interest* that can be used to determine what the camera looks at. By default, the camera's point of interest is the center of the composition. That's where your text currently is, so that point of interest works well.

Make sure the current-time indicator is at the beginning of the time ruler. Select the Camera 1 layer, and press the P key to reveal the Position property for the layer. Create an initial keyframe by clicking the stopwatch icon (🖎) next to the Position property.

Set the z-axis value to **–1000**.

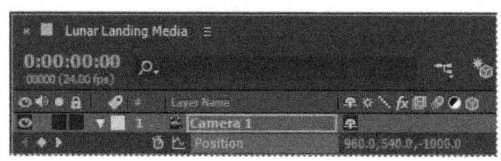
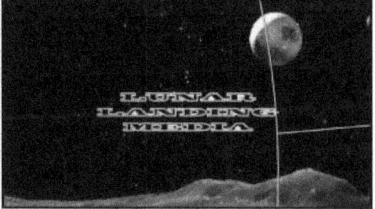

The camera moves slightly closer to the text.

Go to 1:00.

Change the z-axis value to **–500.**

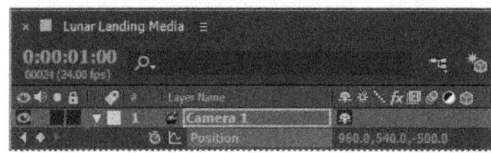

The camera moves much closer to the text.

Right-click (Windows) or Control-click (Mac OS) the second Position keyframe, and choose Keyframe Assistant > Easy Ease In.

Move the current-time indicator through the timeline to 1:00. As the camera moves through the scene, notice how the light reflects off the text layer, and how the overall image is influenced by the wider camera lens.

Hide the Position property for the Camera 1 layer, and choose File > Save.

Repositioning layers

At 1:00, the text sits low on the screen. You want to add text below it, so you'll need to make some adjustments. Also, now that the camera is in place, you'll reposition the background layer so that more of the moonscape is visible.

Press the Home key, or move the current-time indicator to the beginning of the time ruler.

Select the Lunar Landing Media layer in the Timeline panel, and press P to see its Position property. Change the y-axis value for the Position property to **470.**

Select the Background layer in the Timeline panel, and press P to show its Position property. Then change the z-axis value for the Position property to **700**.

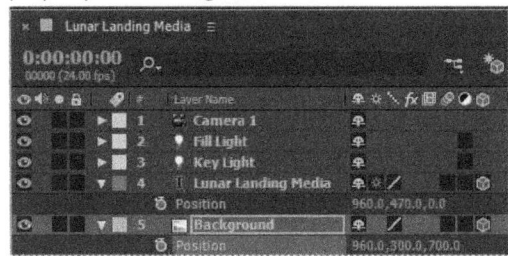 

Hide the Position properties for the Background and Lunar Landing Media layers.

Click an empty area in the Timeline panel to deselect all layers.

Adding a text layer

Now that there's space below the text, you'll create a new text layer to go there.

Select the Horizontal Type Tool (T) in the Tools panel. In the Character panel, select the following settings:

Font: Chaparral Pro

⬤ **Note**

If Chaparral Pro is not available, install it using Typekit. Choose File > Add Fonts From Typekit, search for Chaparral Pro, and sync it using Creative Cloud. Once you've synced the font, it will be available in all applications on your system.

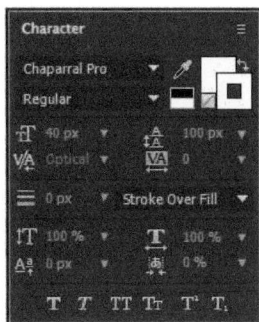

Font Style: Regular

Fill Color: White

Font Size: **40** px

Leading: **100** px

Tracking Value: **0%**

Stroke Width: **0** px

Vertical Scale: **100%**

Deselect All Caps in the Character panel.

In the Composition panel, click an insertion point, and type **A Space Pod LLC**.

Select the Selection tool (➤) in the Tools panel.

In the Timeline panel, click the 3D Layer switch (◉) for the A Space Pod LLC layer to convert it to 3D.

Press the P key to display the Position property for the layer. Then type **960**, **675**, **0** for the Position property to situate the new text below *Lunar Landing Media*. Press P to hide the Position property.

◉ Note

You can use the onscreen widget to position the layer if you prefer.

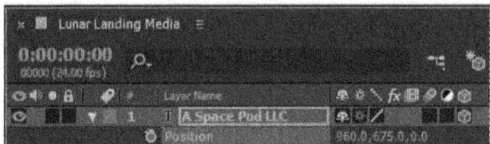 

Move to 1:04 in the timeline. Expand the A Space Pod LLC layer, and choose Opacity from the Animate pop-up menu.

Change the Opacity value under Range Selector 1 to **0**%.

Expand Range Selector 1, and make sure the Start value is 0%. Then click the stopwatch icon (🕭) to create an initial keyframe for the Start value.

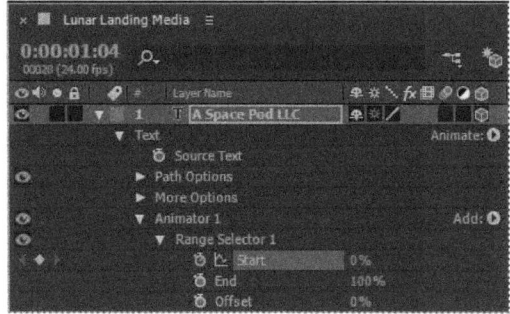 

Move to 1:12 in the timeline, and change the Start value to **100**%.

Manually scrub through the timeline to 1:12 to preview the animation.

Hide all open properties, and choose File > Save to save your work.

Working with Cinema 4D Lite

After Effects installs a version of Maxon Cinema 4D that allows motion graphic artists and animators to insert 3D objects directly into an After Effects scene without pre-rendering passes and potentially complicated file exchanges. You can import, create, and edit 3D objects in a variety of formats.

You'll use Cinema 4D Lite to create extruded text, which you'll add to the After Effects scene, replacing the initial text.

Exporting a scene file

After Effects and Cinema 4D measure coordinates from different places in a scene. In After Effects, the 0, 0, 0 position is in the upper left corner of the scene; in Cinema 4D, the same coordinates are in the center. Keep this in mind when you move between the two applications. You can open an After Effects composition in Cinema 4D without a problem, but it's easier if you line everything up initially. You'll use a null object to do that.

Make sure the Timeline panel is active, and then choose Layer > New > Null Object.

A null object is an invisible layer that has all the properties of a visible layer, so that it can be a parent to any layer in the composition. You'll use a null object to reposition the scene to 0, 0, 0.

In the Timeline panel, select the Null 1 layer, and click the 3D switch (⬤) to make it a 3D layer.

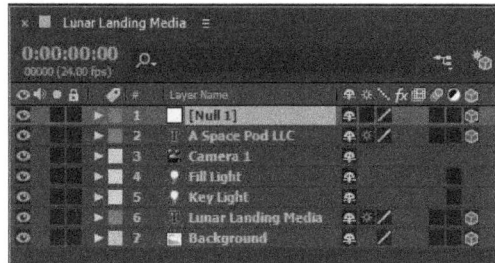 

Select the A Space Pod LLC layer, and then Shift-click the Background layer to select all the layers except the Null 1 layer.

Choose 1. Null 1 from the Parent pop-up menu for the Background layer.

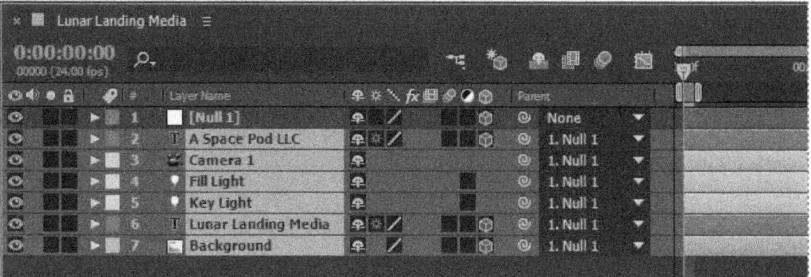

All the selected layers are parented to the Null 1 layer. Any changes to the null object affect them all.

Select the Null 1 layer, and press P to reveal its Position property. Then change the x and y values to **0**.

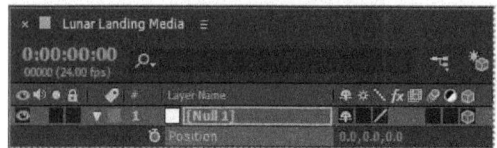

Nothing appears to happen in the Active Camera view in the Composition panel, but in the Right view, the contents of the scene appears to shift.

Hide the Position property for the Null 1 layer, and then choose File > Save.

Select the Lunar Landing Media composition in the Project panel, and then choose File > Export > Maxon Cinema 4D Exporter.

In the Save As dialog box, name the file **Lesson11.c4d**, and save it in the Lesson11 folder. Click Save to export the file.

The Cinema 4D exporter exports the lights, cameras, and certain layers from your After Effects scene into a Cinema 4D file. You can also import the resulting C4D file directly into After Effects for compositing into an After Effects scene.

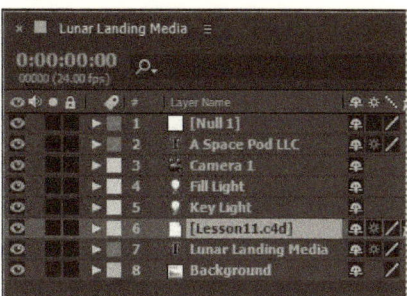

Choose File > Import > File, select the Lesson11.c4d file you just saved, and click Import or Open.

Drag the Lesson11.c4d file from the Project panel to the Timeline panel, placing it between the Key Light and Lunar Landing Media layers.

When you add a C4D file to the Timeline panel, After Effects opens the Cineware effect.

Cineware creates and manages the link between After Effects and Cinema 4D.

While you're working with a Cinema 4D file in After Effects, you should usually choose Software or Standard (Draft) from the Renderer menu in the Cineware effect. However, when you prepare to render your final project, choose Standard (Final) from the Renderer menu.

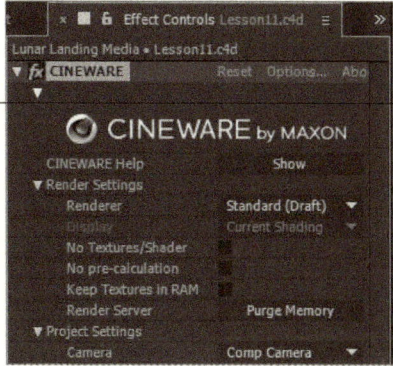

Choose Standard (Draft) from the Renderer menu in the Cineware effect in the Effect Controls panel.

The Software option creates a low-resolution version of the file. The Standard (Draft) option gives you a better view of what the Cinema 4D file looks like.

Choose Comp Camera from the Camera menu in the Effect Controls panel.

The Comp Camera option lets you use the After Effects camera you created earlier in this composition to make any refinements to your camera motion. Cineware will automatically adjust the 3D objects from the Cinema 4D scene.

Creating 3D Text in Cinema 4D

After Effects didn't export the text layers into Cinema 4D, but it did export the background solid object, the two lights you created, and the camera layer. You will use Cinema 4D Lite to create extruded text for this project.

In the Project panel, select the Lesson11.c4d file, and then choose Edit > Edit Original.

Note

When you open Cinema 4D Lite, you may be prompted to update the application.

The Lesson11.c4d file opens in Cinema 4D Lite.

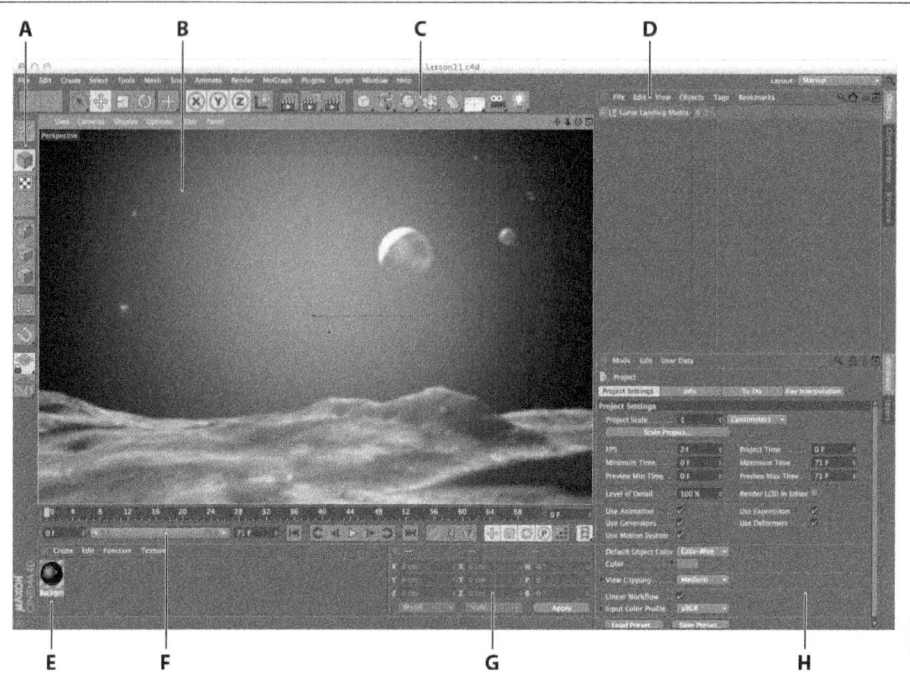

A. Modes icon palette B. Viewport C. Tools icon palette D. Object Manager E. Material Manager F. Timeline G. Coordinates Manager H. Attribute Manager

In the Cinema 4D Timeline, change the clip length to **72** frames: Increase the value in the box on the right, and then extend the timeline to 72 frames.

In the Tools icon palette (below the menu bar), click and hold the triangle in the lower right corner of the Freehand icon ( ) to display its menu, and then select the Text tool (𝕋).

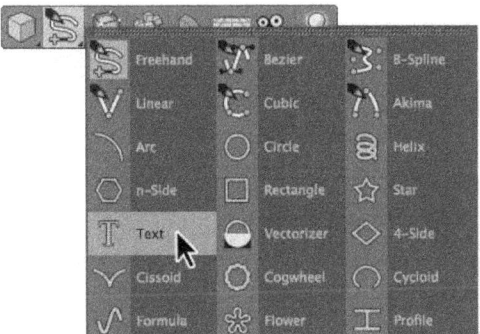

A basic text spline appears in the middle of the scene.

In the text box in the Attribute Manager, type **LUNAR LANDING MEDIA**, with each word on its own line.

In the Attribute Manager, change the text settings as follows:

Font: Blackoak Std

Align: Middle

Height: **70** cm

Vertical Spacing: **−10** cm

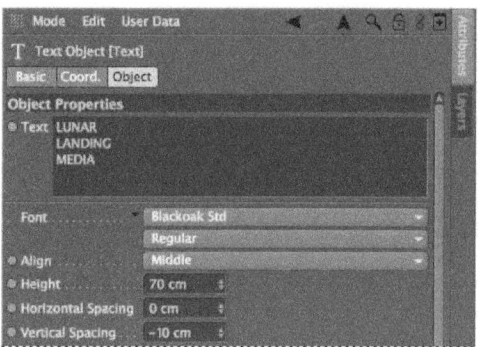

Drag the playhead in the Timeline to frame 24 (1:00).

The camera moves just as it did in After Effects. There's also a 3D axis in the Viewport similar to the one in the Composition panel in After Effects.

Click the y-axis arrow (the green one), and drag the text object until its position is similar to the one in the image. Your goal is to make sure there's room for the other text below it.

Note

If you are unable to select the y-axis arrow, select the Move tool first.

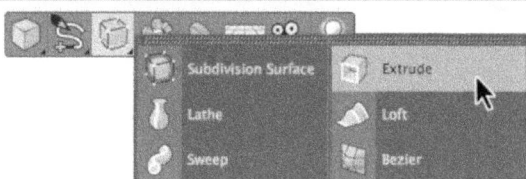

In the Tools icon palette, click and hold the triangle in the lower right corner of the Subdivision Surface icon (⬡) to view its menu, and then select Extrude (▱).

In the Object Manager, select the Text object, and then drag it to the middle column to the right of Extrude to parent it. You'll know you've positioned it correctly when the cursor becomes a box with an arrow pointing down (⬂).

In the Object Manager, the Text object appears nested below the Extrude object, indicating the parent relationship. In the Viewport, the text is now extruded.

In the Object Manager, click the Extrude object to make it active (it turns bright orange).

In the Attribute Manager, select the Object tab, and then change the z-axis Movement value to **70** cm.

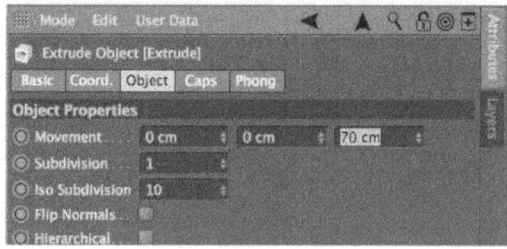

The extruded text looks much better. You'll enhance the text further by beveling the edges and making some adjustments.

In the Attribute Manager, select the Caps tab, and do the following:

Choose Fillet Cap from the Start menu.

Increase the Steps value to **2**.

Decrease the Radius value to **3** cm.

Choose Concave from the Fillet Type menu. The changes you made give the text an interesting edge.

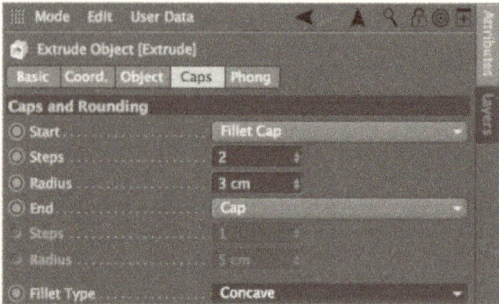

Surfacing the object

Cinema 4D Lite comes with a number of preset surfaces you can apply to 3D objects.

You'll add a metallic surface to the text.

In the Materials Manager, click Create, and then choose Load Material Preset > Lite > Materials > Effects > Mazzie B-Blue.

In the Materials Manager, click the surface you just added, and drag it onto the text in the Viewport.

Choose File > Save.

Updating the project in After Effects

You've made all the changes you need to make in Cinema 4D Lite, so you can now return to After Effects to see how it works in your project. As a final touch, you'll add an audio file for the title card.

Return to After Effects.

After Effects updates, and the Cinema 4D object appears in the Active Camera view in the Composition panel.

Choose 1 View from the Select View Layout pop-up menu at the bottom of the Composition panel. Choose Active Camera from the 3D View pop-up menu, if it isn't already selected.

In the Timeline panel, deselect the Video switch for the Lunar Landing Media text layer to hide it.

The original text layer was a placeholder for the 3D text you created in Cinema 4D Lite.

You don't need it in the final project.

If you need to reposition the text in the Cinema 4D file, return to Cinema 4D Lite, adjust the text, and choose File > Save. Then return to After Effects again.

You can move back and forth between After Effects and Cinema 4D Lite.

Double-click an empty area of the Project panel, and then navigate to the Lesson11/Assets folder. Double-click the Lunar.mp3 file to import it.

Drag the Lunar.mp3 file from the Project panel to the bottom of the layer stack in the Timeline panel.

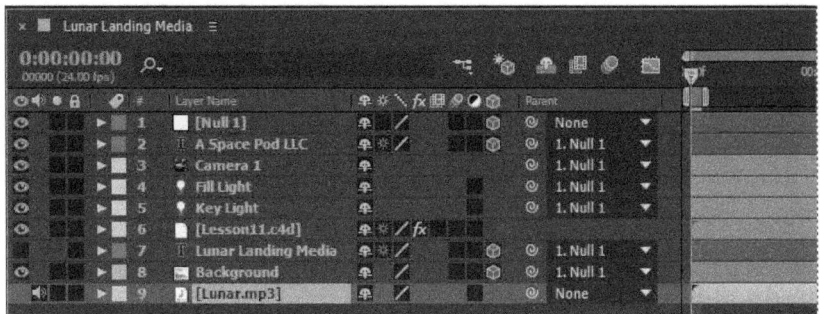

Choose File > Save.

(Optional) Preview the project before you render. To cache the frames in RAM faster, expand the properties for the Lesson11.c4d layer in the Timeline panel, and click CINEWARE under Effects. Then, in the Effect Controls panel, select both No Pre-calculation and Keep Textures In RAM.

You're ready to render the file.

Select the Lunar Landing Media composition in the Project panel, and choose Composition > Add To Render Queue.

In the Render Queue panel, click Best Settings to open the Render Settings dialog box. Then choose Half from the Resolution menu. (If your system is very slow, you may want to choose Quarter or Third.) Click OK.

Click the blue text next to Output To, and navigate to the

Lesson11/Finished_Project folder. Then click Save.

Click Render in the Render Queue panel.

When your project has rendered, open it in QuickTime to see your handiwork!

You've only just scratched the surface of what is possible when working with a 3D scene in After Effects, as well as what you can do with the workflow between Adobe After Effects and Maxon Cinema 4D Lite.

Review questions

1. What happens to a layer when you select its 3D Layer switch?

2. Why is it important to look at multiple views of a composition that contains 3D layers?

3. What is a camera layer?

4. What is a 3D light in After Effects?

Review answers

1. When you select a layer's 3D Layer switch in the Timeline panel, After Effects adds a third axis, the z axis, to the layer. You can then move and rotate the layer in three dimensions. In addition, the layer takes on new properties that are unique to 3D layers, such as the Materials Options property group.

2. The appearance of 3D layers can be deceptive, depending on the view in the Composition panel. By enabling 3D views, you can see the true position of a layer relative to other layers in the composition.

3. You can view After Effects 3D layers from any number of angles and distances using layers called *cameras*. When you set a camera view for your composition, you look at the layers as though you were looking through that camera. You can choose between viewing a composition through the active camera or through a named, custom camera. If you have not created a custom camera, then the active camera is the same as the default composition view.

4. In After Effects, a light is a type of layer that shines light on other layers. You can choose from among four different types of lights—Parallel, Spot, Point, and Ambient—and modify them with various settings.

Working with the 3D Camera Tracker

Track footage using the 3D Camera Tracker.

Add camera and text elements to a tracked scene.

Set a ground plane and origin.

Create realistic shadows for new 3D elements.

Lock elements to planes using null objects.

Adjust camera settings to match real-world footage.

Remove rolling shutter distortions from DSLR footage.

PROJECT: OPENING SEQUENCE FOR TV SHOW

The 3D Camera Tracker effect analyzes two-dimensional footage to create a virtual 3D camera that matches the original. You can use this data to add 3D objects that merge realistically with your scene.

About the 3D Camera Tracker effect

The 3D Camera Tracker effect automatically analyzes the motion present in existing 2D footage, extracts the position and lens type of the real camera that shot the scene, and creates a new 3D camera in After Effects to match it. The effect also overlays 3D track points onto the 2D footage, so you can easily attach new 3D layers onto the original footage.

These new 3D layers have the same movement and perspective changes as the original footage. The 3D Camera Tracker effect even helps create "shadow catchers," so your new 3D layers can appear to cast realistic shadows and reflections onto the existing footage.

The 3D Camera Tracker performs its analysis in the background. Therefore, you can work on other compositions while the footage is being analyzed.

Getting started

In this lesson, you'll create the opening scene for a fictional reality show that estimates the value of everyday objects found on office desks. You'll begin by importing the footage and tracking it with the 3D Camera Tracker effect. Then you'll add 3D text elements that track precisely with the scene. Finally, you'll animate the text, add audio, and enhance the footage to complete the show's introduction.

First, you'll preview the final movie and set up your project.

Make sure the following files are in the Lessons/Lesson12 folder on your hard disk, or download them from your Account page at www.peachpit.com now:

In the Assets folder: DesktopC.mov, Treasures_Music.aif, Treasures_Title.psd

In the Sample_Movie folder: Lesson12.mov

Open and play the Lesson12.mov file to see what you will create in this lesson. When you're done, quit QuickTime Player. You may delete the sample movie from your hard disk if you have limited storage space.

When you begin this lesson, restore the default application settings for After Effects. See "Restoring default preferences" on page 2.

Start After Effects, and then immediately hold down Ctrl+Alt+Shift (Windows) or Command+Option+Shift (Mac OS). When prompted, click OK to delete your preferences. Close the Start window.

After Effects opens to display an empty, untitled project.

Choose File > Save As > Save As.

In the Save As dialog box, navigate to the Lessons/Lesson12/Finished_Project folder.

Name the project **Lesson12_Finished.aep**, and then click Save.

Importing the footage

You need to import three footage items for this lesson.

Choose File > Import > File.

Navigate to the Lessons/Lesson12/Assets folder, Shift-click to select the DesktopC.mov, Treasures_Music.aif, and Treasures_Title.psd files, and then click Import or Open.

Choose File > New > New Folder to create a new folder in the Project panel, or click the Create A New Folder button (📁) at the bottom of the panel.

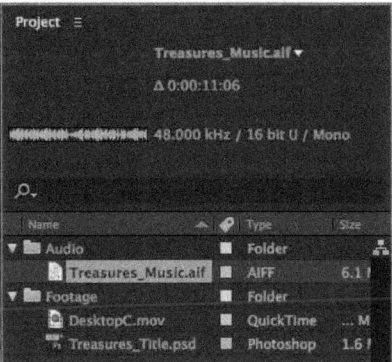

Type **Footage** to name the folder, press Enter or Return to accept the name, and then drag the DesktopC.mov and Treasures_Title.psd items into the Footage folder.

Make sure nothing is selected. Then create another folder, name it **Audio**, and drag the Treasures_Music.aif item into it.

Expand the folders so that you can see their contents.

Creating the composition

Now, you will create a new composition based on the aspect ratio and duration of the DesktopC.mov file.

Drag the DesktopC.mov item onto the Create A New Composition button (🎞) at the bottom of the Project panel. After Effects creates a new composition named DesktopC and displays it in the Composition and Timeline panels.

Drag the DesktopC composition to an empty area of the Project panel to move it out of the Footage folder.

Drag the current-time indicator across the time ruler to preview the shot.

The camera moves around a desktop so that you can see the objects on it. You'll add labels and dollar amounts, animated in time with background music.

Choose File > Save to save the file.

Repairing rolling shutter distortions

Digital cameras with CMOS sensors—including video-capable DSLRs, which are becoming increasingly popular for the creation of films, commercials, and television shows—typically have what is commonly known as a "rolling" shutter, which captures a frame of video one scan line at a time. Due to time lag between scan lines, not all parts of the image are recorded at exactly the same time, causing motion to ripple down the frame. If the camera or the subject is moving, the rolling shutter can cause distortions, such as leaning buildings and other skewed images.

The Rolling Shutter Repair effect attempts to correct this problem automatically. To use it, select the problem layer in the Timeline panel, and choose Effect > Distort > Rolling Shutter Repair.

Due to a rolling shutter distortion, the pillars of the building appear to be leaning.

After applying the effect, the building looks much more stable.

The default settings usually do the trick, but you may need to change the Scan Direction or the Method being used to analyze the footage.

If you plan to use the 3D Camera Tracker effect with footage on which you've used the Rolling Shutter Repair effect, precompose the footage first.

Tracking the footage

The 2D footage is in place. Now you'll have After Effects track it and interpolate where a 3D camera should be placed.

In the Timeline panel, click the Audio icon for the DesktopC.mov layer to mute the audio.

You'll add a soundtrack later, and you don't want any ambient noise from this clip.

Right-click (Windows) or Control-click (Mac OS) the DesktopC.mov layer in the Timeline panel, and choose Track Camera.

After Effects opens the Effect Controls panel and displays its progress as it analyzes the footage in the background. When the analysis is complete, many tracking points appear in the Composition panel. The size of a tracked point indicates its proximity to the virtual camera: Larger points are closer, and smaller points are further away.

The default analysis of the footage often yields satisfactory results, but you can perform a more detailed analysis to better solve the camera position.

In the Effect Controls panel, expand the Advanced category, and then select Detailed Analysis.

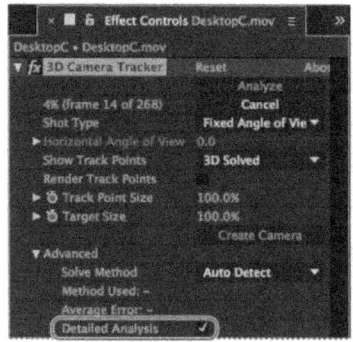

Depending on your system, this may take a while.

After Effects analyzes the footage again. If you're working with a slower machine and you suspect you'll need a detailed analysis, you can save time by selecting Detailed Analysis while the 3D Camera Tracker is performing its initial analysis. The detailed analysis may take a few minutes, depending on your system. Because the analysis is performed in the background, you could work on other aspects of your project while it progresses.

When the analysis is complete, choose File > Save to save your work so far.

Creating a ground plane, a camera, and the initial text

You have a 3D scene, but it needs a 3D camera. You'll add a camera when you create the first text element, and then you'll add a second text element related to the first.

Press the Home key, or move the current-time indicator to the beginning of the time ruler.

In the Composition panel, hover the cursor over the hole in the record on the desk until the displayed target is in line with the plane and the perspective matches. (If you don't see the track points and target, click the 3D Camera Tracker effect in the Effect Controls panel to make it active.)

When you hover the cursor between three or more neighboring track points that can define a plane, a semitransparent triangle appears between the points. Additionally, a red target shows the orientation of the plane in 3D space.

Right-click (Windows) or Control-click (Mac OS) the plane, and choose Set Ground Plane And Origin.

The ground plane and origin provide a reference point, setting a point where the coordinates are (0, 0, 0). Though nothing appears to change in the Composition panel using the Active Camera View, the ground plane and origin make it easier to change the camera's rotation and position.

Right-click (Windows) or Control-click (Mac OS) the same plane, and choose

Create Text And Camera.

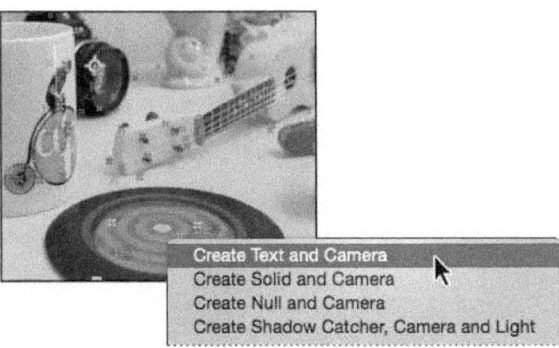

After Effects displays a large text item lying flat in the Composition panel. It also adds two layers to the Timeline panel: Text and 3D Tracker Camera. The 3D switch is enabled for the Text layer, but the DesktopC.mov layer remains 2D. Because the text elements are the only ones that need to be positioned in 3D space, there is no reason to make the background footage layer a 3D layer.

Move the current-time indicator along the time ruler. The text remains in position, tracking with the camera. Return the current-time indicator to the beginning of the time ruler.

Double-click the Text layer in the Timeline panel to add the Character and Paragraph panels to the stacked panels on the right.

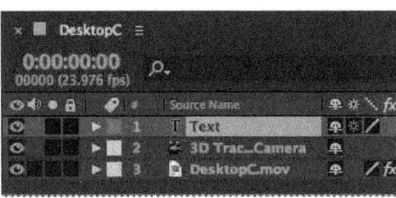

Open the Paragraph panel, and select Center Text for the alignment. The text is centered over the record.

 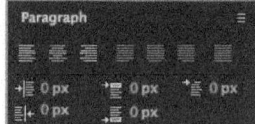

Open the Character panel. Change the font to a sans serif font such as Arial Narrow or Helvetica Light. Then change the font size to **20** px, the stroke width to **1** px, and the stroke type to Fill Over Stroke. Make sure the fill color is white and the stroke color is black (the default colors).

 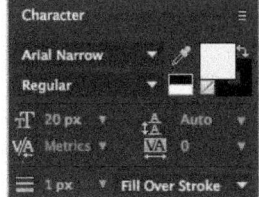

The text looks great, but you want it to stand on end. You'll change its location in space, and then replace it with the price of the object.

Select the Text layer in the Timeline panel to exit text-editing mode. Then, press the R key to display the Rotation property of the layer, and change the Orientation values to **0**, **350**, **0** degrees.

Any new 3D layer you create uses the ground plane and origin to orient the layer in the scene. The Text layer was originally flat, with the Orientation of 270 degrees on the x axis. When you change that value to 0, the text becomes vertical.

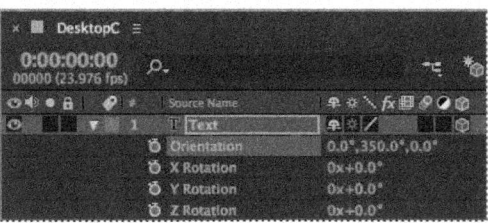 

Double-click the Text layer in the Timeline panel to make it active in the Composition panel.

When the text is editable, it appears to have a light red mask surrounding it.

With the text selected in the Composition panel, type **$35.00** to replace it.

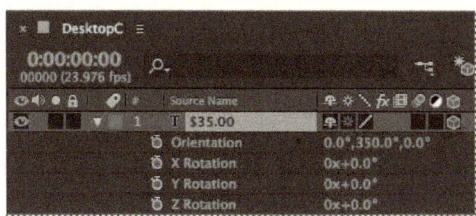 

So far, so good. Next, you want to label the item, and the label needs to stay with the price as the camera moves. You'll duplicate the layer, modify it, and then parent one layer to the other.

Select the $35.00 layer in the Timeline panel, and press Ctrl+D (Windows) or Command+D (Mac OS) to duplicate it.

Double-click the $35.2 layer, and type **HENDRIX 45 RPM** (in all capital letters) in the Composition panel.

The text is too large; it's the same size as the price text. You'll parent it to the $35.00 layer and then scale it.

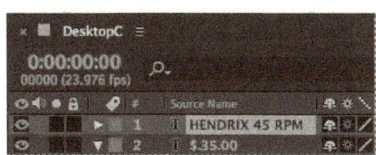 

Select the Hendrix 45 RPM layer in the Timeline panel, and press the P key to reveal the Position property for the layer. Drag the pick whip from the Hendrix layer to the $35.00 layer.

The Position value for the Hendrix layer changes to 0, 0, 0, because its position is related to the parent layer. However, you want the Hendrix layer to appear above the $35.00 layer, not in front of it.

Change the y-axis position value to **−18** to move the Hendrix label above the price text.

With the Hendrix layer selected, press the S key to reveal the Scale property, and change the Scale values to **37.4**, **37.4**, **37.4%**.

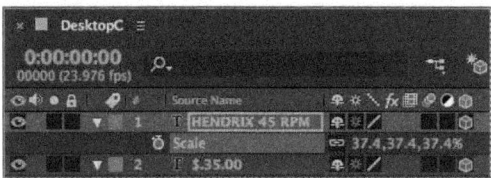

Close the open properties, and then choose File > Save to save your work so far.

Creating realistic shadows

You've set up your first text elements, but unlike true 3D objects, they aren't casting any shadows. You'll create a shadow catcher and a light to add depth to your video.

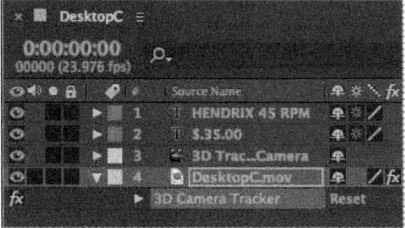

Press the Home key, or move the current-time indicator to the beginning of the time ruler.

Select the DesktopC.mov layer in the Timeline panel, press the E key to display the 3D Camera Tracker effect, and then select the 3D Camera Tracker effect.

Select the Selection tool (▶) in the Tools panel. Then, in the Composition panel, hover until you find the same plane you used to create the text layer.

Right-click (Windows) or Control-click (Mac OS) the target, and choose Create Shadow Catcher And Light.

After Effects adds a light source to the scene. The default settings are applied, so a shadow appears in the Composition panel. However, you'll need to reposition the light to match the light in the source footage. The Shadow Catcher 1 layer that After Effects adds to the Timeline panel is a shape layer that has its material options set so that it accepts shadows only from the scene.

Select the Light 1 layer in the Timeline panel, and press the P key to reveal the Position property for the layer.

Enter the following values for the Position property to reposition the light: **1900**, **−2500**, **−375**.

▷ **Tip**

In a real-world project, it's ideal to work with the lighting plan that was used to shoot the original 2D scene. The goal is to have the new 3D lights match the original source lighting as closely as possible.

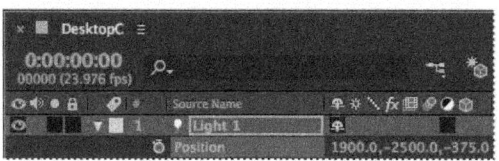 

Choose Layer > Light Settings.

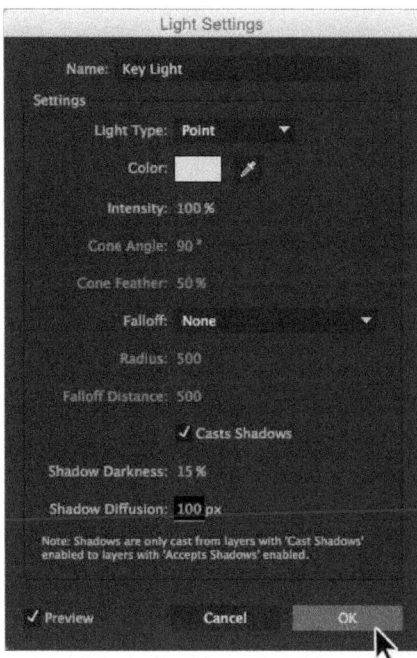

You can change the intensity, color, and other attributes of the light in the Light Settings dialog box.

Name the light **Key Light**. Choose Point from the Light Type menu, and then select a slightly red color (we used R=232, G=214, B=213) to match the slight color cast in the room. Then change the Shadow Darkness to **15%** and the Shadow Diffusion to **100** px. Click OK.

Select the Shadow Catcher 1 layer in the Timeline panel, and press the S key to reveal the Scale property.

Change the Scale value to **340%**.

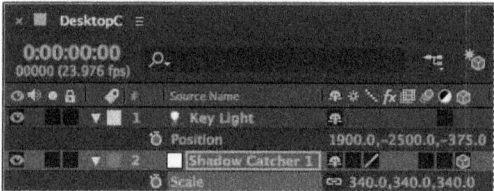 

Scaling the Shadow Catcher 1 layer changes the area in which shadows can appear for the light that was created with it.

Adding ambient light

The shadow looks better after the adjustments you made to the light, but it's now causing the text to appear black. You'll add ambient light to address this. Unlike a point light, ambient light creates a more diffuse light throughout the scene.

Deselect all layers, and then choose Layer > New > Light.

Name the light **Ambient Light**, choose Ambient from the Light Type menu, and change its Intensity value to **80%**. The light color should be the same as the color you selected for the point light.

Click OK to add the light to the scene.

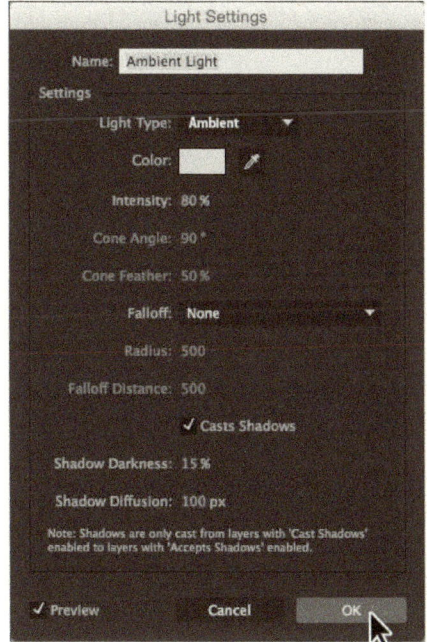

Hide the properties for all layers in the Timeline panel, except for the DesktopC.mov layer.

Creating additional text elements

You created the label for the Hendrix record. Now you need to perform the same tasks to create labels for the camera, gold statue, pocket knife, and ukulele. You'll use the same steps to create each label, but because the objects are in different places on the table, you'll need to use different orientation and scaling values, as listed in the following chart. You'll find it easiest to attach the label for each to the correct plane at different points in the time ruler.

OBJECT	POSITION IN TIME RULER (STEP 1)	ORIENTATION (STEP 5)	PRICE (STEP 6)	PRICE SCALE (STEP 7)	LABEL (STEP 9)
camera	3:00	0, 310, 0	$298.00	3000	35MM CAMERA
statue	5:00	0, 325, 0	$612.00	2000	GOLD STATUE
knife	7:00	0, 340, 0	$75.00	2500	POCKET KNIFE
ukulele	9:00	0, 310, 0	$500.00	3000	1942 UKULELE

▷ **Tip**

If a 3D object should be obscured by an object in the background, duplicate the background layer, move it to the top of the layer stack, and then use the Mask tool to create masks around portions of the foreground elements. You will need to animate these masks over time, but if you do it carefully, you can create a seamless composition.

Move the current-time indicator to get a better view of the object.

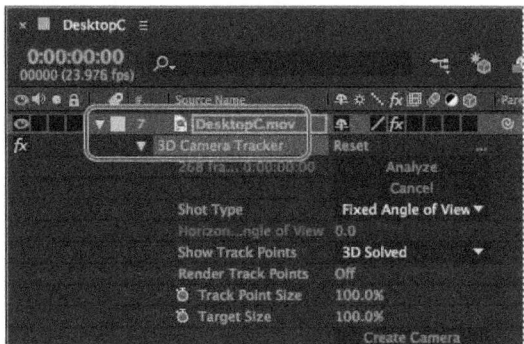

In the Timeline panel, select the 3D Camera Tracker (under the DesktopC.mov layer) to make it active. (If you don't see the 3D Camera Tracker, press the E key to reveal it.)

◉ Note

Make sure you select the 3D Camera Tracker effect in the DesktopC.mov layer, not the 3D Tracker Camera layer.

Make sure the Selection tool (▶) is selected. Then, in the Composition panel, hover over an area so that the red target is parallel to the front of the object.

Right-click (Windows) or Control-click (Mac OS) the target, and choose Create Text.

Select the Text layer in the Timeline panel, and press the R key to reveal the

Rotation values. Then change the Orientation values.

Double-click the Text layer to make it editable, and then type the price in the Composition panel.

Select the price layer in the Timeline panel, and press S to reveal the Scale property. Change the Scale value.

With the price layer selected, press Ctrl+D (Windows) or Command+D (Mac OS) to duplicate the layer.

Double-click the duplicate layer in the Timeline panel, and then type the label in the Composition panel.

Select the label layer in the Timeline panel, and press P to reveal its Position property. Then drag the pick whip from the label layer (e.g., 35MM CAMERA) to the price layer (e.g., $298.00).

Note

If you turn on Caps Lock to type the label, be sure to turn it off again. Otherwise, you'll get unexpected results, and After Effects won't be able to update the layer name.

Change the y value of the Position property for the label layer to **–18** to move the label above the price.

Select the label layer again, and press S to reveal the Scale property. Change its Scale values to **50, 50, 50%**.

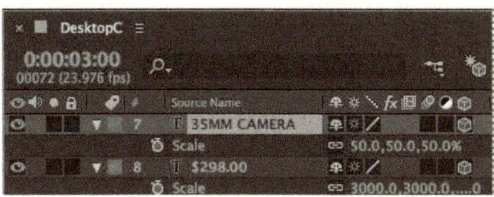 

Hide the properties for the layers you just created.

Repeat steps 1–13 to label the additional objects, using the values in the chart on the previous page.

The labels all look good, but they may overlap in places that can make them hard to read.

You can reposition them as necessary.

If you need to adjust a label, select the price layer for the object, and then use the Selection tool to adjust its position. Because you've parented the label layer to the price layer, adjusting the price moves both text layers.

Choose File > Save to save your work so far.

Locking a layer to a plane with a null object

The title card for the show should be flat on the table, using the same plane you used to attach text to the record. You'll use a null object to attach the title card to that plane. The title card is an Adobe Photoshop file.

Press the Home key, or move the current-time indicator to the beginning of the time ruler.

In the Timeline panel, select the 3D Camera Tracker (under the DesktopC.mov layer) to make it active. (If you don't see the 3D Camera Tracker, press the E key to reveal it.)

Select the Selection tool, and then move the cursor so that the target is lying flat over the record.

Right-click (Windows) or Control-click (Mac OS) the target, and choose Create Null.

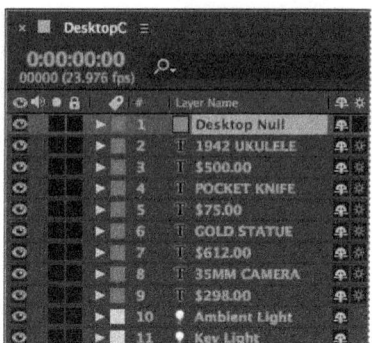

After Effects adds a Track Null 1 layer to the top of the layer stack in the Timeline panel. Because you know that the record is on the same plane as the desktop, you can use this null object to position the title of the show in the open area of the desk, and still have it move correctly in relation to other elements and the camera in the scene.

Select the Track Null 1 layer in the Timeline panel, press Enter or Return, and change the name to **Desktop Null**. Press Enter or Return again to accept the name change.

From the Project panel, drag the Treasures_Title.psd asset to the Timeline panel, placing it directly above the Desktop Null layer.

▷ **Tip**

Instead of dragging the pick whip, you could choose 2. Desktop Null from the Parent menu in the Treasures_Title layer.

Drag the pick whip from the Treasures_Title layer to the Desktop Null layer to parent the layer.

Click the 3D switch for the Treasures_Title layer to make it a 3D layer.

Because you've parented the title layer to the null object, when it becomes a 3D layer it is automatically oriented to be flat on the desktop.

Move to the end of the time ruler so you can see how the title card is positioned. You need to move the title to the empty area of the desktop, and then rotate it and resize it.

Select the Treasures_Title layer in the Timeline panel, and press R to reveal its Rotation property. Then change its Z Rotation value to **305** degrees.

Press the S key to reveal the Scale property, and change the Scale amount to **625%**.

With the Selection tool, move the title text into position, as in the image at the bottom of this page. If you need to resize the text, use the Selection tool to adjust the object's corner handles.

Click the Toggle Switches/Modes button at the bottom of the Timeline panel. Choose Luminosity from the Mode menu for the Treasures_Title layer.

Click the Toggle Switches/Modes button again to return to displaying switches.

Choose File > Save to save your work so far.

Animating the text

The 3D text elements, camera, and lighting are all complete, but you can make the introduction more interesting by animating the text to appear according to cues in the soundtrack. You'll add an audio track, and then animate the labels to appear when cash register sounds occur.

Animating the first text elements

You'll animate the record label and price to appear early in the intro, with the price cycling through characters until it arrives at the final text.

In the Project panel, drag the Treasures_Music.aif file from the Audio folder to the bottom of the layer stack in the Timeline panel.

Move the current-time indicator to the beginning of the timeline, and then press the spacebar to move the first few seconds of the composition into RAM. Press the spacebar to stop caching, go to the beginning of the time ruler, and press the spacebar again to preview what you cached.

Notice that the cash register sound occurs periodically. You'll animate the text to appear at those points.

Go to 1:00, and select the $35.00 layer. Press the S key to reveal the Scale property, and then change the Scale amount to **0%**. Click the stopwatch icon (⏱) to create an initial keyframe.

Go to 1:08, and change the Scale amount for the $35.00 layer to **3200%** so that the text is larger than its final size.

Go to 1:10, and change the Scale amount to **3000%**, the final value for the text.

Go to 1:00, and press S to hide the Scale property. Then click the arrow next to the $35.00 layer to reveal all its properties.

Next to the Text property, choose Character Offset from the Animate menu.

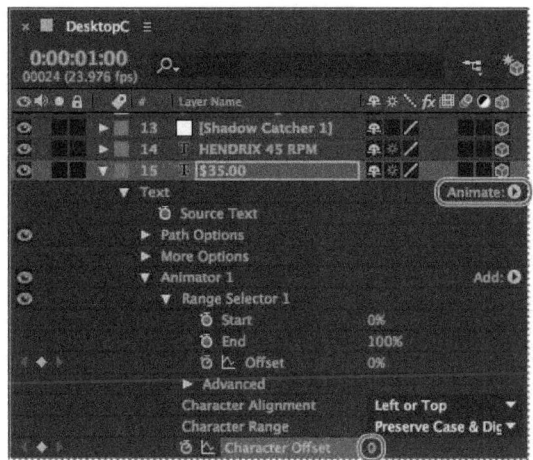

Expand Range Selector 1 in the Animator 1 properties. Then click the stopwatch next to Offset to create an initial keyframe, and make sure the value is **0%**.

Create an initial keyframe for Character Offset (under Character Range), and make sure its value is **0**.

Go to 1:12, and change the Range Selector 1 Offset value to **–100%**.

Click the word *Offset* to select both keyframes, right-click (Windows) or Control-click (Mac OS) one of the keyframes, and then choose Keyframe Assistant > Easy Ease.

Go to 1:17, and change the Character Offset value to **20**.

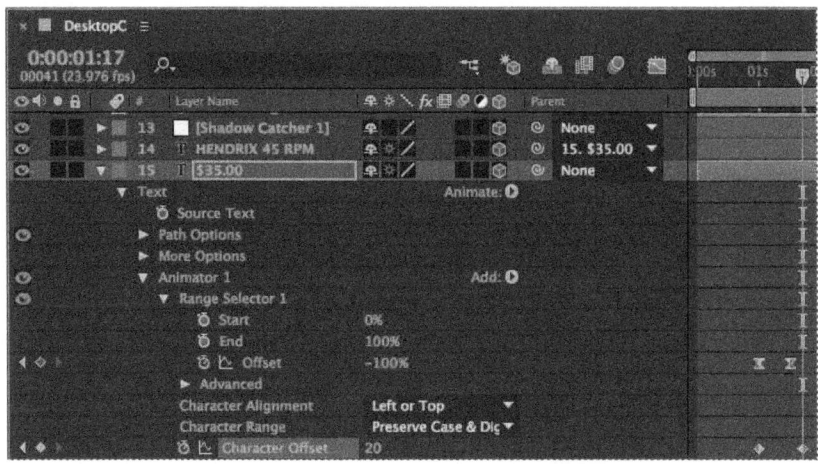

Preview the first two seconds of the composition.

The title of the record pops up as the text cycles through to the estimated price. The character offset values determine how the text cycles through characters to arrive at the final one.

Copying the animation to other text elements

Now that you've animated the text for the record, you can copy the animation for the other objects, placing the keyframes at the appropriate points in the time ruler.

Select the $35.00 layer, and press the U key to reveal only the properties that have keyframes.

In the time graph, drag a marquee around all the keyframes to select them.

Choose Edit > Copy to copy the keyframes and their values.

Go to 3:00, and select the $298.00 layer. Choose Edit > Paste to paste the keyframes and their values, beginning at the current time.

Go to 5:00, and select the $612.00 layer. Press Ctrl+V (Windows) or Command+V (Mac OS) to paste the keyframes and their values.

Go to 7:00, select the $75.00 layer, and press Ctrl+V (Windows) or Command+V (Mac OS).

Go to 9:00, select the $500.00 layer, and press Ctrl+V (Windows) or Command+V (Mac OS).

Hide the properties for all the layers, and then choose File > Save.

Adjusting the camera's depth of field

The intro is looking pretty good, but you can make the computer-generated elements more closely match the source footage if you adjust the depth of field for the 3D camera. You'll use the values that were used in the camera that shot the original footage, so the text that is further away from the camera appears to be more out of focus.

Select the 3D Tracker Camera layer in the Timeline panel.

Choose Layer > Camera Settings.

In the Camera Settings dialog box, do the following, and then click OK:

Select Enable Depth of Field.

Set the Focus Distance to **200** mm.

Change the F-Stop value to **5.6**.

Set the Focal Length to **27.2**.

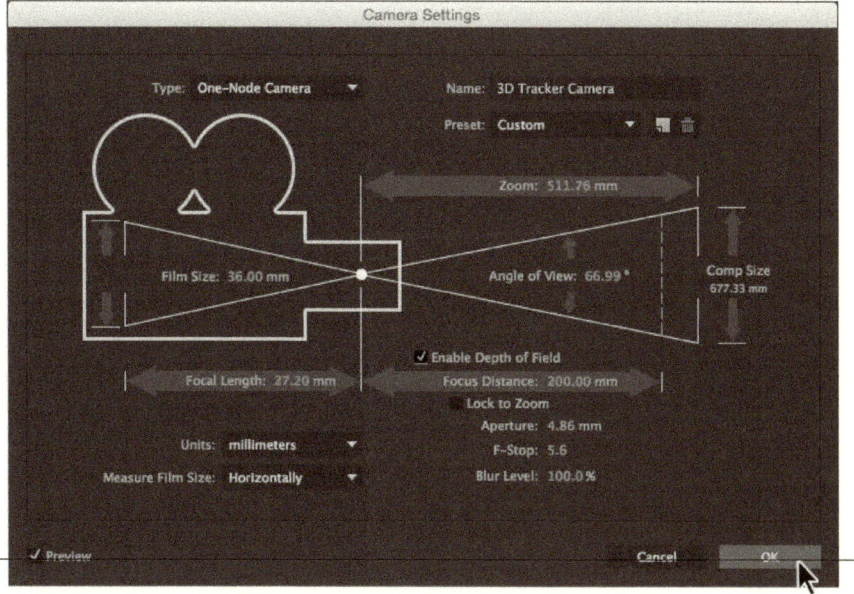

In the Timeline panel, select all of the layers except the audio layer. Then select the Motion Blur switch for one of the layers, applying it to all selected layers.

Click the Enable Motion Blur button (𝒪) at the top of the Timeline panel to enable motion blur for all layers.

Choose File > Save to save your project.

Rendering the composition

You've done some complex work to create a scene that merges the added components with an existing tableau. To see the final results, you'll render the project. You'll learn more about rendering in Lesson 14, "Rendering and Outputting."

Choose Window > Render Queue to open the Render Queue panel.

Drag the DesktopC composition from the Project panel to the Render Queue panel.

Click the blue words next to Render Settings. Then, in the Render Settings dialog box, choose Half from the Resolution menu, and click OK.

Click the blue text next to Output Module. Then, in the Output Module Settings dialog box, choose QuickTime from the Format menu.

Click Format Options in the Output Module Settings dialog box. Then do the following in the QuickTime Options dialog box, and click OK:

Choose H.264 from the Video Codec menu.

Select Limit Data Rate To in the Bitrate Settings area.

Change the data rate limit to **8000** kbps.

In the Output Module Settings dialog box, make sure Audio Output Auto is chosen in the Audio Output pop-up menu. Then click OK.

When Audio Output Auto is selected, After Effects automatically detects active audio in the composition.

Click the blue text next to Output To, navigate to the Lesson12/Finished_Project folder, and click Save.

Click Render in the Render Queue panel to render the composition.

When After Effects has finished rendering the composition, play the QuickTime movie to admire your work!

Advanced Editing Techniques

Stabilize a shaky camera shot.

Use single-point motion tracking to track one object in a shot to another object in a shot.

Perform multipoint tracking using perspective corner-pinning.

Use Imagineer Systems mocha for After Effects to track motion.

Create a particle system.

Use the Timewarp effect to create slow-motion video.

PROJECT: SPECIAL EFFECTS AND EDITING TECHNIQUES

After Effects provides advanced motion stabilization, motion tracking, high-end effects, and other features for the most demanding production environments.

Getting started

In previous lessons, you've used many of the essential 2D and 3D tools you need for motion graphics design. But Adobe After Effects also offers motion stabilization, motion tracking, advanced keying tools, distortion effects, the capability to retime footage using the Timewarp effect, support for high dynamic range (HDR) color images, network rendering, and much more. In this lesson, you will learn how to use Warp Stabilizer VFX to stabilize a handheld camera shot, how to track one object to another in an image so that their motion is synchronized, and how to use corner-pinning to track an object with perspective. Finally, you will explore two of the high-end digital effects available in After Effects: a particle system generator and the Timewarp effect.

This lesson includes multiple projects. Take a peek at all of them before beginning.

Make sure the following files are in the Lessons/Lesson13 folder on your hard disk, or download them from your Account page at www.peachpit.com now:

In the Assets folder: flowers.mov, Group_Approach[DV].mov, majorspoilers.mov, metronome.mov, mocha_tracking.mov, multipoint_tracking.mov

In the Sample_Movies folder: Lesson13_Multipoint.mov,

Lesson13_Particles.mov, Lesson13_Stabilize.mov, Lesson13_Timewarp.mov, Lesson13_Tracking.mov

Open and play the sample movies in the Lesson13/Sample_Movies folder to see the projects you will create in this lesson.

Note

You can view these movies all at once or, if you don't plan to complete these exercises in one session, you can watch each sample movie just before you are ready to complete the associated exercise.

When you're done, quit QuickTime Player. You may delete these sample movies from your hard disk if you have limited storage space.

Using Warp Stabilizer VFX

If you shoot footage using a handheld camera, you will probably end up with shaky shots. Unless this look is intentional, you'll want to stabilize your shots to eliminate unwanted motion.

Warp Stabilizer VFX in After Effects automatically removes extraneous jitters. When played back, the motion appears smooth, because the layer itself is scaled and moves incrementally to offset the unwanted movement.

Bicubic scaling

When you scale video footage or an image to a larger size, After Effects must sample data to add information where none existed before. You can choose which sampling method After Effects uses when scaling a layer. For details, see After Effects help.

Bilinear sampling is the method After Effects traditionally used. However, bicubic sampling uses a more complex algorithm that typically provides better results when color transitions are more gradual, as in nearly all real-world photographic images. Bilinear scaling may be a better option for sharp-edged graphics.

To choose a sampling method for a layer, select the layer, and choose Layer > Quality > Bicubic or Layer > Quality > Bilinear. Bicubic and bilinear sampling are available only for layers that are set to Best quality. (To change a layer's quality setting to Best, choose Layer > Quality > Best.)

If you need to scale an image by a large amount while preserving details, use the Detail-preserving Upscale effect instead. The effect preserves the sharpness of sharp lines and curves. For example, you can scale up from SD frame sizes to HD frame sizes, or from HD frame sizes to digital cinema frame sizes. This effect is very closely related to the Preserve Details resampling option in the Image Size dialog box in Photoshop. Note that using the Detail-preserving Upscale effect is slower than using either bilinear or bicubic scaling for the layer.

Setting up the project

As you start After Effects, restore the default application settings for After Effects. See "Restoring default preferences" on page 2.

Start After Effects, and then immediately hold down Ctrl+Alt+Shift (Windows) or Command+Option+Shift (Mac OS) to restore default preferences settings. When prompted, click OK to delete your preferences.

Close the Start window.

After Effects opens to display a new, untitled project.

Choose File > Save As > Save As.

In the Save As dialog box, navigate to the Lessons/Lesson13/Finished_Projects folder.

Name the project **Lesson13_Stabilize.aep**, and then click Save.

Importing the footage

You need to import one footage item to start this project.

Double-click an empty area of the Project panel to open the Import File dialog box.

Navigate to the Lessons/Lesson13/Assets folder. Select the flowers.mov file, and click Import or Open.

Creating the composition

You'll start by creating the composition.

Drag the flowers.mov clip in the Project panel onto the Create A New Composition button () at the bottom of the panel.

After Effects creates a new composition named Flowers with the same pixel size, aspect ratio, frame rate, and duration of the source clip.

Click the Play button in the Preview panel to preview the footage. Press the spacebar to stop the preview when you've seen the whole clip.

This clip was shot with a handheld camera in the late afternoon. A slight breeze rustles the vegetation, and the camera moves unsteadily.

Applying Warp Stabilizer VFX

Warp Stabilizer VFX starts analyzing footage as soon as you apply it. Stabilization is a background process, so you can work on other compositions while it finishes. How long it takes depends on your system. After Effects displays a blue banner while it analyzes the footage and an orange banner while it applies stabilization.

Select the flowers.mov layer in the Timeline panel, and choose Animation > Warp Stabilizer VFX. The blue banner appears immediately.

When Warp Stabilizer VFX has finished stabilizing, and the orange banner has disappeared, press the spacebar to preview the changes.

Press the spacebar to stop the preview.

The clip is still shaky, but it's smoother than it was initially. Warp Stabilizer VFX moved and repositioned the footage. To see how it applied changes, view the effects in the Effect Controls panel. For example, the clip's borders were scaled up (to about 103%) to hide black gaps that occur when the image is repositioned in the stabilization process. You'll adjust the settings that Warp Stabilizer VFX uses.

Adjusting the Warp Stabilizer VFX settings

You'll change the settings in the Effect Controls panel to make the shot smoother.

In the Effect Controls panel, increase the Smoothness amount to **75%**.

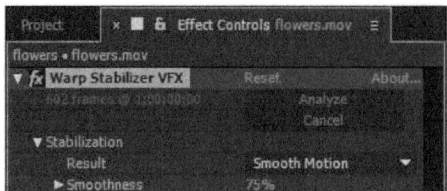

Warp Stabilizer VFX immediately begins stabilizing again. It doesn't need to analyze the footage, because the initial analysis data is stored in memory.

Warp Stabilizer VFX settings

This is a summary of the Warp Stabilizer VFX settings to help you get started. To learn more about the settings, and to read more tips for using the effect successfully, see After Effects Help.

Result controls the intended result. Smooth Motion makes camera movement smoother, but doesn't eliminate it; use the Smoothness setting to control how smooth the movement becomes. No Motion attempts to remove all of the camera motion.

Method specifies the most complex operation the Warp Stabilizer VFX performs on the footage to stabilize it: Position, which is based on position data only; Position, Scale, Rotation, which uses these three types of data; Perspective, which effectively corner-pins the entire frame; or Subspace Warp (the default), which attempts to warp various parts of the frame differently to stabilize the entire frame.

Borders settings adjust how borders (the moving edges) are treated for footage that is stabilized. Framing controls how the edges appear in a stabilizing result, and determines whether the effect crops, scales, or synthesizes edges using material from other frames.

Auto-scale displays the current auto-scale amount, and allows you to set limits on the amount of auto-scaling.

Advanced settings give you even greater control over the actions of the Warp Stabilizer VFX effect.

When Warp Stabilizer VFX has finished, preview the changes.

Press the spacebar to stop playback when you're done.

It's better, but still a little rough. The Auto-scale setting in the Effect Controls panel now displays 103.7%; the effect moved the frames more dramatically, requiring more scaling to eliminate black gaps around the edges.

Rather than change the amount Warp Stabilizer VFX smooths the footage, now you'll change its goal.

In the Effect Controls panel, choose No Motion from the Result menu.

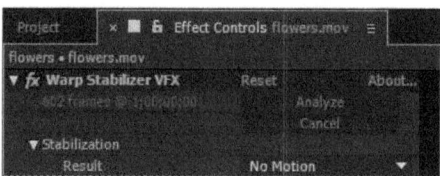

With this setting, Warp Stabilizer VFX attempts to lock the camera in position. This requires even more scaling. When No Motion is selected, the Smoothness option is dimmed.

When the orange banner disappears, preview the changes again. Press the spacebar to stop the playback.

Now the camera stays in position, so that the movement you notice is the rustling of the flowers in the wind, not the shakiness of the camera. In order to achieve this effect, Warp Stabilizer VFX had to scale the clip to about 112% of its original size.

Fine-tuning the results

The default analysis works well most of the time, but sometimes you may need to massage the end results even further. In this project, the clip skews subtly in a few places, most noticeably at about the five-second mark. Casual viewers may not notice the problem, but a keen producer will. You'll change the method that Warp Stabilizer VFX uses to remove the skew.

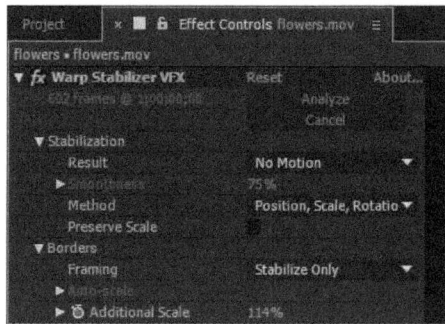

In the Effect Controls panel, choose Position, Scale, Rotation from the Method menu.

Choose Stabilize Only from the Framing menu.

Increase the Additional Scale to **114%**.

Note

Scaling a video layer up degrades the image. A good rule of thumb is to increase the layer to no more than 115% the size of the original source.

Preview the changes.

Now the shot looks rock-steady. The only movement is that caused by the wind rustling the flowers.

Press the spacebar to stop the playback when you're done.

Choose File > Save to save your work.

Choose File > Close Project.

As you have discovered, stabilizing a shot is not without its drawbacks. To compensate for the movement or rotation data applied to the layer, the frames must be scaled, which could ultimately degrade the footage. If you really need to use the shot in your production, this may be the best compromise.

Using single-point motion tracking

With the increase in the number of productions that incorporate digital elements into final shots, compositors need an easy way to synchronize computer-generated effects with film or video backgrounds. After Effects lets you do this with the capability to follow, or track, a defined area in the shot, and to apply that movement to other layers. These layers can contain text, effects, images, or other footage. The resulting visual effect precisely matches the original moving footage.

When you track motion in an After Effects composition that contains multiple layers, the default tracking type is Transform. This type of motion tracking tracks position and/or rotation to apply to another layer. When tracking position, this option creates one track point, and generates Position keyframes. When tracking rotation, this option creates two track points, and produces Rotation keyframes.

In this exercise, you will track a shape layer to the weighted arm of a metronome. This will be especially challenging, as the camera operator chose not to use a tripod.

Setting up the project

If you've just completed the first project, and After Effects is open, skip to step 3. Otherwise, restore the default application settings for After Effects. See "Restoring default preferences" on page 2.

Start After Effects, and then immediately hold down Ctrl+Alt+Shift (Windows) or Command+Option+Shift (Mac OS) to restore default preferences settings. When prompted, click OK to delete your preferences.

Close the Start window.

After Effects opens to display a new, untitled project.

Choose File > Save As > Save As.

In the Save As dialog box, navigate to the Lessons/Lesson13/Finished_Projects folder.

Name the project **Lesson13_Tracking.aep**, and then click Save.

Creating the composition

You need to import one footage item to start this project. You'll use it to create the composition.

Double-click an empty area of the Project panel to open the Import File dialog box.

Navigate to the Lessons/Lesson13/Assets folder. Select the metronome.mov file, and then click Import or Open.

In the Project panel, drag the metronome.mov clip onto the Create A New Composition button at the bottom of the panel.

After Effects creates a new composition named Metronome, with the same pixel size, aspect ratio, frame rate, and duration of the source clip.

Drag the current-time indicator across the time ruler to manually preview the footage.

Creating a shape layer

You're going to attach a star to the end of the metronome. First, you need to create the star.

You'll use a shape layer.

Press the Home key, or move the current-time indicator to the beginning of the time ruler.

Click an empty area of the Timeline panel to deselect the layer.

Select the Star tool (✷), hidden behind the Rectangle tool (▢) in the Tools panel.

Click the Fill Color swatch, and select a light yellow such as R=**220**, G=**250**, B=**90**. Click the word *Stroke*, select None in the Stroke Options dialog box, and click OK.

⬤ Note

If you don't see the Fill Color swatch, make sure you don't have a layer selected. When a layer is selected, shape tools draw masks.

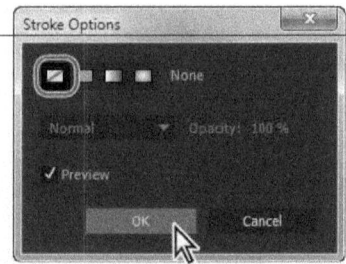

In the Composition panel, draw a small star.

Use the Selection tool to position the star over the weighted end of the pendulum arm.

Select Shape Layer 1 to see the layer's anchor point. Use the Pan Behind tool (⌖) to move the anchor point to the center of the star shape, if it isn't already there.

Positioning the track point

After Effects tracks motion by matching pixels from a selected area in a frame to pixels in each succeeding frame. You create tracking points to specify the area to track. A track point contains a feature region, a search region, and an attach point. After Effects displays the track point in the Layer panel as it tracks.

You will track the metronome weight (the rhombus at the end of its arm) by placing tracking regions around the area that you'll track another layer to. With the star shape added to the Tracking composition, you are ready to position the track point.

Select the metronome.mov layer in the Timeline panel.

Choose Animation > Track Motion. The Tracker panel opens; increase its size if you can't see all the options.

After Effects opens the selected layer in the Layer panel. The Track Point 1 indicator is in the center of the image.

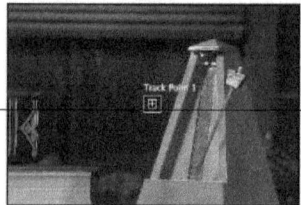 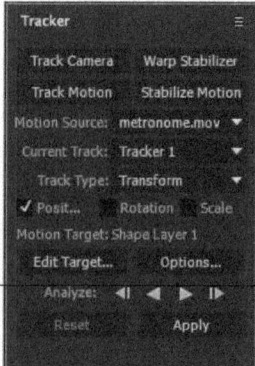

Notice the settings in the Tracker panel: Metronome.mov is selected in the Motion Source menu. The Current Track is Tracker 1, and the Motion Target is Shape Layer 1, because After Effects automatically sets the Motion Target to the layer immediately above the source layer.

Now, you'll position your track point.

Using the Selection tool (▸), move the Track Point 1 indicator (drag the empty portion of the inner box) in the Layer panel over the metronome weight.

● **Note**

In this exercise, you want the star to move atop the metronome weight. However, if you wanted an object to move in relationship to the tracked area but not on top of it, you could reposition the attach point accordingly.

Enlarge the search region (the outer box) to encompass the area around the pendulum. Then adjust the feature region (the inner box) within the weight.

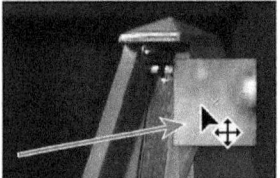  

Analyzing and applying tracking

Now that the search and feature regions are defined, you can apply the tracker.

● **Note**

The tracking analysis may take quite a while. The larger the search and feature regions, the longer After Effects takes to analyze tracking.

Click the Analyze Forward button (▶) in the Tracker panel. Watch the analysis to ensure the track point stays with the metronome weight. If it doesn't, press the spacebar to stop the analysis, and reposition the feature region. (See the sidebar "Checking for drift.")

When the analysis is complete, click the Apply button.

In the Motion Tracker Apply Options dialog box, click OK to apply the tracking to the x and y dimensions.

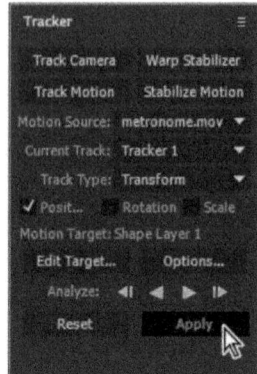 

Checking for drift

As an image moves in a shot, the lighting, surrounding objects, and angle of the object can all change, making a once-distinct feature no longer identifiable at the subpixel level. It takes time to develop an eye for choosing a trackable feature. Even with careful planning and practice, you may often find that the feature region drifts away from the desired feature. Readjusting the feature and search regions, changing the tracking options, and trying again are all standard parts of digital tracking. When you notice drifting occurring, try the following:

Immediately stop the analysis by pressing the spacebar.

Move the current-time indicator back to the last good tracked point. You can see this in the Layer panel.

Reposition and/or resize the feature and search regions, being careful not to accidentally move the attach point. Moving the attach point will cause a noticeable jump in your tracked layer.

Click the Analyze Forward button to resume tracking.

The motion-tracking data is added to the Timeline panel, where you can see that the track data is in the metronome layer, but the results are applied to the Position property of the Shape Layer 1 layer.

Press the spacebar to preview the movie. The star not only follows the pendulum; it moves with the camera's movement.

When you're ready, press the spacebar to stop playback.

Hide the properties for both layers in the Timeline panel, choose File > Save, and then choose File > Close Project.

Motion tracking an element onto background footage can be fun. As long as you have a stable feature to track, single-point motion tracking can be quite easy.

Moving and resizing the track points

In setting up motion tracking, it's often necessary to refine a track point by adjusting its feature region, search region, and attach point. You can resize or move these items independently or in groups by dragging with the Selection tool. The pointer icon changes to reflect one of many different activities.

*Track point components (left) and Selection tool pointer icons (right): **A.** Search region **B.** Feature region **C.** Attach point **D.** Moves search region **E.** Moves both regions **F.** Moves entire track point **G.** Moves attach point **H.** Moves entire track point **I.** Resizes region*

To turn feature region magnification on or off, choose Magnify Feature When Dragging from the Tracker panel menu. A check mark appears next to the option when it's on.

To move only the search region, using the Selection tool, drag the edge of the search region; the Move Search Region pointer (⌕) appears (D, above).

To move just the feature and search regions together, Alt-drag (Windows) or Option-drag (Mac OS) with the Selection tool inside the feature or search region; the Move Both Regions pointer (⌖) appears (E, above).

To move only the attach point, using the Selection tool, drag the attach point; the Move Attach Point pointer (⯈ₒ) appears (G, above).

To resize the feature or search region, drag a corner handle (I, above).

To move the feature region, search region, and attach point together, drag with the Selection tool inside the track point area (avoiding the region edges and the attach point); the Move Track Point pointer (⯈✛) appears.

For more information about track points, see After Effects Help.

Using multipoint tracking

After Effects also offers two more advanced types of tracking that use multiple tracking points: parallel corner-pinning and perspective corner-pinning.

When you track using parallel corner-pinning, you simultaneously track three points in the source footage. After Effects calculates the position of a fourth point to keep the lines between the points parallel. When the movement of the points is applied to the target layer, the Corner Pin effect distorts the layer to simulate skew, scale, and rotation, but not perspective. Parallel lines remain parallel, and relative distances are preserved.

When you track using perspective corner-pinning, you simultaneously track four points in the source footage. When applied to the target footage, the Corner Pin effect uses the movement of the four points to distort the layer, simulating changes in perspective.

You'll attach an animation to a computer monitor using perspective corner-pinning. The effect is similar to the Lesson 7 project, but you'll use a different technique. If you haven't already watched the sample movie for this exercise, do so now.

Setting up the project

Start by launching After Effects and creating a new project.

If it's not already open, start After Effects, and then immediately hold down Ctrl+Alt+Shift (Windows) or Command+Option+Shift (Mac OS) to restore default preferences settings. When prompted, click OK to delete your preferences, and close the Start window.

After Effects opens to display an empty, untitled project.

Choose File > Save As > Save As.

In the Save As dialog box, navigate to the Lessons/Lesson13/Finished_Projects folder.

Name the project **Lesson13_Multipoint.aep,** and then click Save.

Double-click an empty area of the Project panel to open the Import File dialog box, and then navigate to the Lessons/Lesson13/Assets folder.

Ctrl-click (Windows) or Command-click (Mac OS) both the majorspoilers.mov and multipoint_tracking.mov files, and then click Import or Open.

Press Ctrl+N (Windows) or Command+N (Mac OS) to create a new composition.

In the Composition Settings dialog box, do the following, and then click OK:

Type **Multipoint_Tracking** in the Composition Name field.

Choose NTSC DV from the Preset menu.

Set the Duration to **7:05**—the length of the majorspoilers.mov file.

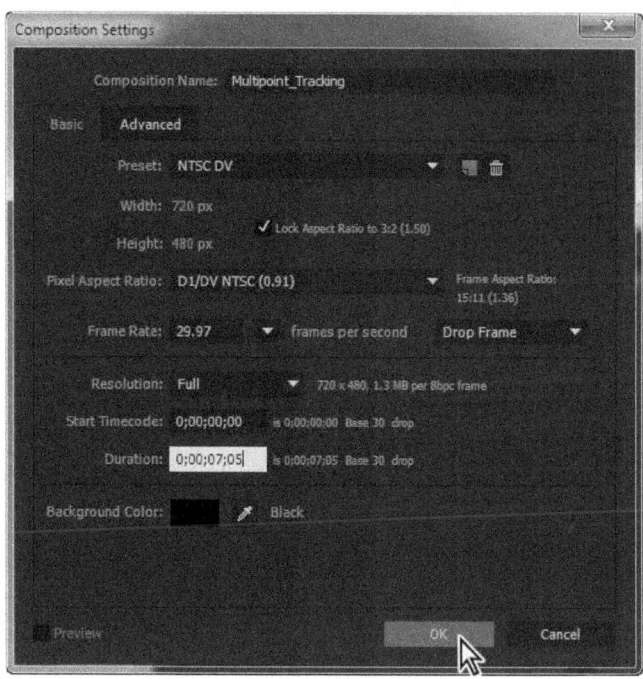

Drag the multipoint_tracking.mov item from the Project panel to the Timeline panel. Manually preview the footage, which is shaky because it was shot with a handheld camera.

Because you're positioning the majorspoilers.mov layer on the computer monitor, it will be fairly easy to place tracking markers on the flat plane. By default, the tracker tracks by luminance, so you will use the areas around the screen that have high contrast differences for tracking.

Press the Home key, or move the current-time indicator to the beginning of the time ruler.

Drag the majorspoilers.mov footage item from the Project panel to the Timeline panel, placing it at the top of the layer stack.

To make it easier to see the underlying movie as you place the tracking points, turn off the Video switch for the majorspoilers.mov layer in the Timeline panel.

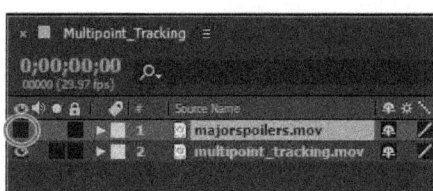 

Positioning the track points

You're ready to add the track points to the multipoint_tracking.mov layer.

Select the multipoint_tracking.mov layer in the Timeline panel.

Choose Window > Tracker to open the Tracker panel, if it isn't open.

In the Tracker panel, choose multipoint_tracking.mov from the Motion Source menu.

Select the multipoint_tracking.mov layer again, and then click Track Motion.

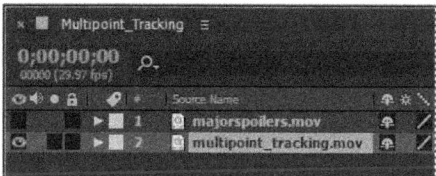
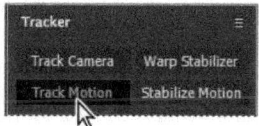

The desk scene opens in the Layer panel, with a track point indicator in the center of the image. However, you will be tracking four points in order to attach the animated movie to the computer screen.

Choose Perspective Corner Pin from the Track Type menu. Three more track point indicators appear in the Layer panel.

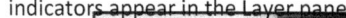

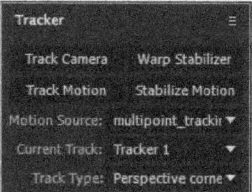

Drag the track points to four different high-contrast areas of the image. The four corners of the computer screen provide excellent contrast. Use the following image as a guide. (Because the areas of high contrast are also where you want to attach the majorspoilers layer, you don't need to move the attach points.)

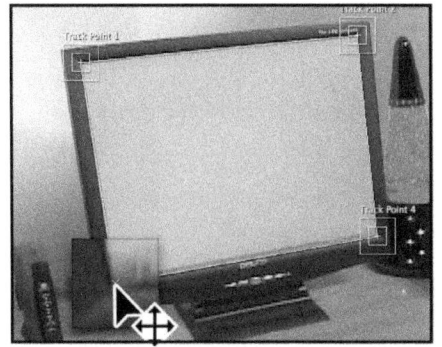 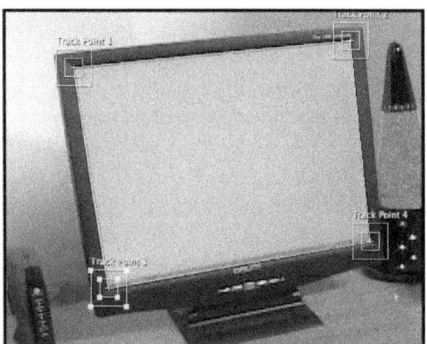

▶ Tip

It may be helpful to zoom in when placing and adjusting the track points.

Zoom out again when you have finished.

Applying the multipoint tracker

You're ready to analyze the data and apply the tracker.

Click the Analyze Forward button (▶) in the Tracker panel. When the analysis is complete, click the Apply button to calculate the tracking.

● **Note**

If the composition doesn't appear in the Composition panel, click in the Timeline window to move the current-time indicator and refresh the display.

Notice the results in the Timeline panel: You can see the Corner Pin and Position property keyframes for the majorspoilers layer and the track point data for the motion_tracking layer.

Make the majorspoilers layer visible again, move the current-time indicator to the beginning of the timeline, and preview the movie to see the results of the tracker.

When you're done watching the preview, press the spacebar to stop playback.

If you don't like the results, return to the Tracker panel, click the Reset button, and try again. With practice, you will become adept at identifying good feature regions.

Hide the layer properties to keep the Timeline panel neat, and choose File > Save to save your work.

Choose File > Close Project.

mocha for After Effects

In most cases, you'll get better and more accurate tracking results using mocha from Imagineer Systems to track points in video. A version of mocha is included with After Effects. To track using mocha, choose Animation > Track In Mocha AE.

One advantage of mocha for After Effects is that you don't have to accurately place tracking points to obtain a perfect track. Rather than using tracking points, mocha for After Effects uses a planar tracker, which attempts to track an object's translation, rotation, and scaling data based on the movement of a user-defined plane. Planes provide more detail to the computer than is possible with single-point and multipoint tracking tools.

When you work with mocha for After Effects, you need to identify planes in a clip that coincide with movement you want to track. Planes don't have to be tabletops or walls. For example, if someone is waving goodbye, you can use their upper and lower limbs as two planes. After you track the planes, you can export the tracking data for use in After Effects.

mocha for After Effects uses two different spline technologies for tracking: X splines and Bezier splines. X splines may work better for tracking, especially with perspective motion, but Bezier splines work well, too, and are the industry standard.

To learn more about mocha for After Effects, choose Help > Online Help or Help > Offline Help in mocha.

We've saved some tracking data for the computer monitor in mocha for After Effects, so that you can apply it in After Effects if you'd like. To apply the data, follow these steps:

Create a new project in After Effects, and import the majorspoilers.mov and mocha_tracking.mov files from the Lesson13/Assets folder. Create a new composition from the mocha_tracking.mov file, and then drag the majorspoilers.mov file to the top of the layer stack in the Timeline panel.

Open the mocha_data.txt file (in the Lesson13/Optional_Mocha_Tutorial folder) in a text editor such as WordPad or TextEdit. (Don't use Notepad on Windows. It doesn't retain the mocha formatting, so After Effects doesn't recognize its content on the clipboard.) Choose Edit > Select All, and then Edit > Copy to copy all the data.

Select the majorspoilers.mov layer in the Timeline panel, and choose Edit

Paste. All the data is applied to the layer.

Preview the results.

Creating a particle simulation

After Effects includes several effects that do an excellent job of creating particle simulations. Two of them—CC Particle Systems II and CC Particle World—are based on the same engine. The major difference between the two is that Particle World enables you to move the particles in 3D space, rather than in a 2D layer.

In this exercise, you'll learn how to use the CC Particle Systems II effect to create a supernova that could be used as the opening of a science program or as a motion background. If you haven't already watched the sample movie for this exercise, do so now before continuing.

Setting up the project

Start by launching After Effects and creating a new composition.

If it's not already open, start After Effects, and then immediately hold down Ctrl+Alt+Shift (Windows) or Command+Option+Shift (Mac OS) to restore default preferences settings. When prompted, click OK to delete your preferences, and close the Start window.

After Effects opens to display an empty, untitled project.

Choose File > Save As > Save As.

In the Save As dialog box, navigate to the Lessons/Lesson13/Finished_Projects folder.

Name the project **Lesson13_Particles.aep**, and then click Save.

You don't need to import any footage items for this exercise. However, you do need to create the composition.

In After Effects, press Ctrl+N (Windows) or Command+N (Mac OS).

In the Composition Settings dialog box, do the following, and then click OK:

Type **Supernova** in the Composition Name field.

Choose NTSC D1 from the Preset pop-up menu.

Set the Duration to **10:00**.

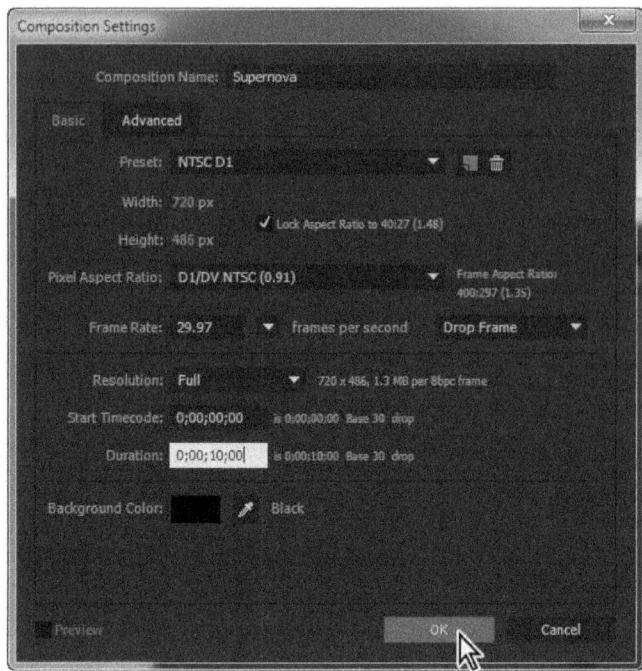

Creating a particle system

You will build the particle system from a solid layer, so you'll create that next.

Choose Layer > New > Solid to create a new solid layer.

In the Solid Settings dialog box, type **Particles** in the Name box.

Click Make Comp Size to make the layer the same size as the composition. Then click OK.

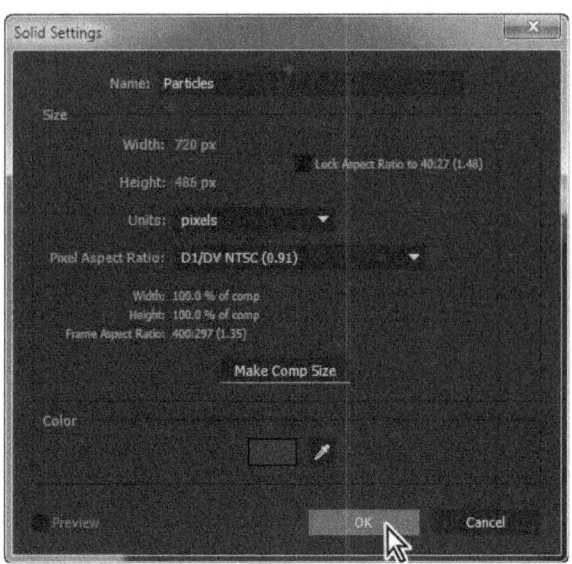

Understanding Particle Systems II properties

Particle systems have a unique vocabulary. Some of the key settings are explained here for your reference. They're listed in the order in which they appear (top to bottom) in the Effect Controls panel.

Birth Rate Controls the number of particles generated per second. The value itself is arbitrary and does not equal the actual number of particles being generated. However, the higher the number, the more densely packed the particles become.

Longevity Determines how long the particles are visible.

Producer Position Controls the center point or origin of the particle system. The position is set based on the x, y coordinates. All particles emanate from this single point. You can control the size of the producer by making adjustments to the x and y radius settings. The higher these values, the larger the producer point will be. A high x value and a y value of zero (0) result in a line.

Velocity Controls the speed of particles. The higher the number, the faster the particles move.

Inherent Velocity % Determines how much of the velocity is passed along to the particles when the Producer Position is animated. A negative value causes the particles to move in the opposite direction.

Gravity Determines how fast particles fall. The higher the value, the faster the particles fall. A negative value causes particles to rise.

Resistance Simulates particles interacting with air or water, slowing over time.

Direction Determines which direction the particles flow. Use with the Direction Animation type.

Extra Introduces randomness into the movement of the particles.

Birth/Death Size Determines the size of the particles when they are created and when they expire.

Opacity Map Controls opacity changes for the particle over its lifetime.

Color Map Use with the Birth and Death colors to shade the particles over time.

With the Particles layer selected in the Timeline panel, choose Effect > Simulation > CC Particle Systems II.

Go to 4:00 to see the particle system.

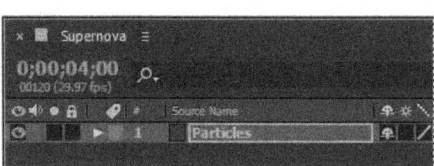 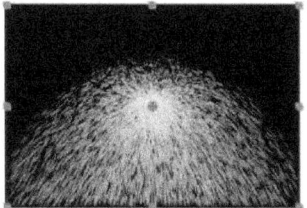

A large stream of yellow particles appears in the Composition panel.

Customizing the particle effect

You will turn this stream of particles into a supernova by customizing the settings in the Effect Controls panel.

Expand the Physics property group in the Effect Controls panel. The Explosive Animation setting works fine for this project, but instead of the particles falling down, you want them to flow out in all directions, so change the Gravity value to **0.0**.

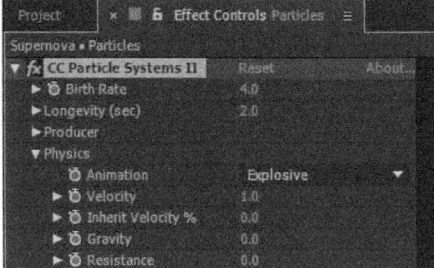 

Hide the Physics property group, and expand the Particle property group. Then choose Faded Sphere from the Particle Type menu.

Now the particles look intergalactic. Don't stop there, though.

Change the Death Size to **1.50**, and increase the Size Variation to **100%**. This allows the particles to change birth size randomly.
Reduce the Max Opacity to **55%** to make the particles semitransparent.

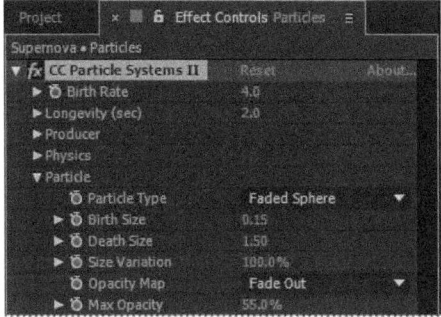

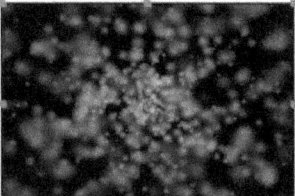

Click the Birth Color swatch, and change the color to R=**255**, G=**200**, B=**50** to give the particles a yellow hue at birth.

Click the Death Color swatch, and change the color to R=**180**, G=**180**, B=**180** to give the particles a light gray hue as they fade out.

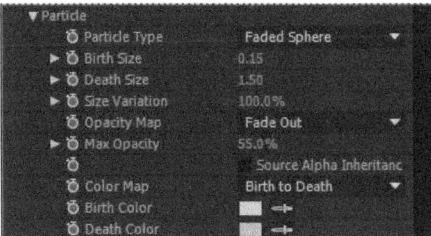

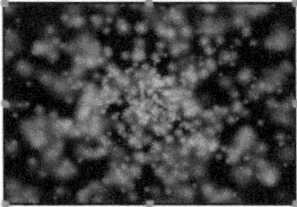

Note

Even though they're at the top of the Effect Controls panel, it is often easier to adjust the Longevity and Birth Rate settings after you have set the other particle properties.

To keep the particles from staying onscreen too long, decrease the Longevity value to **0.8** seconds.

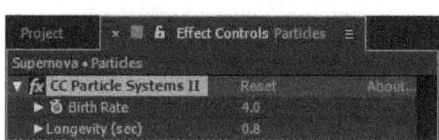 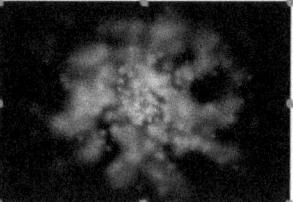

The Faded Sphere particle type softens the look, but the particle shapes are still too sharply defined. You will fix that by blurring the layer to blend the particles with one another.

Hide the CC Particle Systems II effect properties.

Choose Effect > Blur & Sharpen > Fast Blur.

In the Fast Blur area of the Effect Controls panel, increase the Blurriness value to **10**. Then select Repeat Edge Pixels to keep the particles from being cropped at the edge of the frame.

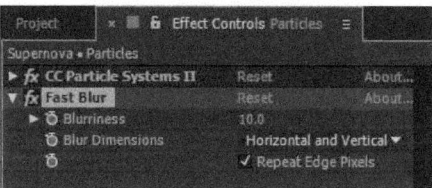 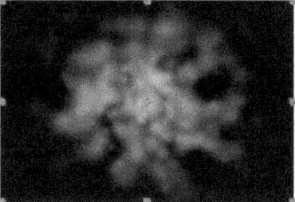

Creating the sun

You will now create a bright halo of light that will go behind the particles.

Go to 7:00.

Press Ctrl+Y (Windows) or Command+Y (Mac OS) to create a new solid layer.

In the Solid Settings dialog box, do the following:

Type **Sun** in the Name box.

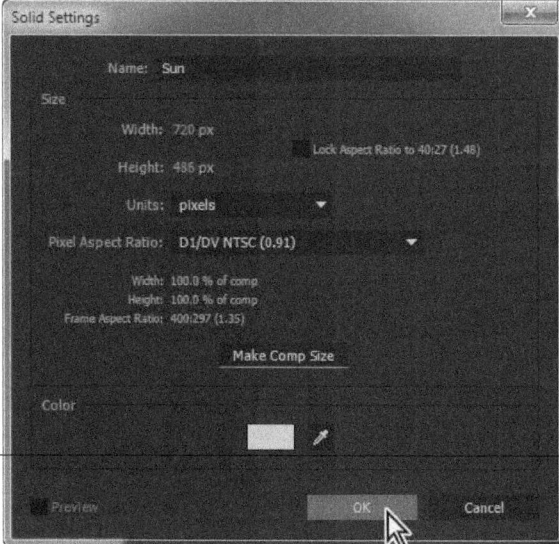

Click Make Comp Size to make the layer the same size as the composition.

Click the color swatch to make the layer the same yellow as the Birth Color of the particles (**255**, **200**, **50**).

Click OK to close the Solid Settings dialog box.

Drag the Sun layer below the Particles layer in the Timeline panel.

Select the Ellipse tool (⬭), which is hidden behind the Rectangle tool (▭) or the Star tool (★) in the Tools panel, and Shift-drag in the Composition panel to draw a circle with a radius of roughly 100 pixels, or one-fourth the width of the composition.

You've created a mask.

Using the Selection tool (▶), drag the mask shape to the center of the Composition panel.

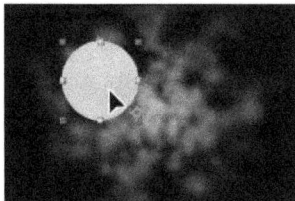 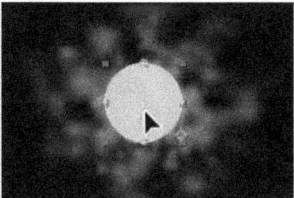

With the Sun layer selected in the Timeline panel, press the F key to reveal its Mask Feather property. Increase the Mask Feather amount to **100, 100** pixels.

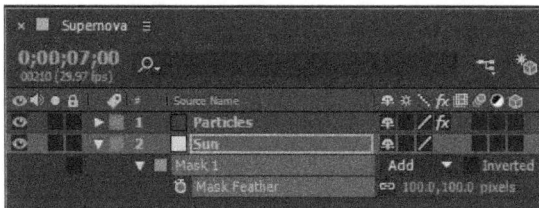 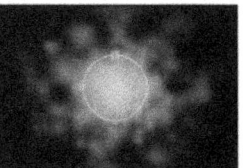

Press Alt+[(Windows) or Option+[(Mac OS) to set the In point of the layer to the current time.

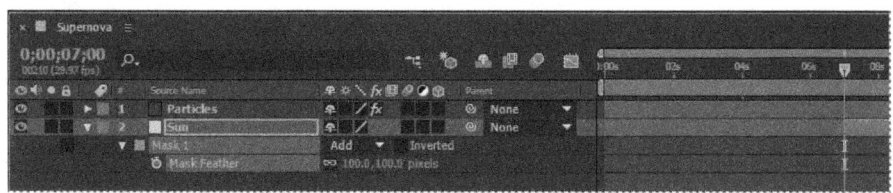

Hide the properties for the Sun layer.

Lighting the darkness

Since the sun is bright, it should illuminate the surrounding darkness.

Make sure the current-time indicator is still at 7:00.

Press Ctrl+Y (Windows) or Command+Y (Mac OS) to create a new solid layer.

In the Solid Settings dialog box, name the layer **Background**, click the Make Comp Size button to make the layer the same size as the composition, and then click OK to create the layer.

In the Timeline panel, drag the Background layer to the bottom position in the layer stack.

With the Background layer selected in the Timeline panel, choose Effect > Generate

Gradient Ramp.

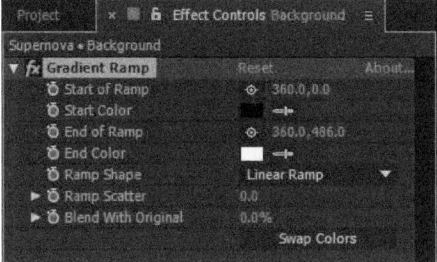 

The Gradient Ramp effect creates a color gradient, blending it with the original image. You can create linear ramps or radial ramps, and vary the position and colors of the ramp over time. Use the Start Of Ramp and End Of Ramp settings to specify the start and end positions. Use the Ramp Scatter setting to disperse the ramp colors and eliminate banding.

In the Gradient Ramp area of the Effect Controls panel, do the following:

Change Start Of Ramp to **360**, **240** and End Of Ramp to **360**, **525**.

Choose Radial Ramp from the Ramp Shape menu.

Click the Start Color swatch, and set the start color to dark blue (R=**0**, G=**25**, B=**135**).

Set the End Color to black (R=**0**, G=**0**, B=**0**).

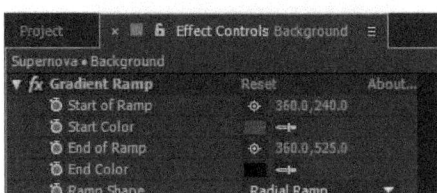 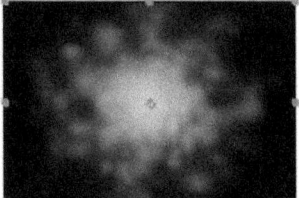

Press Alt+[(Windows) or Option+[(Mac OS) to set the In point of the layer to the current time.

Adding a lens flare

To tie all the elements together, you'll add a lens flare to simulate an explosion.

Press the Home key, or move the current-time indicator to the beginning of the time ruler.

Press Ctrl+Y (Windows) or Command+Y (Mac OS) to create a new solid layer.

In the Solid Settings dialog box, name the layer **Nova**, click the Make Comp Size button to make the layer the same size as the composition, set the Color to black (R=**0**, G=**0**, B=**0**), and then click OK.

Drag the Nova layer to the top of the layer stack in the Timeline panel. Then, with the Nova layer selected, choose Effect > Generate > Lens Flare.

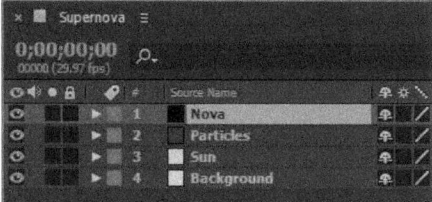 

In the Lens Flare area of the Effect Controls panel, do the following:

Change Flare Center to **360**, **240**.

Make sure 50–300mm Zoom is selected in the Lens Type menu.

Decrease Flare Brightness to **0%**, and then click the Flare Brightness stopwatch icon ( ) to create an initial keyframe.

Go to 0:10.

Increase the Flare Brightness to **240%**.

Go to 1:04, and decrease the Flare Brightness to **100%**.

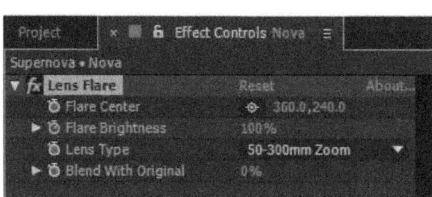 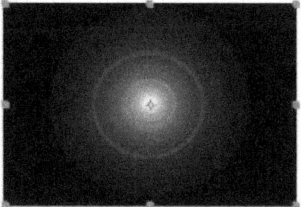

With the Nova layer selected in the Timeline panel, press the U key to see the animated Lens Flare property.

About high dynamic range (HDR) footage

After Effects also supports high dynamic range (HDR) color.

The dynamic range (ratio between dark and bright regions) in the physical world far exceeds the range of human vision and of images that are printed or displayed on a monitor. But while human eyes can adapt to very different brightness levels, most cameras and computer monitors can capture and reproduce only a limited dynamic range. Photographers, motion-picture artists, and others working with digital images must be selective about what's important in a scene, because they're working with a limited dynamic range.

HDR footage opens up a world of possibilities, because it can represent a very wide dynamic range through the use of 32-bit floating-point numeric values. Floating-point numeric representations allow the same number of bits to describe a much larger range of values than integer (fixed-point) values. HDR values can contain brightness levels, including objects as bright as a candle flame or the sun, that far exceed those in 8-bit-per-channel (bpc) or

16-bpc (non-floating-point) mode. Lower dynamic range 8-bpc and 16-bpc modes can represent RGB levels only from black to white, which represents an extremely small segment of the dynamic range in the real world.

After Effects supports HDR images in a variety of ways. For example, you can create 32-bpc projects to work with HDR footage, and you can adjust the exposure, or the amount of light captured in an image, when working with HDR images in After Effects. For more information about support in After Effects for HDR images, see After Effects Help.

Right-click (Windows) or Control-click (Mac OS) the ending Flare Brightness keyframe, and choose Keyframe Assistant > Easy Ease In.

Right-click (Windows) or Control-click (Mac OS) the beginning Flare Brightness keyframe, and choose Keyframe Assistant > Easy Ease Out.

Finally, you need to make the layers under the Nova layer visible in the composition.

Press F2 to deselect all layers, and choose Columns > Modes from the Timeline panel menu. Then choose Screen from the Mode menu for the Nova layer.

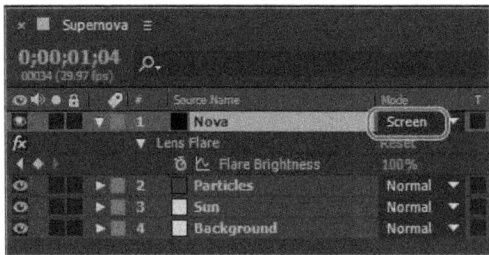 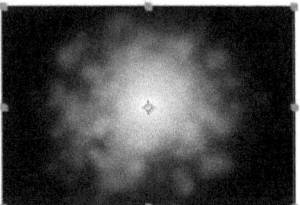

Preview the movie. When you're done, press the spacebar to stop the preview.

Choose File > Save, and then choose File > Close Project.

Retiming playback using the Timewarp effect

The Timewarp effect in After Effects gives you precise control over a wide range of parameters when changing the playback speed of a layer, including interpolation methods, motion blur, and source cropping to eliminate unwanted artifacts.

In this exercise, you will use the Timewarp effect to change the speed of a clip for a dramatic slow-motion playback. If you haven't already watched the sample movie for this exercise, do so now.

Setting up the project

Start by launching After Effects and creating a new project.

If After Effects isn't open, start it, and then immediately hold down Ctrl+Alt+Shift (Windows) or Command+Option+Shift (Mac OS) to restore default preferences settings. When prompted, click OK to delete your preferences, and close the Start window.

After Effects opens to display an empty, untitled project.

Choose File > Save As > Save As.

In the Save As dialog box, navigate to the Lessons/Lesson13/Finished_Projects folder.

Name the project **Lesson13_Timewarp.aep**, and then click Save.

Double-click an empty area of the Project panel to open the Import File dialog box. Then navigate to the Lessons/Lesson13/Assets folder on your hard disk, select the Group_Approach[DV].mov, and click Import or Open.

Click OK in the Interpret Footage dialog box.

Now, you'll create a new composition based on the footage item's aspect ratio and its duration.

Drag the Group_Approach[DV].mov file onto the Create A New Composition button () at the bottom of the Project panel.

After Effects creates a new composition named for the source file, and displays it in the

Composition and Timeline panels.

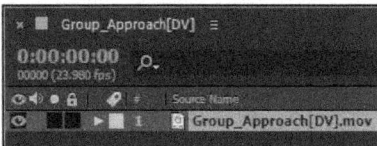 

Choose File > Save to save your work.

Using Timewarp

In the source footage, a group of young people approaches the camera at a steady pace. At around 2 seconds, the director would like the motion to begin to slow down to 10%, and then ramp back up to full speed at 7:00.

With the Group_Approach[DV] layer selected in the Timeline panel, choose Effect > Time > Timewarp.

In the Timewarp area of the Effect Controls panel, make sure Pixel Motion is selected in the Method menu and Speed is selected in the Adjust Time By menu.

With Pixel Motion selected, Timewarp creates new frames by analyzing the pixel movement in nearby frames and creating motion vectors. The Speed option controls the time adjustment by percentage rather than by a specific frame.

Go to 2:00.

In the Effect Controls panel, set the Speed to **100**, and click the stopwatch (⏱) to set a keyframe.

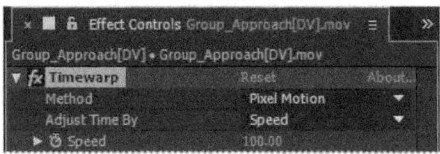 

This tells Timewarp to keep the speed of the clip at 100% until the 2-second mark.

▶ **Tip**

To see the Speed keyframes, select Timewarp in the Timeline panel, and press the U key.

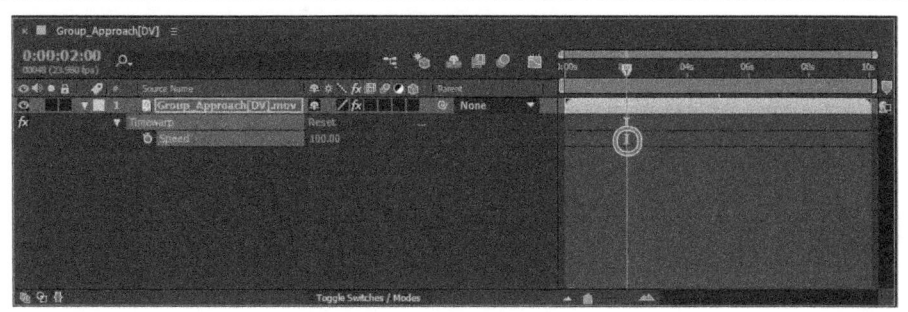

Go to 5:00, and set the Speed to **10**. After Effects adds a keyframe.

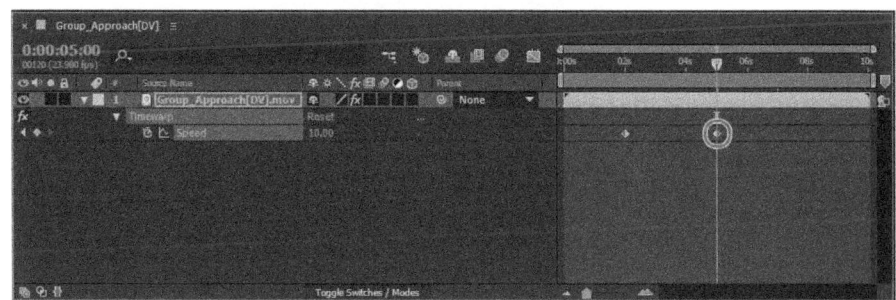

Go to 7:00, and set the Speed to **100**. After Effects adds a keyframe.

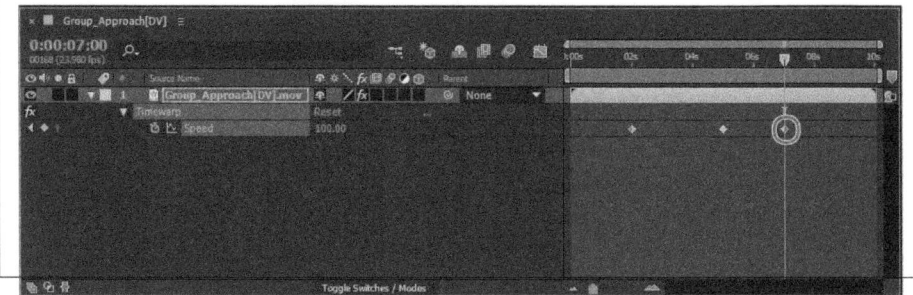

Note

Be patient. The first time through, After Effects is caching information in RAM. The second
time it plays will provide a more accurate playback.

Press the Home key or move the current-time indicator to the beginning of the time ruler,
and then watch a preview of the effect.

The speed adjustments are rather abrupt—not the smooth, slow-motion curve you would
expect to see in a professional effect. This is because the keyframes are linear instead of
curved. You'll fix that next.

Press the spacebar to stop playback when you're ready.

With the Group_Approach[DV] layer selected in the Timeline panel, press the U key to see the animated Timewarp Speed property.

Click the Graph Editor button in the Timeline panel to display the Graph Editor instead of the layer bars. Make sure the Speed property name for the Group_Approach[DV] layer is selected. The Graph Editor displays its graph.

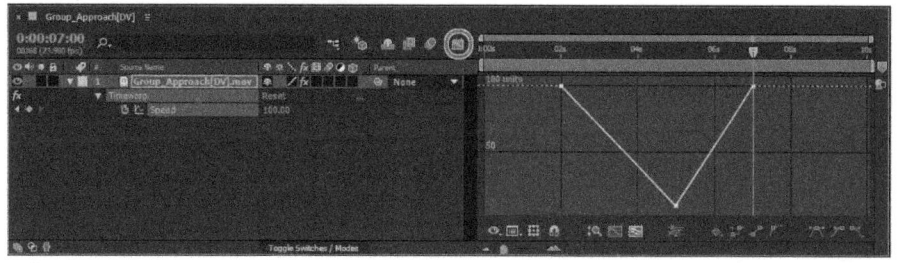

▷ **Tip**

Close columns in the Timeline panel to see more icons in the Graph Editor.

You can also apply an Easy Ease adjustment by pressing the F9 key.

Click to select the first Speed keyframe (at 2:00), and then click the Easy Ease icon (⚲) at the bottom of the Graph Editor.

This adjusts the influence into and out of the keyframe to smooth out sudden changes.

Repeat step 11 for the other two Speed keyframes in the motion graph, at 5:00 and 7:00.

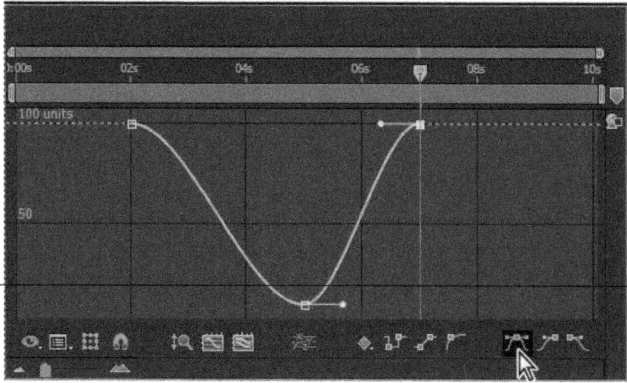

The motion graph is now smoother, but you can tweak it even more by dragging the Bezier handles.

Using the Bezier handles for the keyframes at 2:00 and 5:00, adjust the curve so that it resembles the following image.

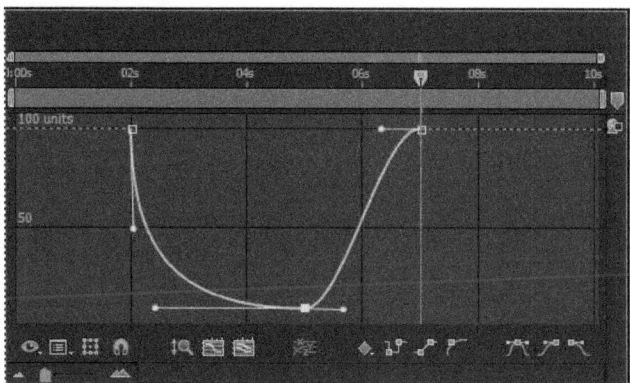

Preview the movie again. This time, the slow-motion Timewarp effect looks professional.

Choose File > Save to save the project, and then choose File > Close Project.

You've now experimented with some of the advanced features in After Effects, including motion stabilization, motion tracking, particle systems, and the Timewarp effect. To render and export any or all of the projects you completed in this lesson, see <u>Lesson 14</u>, "<u>Rendering and Outputting</u>," for instructions.

Review questions

1. What is Warp Stabilizer VFX, and when do you need to use it?

2. Why might drifting occur when you're tracking an image?

3. What is the birth rate in a particle effect?

4. What does the Timewarp effect do?

Review answers

1. Shooting footage using a handheld camera typically results in shaky shots. Unless this look is intentional, you will want to stabilize the shots to eliminate unwanted motion. Warp Stabilizer VFX in After Effects analyzes the movement and rotation of the target layer, and then makes adjustments to it. When played back, the motion appears smooth, because the layer itself moves incrementally to offset the unwanted motion. You can change the way Warp Stabilizer VFX crops, scales, and performs other adjustments by modifying settings for the effect.

2. Drifting occurs when the feature region loses the feature that's being tracked. As an image moves in a shot, the lighting, surrounding objects, and angle of the object can change, making a once-distinct feature unidentifiable at the subpixel level. Even with careful planning and practice, the feature region often drifts away from the desired feature. Readjusting the feature and search regions, changing the tracking options, and trying again are all standard procedures in digital tracking.

3. The birth rate in a particle effect determines how often new particles are created.

4. The Timewarp effect gives you precise control over a wide range of parameters to change the playback speed of a layer, including interpolation methods, motion blur, and source cropping to eliminate unwanted artifacts

Chapter 14: Rendering and exporting

Basics of rendering and exporting

Rendering and exporting overview

What is rendering?

Rendering is the creation of the frames of a movie from a composition. The rendering of a frame is the creation of a composited two-dimensional image from all the layers, settings, and other information in a composition that makes up the model for that image. The rendering of a movie is the frame-by-frame rendering of each of the frames that make up the movie. For more information on how each frame is rendered, see Render order and collapsing transformations.

It is common to speak of rendering as if this term only applies to final output. However, the processes of creating previews for the Footage, Layer, and Composition panels are also kinds of rendering. In fact, it is possible to save a preview as a movie and use that as your final output. (See Preview video and audio .)

After a composition is rendered for final output, it is processed by one or more output modules that encode the rendered frames into one or more output files. This process of encoding rendered frames into files for output is one kind of exporting.

Note:

See Project settingsfor more information about project settings that determine how time is displayed in the project, how color data is treated in the project, and what sampling rate to use for audio.

See Composition settingsto learn how you can specify composition settings such as resolution, frame size, and pixel aspect ratio for your final rendered output.

After Effects provides various rendering options that help you accelerate the rendering process. GPU acceleration offers better speed and precision in rendering your effects. The Video Rendering and Effects dropdown in the Project Settings dialog box gives you the following GPU effect rendering options to choose from:

Software Only: CPU is used to render effects

Mercury GPU Acceleration: GPU is used to render effects. On Mac, Mercury GPU Acceleration can use OpenCL or Metal. On Windows, GPU effect rendering uses either CUDA or OpenCL based on your selection.

Note: GPU-accelerated effects may render with small color precision differences in an 8-bpc project when compared to CPU-only rendering. Set the project to 16-bpc or 32-bpc for accurate results.

After you have completed a composition, you can output a movie file. There are two different methods of outputting a movie file. Choose the one based on your needs.

Last updated 3/8/2018

Rendering and exporting

You might need a movie file for the following reasons:

You need a high-quality movie (with or without an alpha channel) or image sequence that will be placed in a Premiere Pro sequence, or used in another video editing, compositing, or 3D graphics application.

To create a high-quality movie file, render it with the Render Queue. See Render and export with the Render Queue panel

You need a compressed movie that will be played on the web, or used for DVD or Blu-ray disc.

To create a high-quality movie file that is compressed for the web, DVD, or Blu-ray disc, encode it using the Adobe Media Encoder. See Render and export with Adobe Media Encoder

Note: *Some kinds of exporting don't involve rendering and are for intermediate stages in a workflow, not for final output. For example, you can export a project as an Adobe Premiere Pro project by choosing File > Export > Adobe Premiere Pro Project. The project information is saved without rendering. In general, data transferred through Dynamic Link is not rendered.*

A movie can be made into a single output file that contains all the rendered frames, or it can be made into a sequence of still images (as you would do when creating output for a film recorder).

To generate output, you can either render your compositions using the After Effects render queue or add your compositions to the Adobe Media Encoder queue with the render settings that you have chosen in the Render Queue panel.

For the Render Queue, After Effects uses an embedded version of the Adobe Media Encoder to encode most movie formats through the Render Queue panel. When you manage render and export operations with the Render Queue panel, the embedded version of the Adobe Media Encoder is called automatically. The Adobe Media Encoder appears only in the form of the export settings dialog boxes with which you specify some encoding and output settings. (See Encoding and compression options for movies.)

Note: *The embedded version of the Adobe Media Encoder used to manage export settings within After Effects output modules does not provide all the features of the full, stand-alone Adobe Media Encoder application.*

From an expert: Using the Render Queue to export files

From an expert: Using the Render Queue to export files

Render and export with the Render Queue panel

The primary way of rendering and exporting movies from After Effects is through the Render Queue panel.

When you place a composition into the Render Queue panel, it becomes a render item. You can add many render items to the render queue, and After Effects can render multiple items in a batch, unattended. When you click the Render button in the upper-right corner of the Render Queue panel, all items with the status of Queued are rendered and output in the order in which they are listed in the Render Queue panel.

You do not need to render a movie multiple times to export it to multiple formats with the same render settings. You can export multiple versions of the same rendered movie by adding output modules to a render item in the Render Queue panel.When working with multiple render items, it is often useful to add comments in the Comment column in the Render Queue panel. If the Comment column is not visible, right-click (Windows) or Control-click (Mac OS) a column heading, and choose Columns > Comment.

Manage render items

In the Render Queue panel, you can manage several render items at once, each with its own render settings and output module settings.

Last updated 3/8/2018

Rendering and exporting

Render settings determine the following characteristics:

Output frame rate

Duration

Resolution

Layer quality

Output module settings—which are applied after render settings—determine post-rendering characteristics such as the following:

Output format

Compression options

Cropping

Whether to embed a link to the project in the output file

You can create templates that contain commonly used render settings and output module settings.

Using the Render Queue panel, you can render the same composition to different formats or with different settings, all with one click of the Render button:

You can output to a sequence of still images, such as a Cineon sequence, which you can then transfer to film for cinema projection.

You can output using lossless compression (or no compression) to a QuickTime container for transfer to a non-linear editing (NLE) system for video editing.

You can select, duplicate, and reorder render items using many of the same keyboard shortcuts that you use for working with layers and other items. See General.

Note: *To transfer the output rendered from After Effects to film or video, you must have the proper hardware for film or video transfer, or have access to a service bureau that can provide transfer services.*

Render and export a movie using the render queue

Select the composition from which to make a movie in the Project panel, and then do one of the following to add the composition to the render queue:

Choose Composition > Add To Render Queue.

Drag the composition to the Render Queue panel.

To create a composition from a footage item and immediately add that composition to the render queue, drag the footage item from the Project panel to the Render Queue panel. It is a convenient way to convert a footage item from one format to another.

Click the triangle next to the Output To heading in the Render Queue panel to choose a name for the output file based on a naming convention, and then choose a location; or click the text next to the Output To heading to enter any name. (See Specify filenames and locations for rendered output.)

Click the triangle to the right of the Render Settings heading to choose a render settings template, or click the underlined text to the right of the Render Settings heading to customize the settings. (See Render settings.)
Choose a Log type from the Log menu.

When a log file has been written, the path to the log file appears under the Render Settings heading and Log menu.

Last updated 3/8/2018

515

Rendering and exporting

Click the triangle to the right of the Output Module heading to choose an output module settings template, or click the underlined text to the right of the Output Module heading to customize the settings. You use the output module settings to specify the file format of the output movie. In some cases, a format-specific dialog box opens after you choose a format, in which you can choose format-specific settings. (See Output modules and output module settingsand Encoding and compression options for movies.)

When an output name and location have been set, and render settings and an output module have been selected, the entry in the Render column automatically becomes selected (shown by a check mark) and the status changes to Queued. The status Queued means that the render item is in the render queue.

Press Caps Lock before you start rendering to prevent the Composition panel from displaying rendered frames. By not updating the Composition panel, After Effects requires less time to process simple render items with many frames.

Click the Render button in the upper-right corner of the Render Queue panel.

Rendering a composition into a movie can take a few seconds or many hours, depending on the composition's frame size, quality, complexity, and compression method. As After Effects renders the item, you are unable to work in the program. An audio alert indicates when rendering is complete.

See this tutorial to learn how to use the render queue to export files.

When rendering of a render item is complete, it remains in the Render Queue panel with its status changed to Done until you remove the item from the Render Queue panel. You cannot rerender a completed item, but you can duplicate it to create a new item in the queue with the same settings or with new settings.

After an item has been rendered, you can import the finished movie as a footage item by dragging its output module from the Render Queue panel into the Project panel. (See Import footage items.)

Render item statuses

Each render item has a status, which appears in the Status column in the Render Queue panel:

Unqueued The render item is listed in the Render Queue panel but is not ready to render. Confirm that you have selected the desired render settings and output module settings, and then select the Render option to queue the render item.

Queued The render item is ready to render.

Needs Output An output filename has not been specified. Choose a value from the Output To menu, or click the underlined Not Yet Specified text next to the Output To heading to specify a filename and path.

Failed After Effects was unsuccessful in rendering the render item. Use a text editor to view the log file for specific information on why the rendering was unsuccessful. When a log file has been written, the path to the log file appears under the Render Settings heading and Log menu.

User Stopped The rendering process was stopped.

Done The rendering process for the item is complete.

Manage render items and change render statuses

Select the source composition for a render item in the Project panel: Right-click (Windows) or Control-click (Mac OS) the render item and choose Reveal Composition In Project from the context menu.

Remove a render item from the render queue (change its status from Queued to Unqueued): Deselect the item entry in the Render column. The item remains in the Render Queue panel.

Change the status of a render item from Unqueued to Queued: Select the item in the Render column.

Last updated 3/8/2018

Rendering and exporting

Remove a render item from the Render Queue panel: Select the item and press Delete, or choose Edit > Clear.

Rearrange items in the Render Queue panel: Drag an item up or down the queue. A heavy black line appears between render items, indicating where the item will be placed. You can also reorder selected render items by choosing Layer > Arrange, and then choosing Bring Render Item Forward, Send Render Item Backward, Bring Render Item To Front, or Send Render Item To Back

Move selected render items up (earlier) in the render queue: Press Ctrl+Alt+Up Arrow (Windows) or Command+Option+Up Arrow (Mac OS).

Move selected render items down (later): Press Ctrl+Alt+Down Arrow (Windows) or Command+Option+Down Arrow (Mac OS).

Move selected render items to the top of the render queue: Press Ctrl+Alt+Shift+Up Arrow (Windows) or Command+Option+Shift+Up Arrow (Mac OS).

Move selected render items to the bottom (end) of the render queue: Press Ctrl+Alt+Shift+Down Arrow (Windows) or Command+Option+Shift+Down Arrow (Mac OS).

Duplicate a render item: Right-click (Windows) or Control-click (Mac OS) the render item and choose a command from the context menu:

Render with the same filename: Choose Duplicate With File Name.

Render with a new filename: Choose Duplicate, click the underlined filename next to Output To, enter a new filename, and click Save.

Pause or stop rendering

If the disk (to which an output module is writing) runs out of space, After Effects pauses the render operation. You can clear additional disk space and then resume rendering and exporting.

To pause rendering, click Pause. To resume rendering, click Continue.

While rendering is paused, you cannot change settings or use After Effects in any other way.

To stop rendering with the purpose of starting the same render over again, Alt-click (Windows) or Option-click (Mac OS) Stop.

The render item for which rendering was stopped is assigned the status User Stopped, and a new item with the status of Queued is added to the Render Queue panel. The new item uses the same output filename and has the same duration as the original render item.

To stop rendering with the purpose of resuming the same render, click Stop.

The render item for which rendering was stopped is assigned the status User Stopped, and a new item with the status of Unqueued is added to the Render Queue panel. The new item uses an incremented output filename and resumes rendering at the before frame at which rendering was stopped—so the first frame of the new item is the last successfully rendered frame of the stopped item.

Information shown for current render operations

Basic information about the current batch of renders is shown at the bottom of the Render Queue panel:

Message A status message. For example, Rendering 1 of 4.

RAM Memory available for the rendering process.

Renders Started The date and time at which the current batch of renders was started.

Total Time Elapsed The rendering time elapsed (not counting pauses) since the current batch of renders was started.

Last updated 3/8/2018

Rendering and exporting

Most Recent Error The path where the log files are located.

To view more information about the current render operation, click the triangle to the left of the Current Render ▫ heading. The Current Render pane collapses (closes) after a short time. To prevent it from collapsing after a time-out

period, Alt-click (Windows) or Option-click (Mac OS) the triangle next to the Current Render heading. To view details of a completed render, review the log file. When a log file has been written, the path to the log file appears under the Render Settings heading and Log menu.

Change the render-complete sounds

A chime plays when all items in the render queue have been rendered and exported; a different sound plays if a render operation fails. You can change the render-complete sounds by replacing files named rnd_okay.wav and rnd_fail.wav in the sounds folder. The sounds folder is in the following location:

Program Files\Adobe\Adobe After Effects CC 2015\Support Files (Windows)

Applications/Adobe After Effects CC/Contents/Resources (Mac OS)

Online resources for rendering and exporting with the render queue

Lloyd Alvarez provides a script on his After Effects Scripts website that takes items that are ready to render in the render queue and sends them to render in the background using aerender.

Jeff Almasol provides a script on his redefinery website that renders and exports each of the selected layers separately. You might find this script useful if layers represent different versions of an effect or different parts of an effect that you want to render as separate "passes" for flexibility in how they get composited.

Christopher Green provides a script (Queue_Comp_Sections.jsx) on his website with which you can use multiple guide layers to designate multiple time spans to be rendered and exported separately through the render queue.

Render and export with Adobe Media Encoder

From an expert: Export a composition from After Effects to Adobe Media Encoder

From an expert: Export a composition from After Effects to Adobe Media Encoder

You can also export After Effects compositions directly into Adobe Media Encoder, which offers the flexibility to continue working in After Effects while files are being processed. When you use Adobe Media Encoder, you can also use additional presets and options that are not available in the After Effects Render Queue.

You can add your composition to the Adobe Media Encoder Queue using one of the following methods:

Add to Adobe Media Encoder Queue (Composition > Add to Adobe Media Encoder Queue or File > Export > Add to Adobe Media Encoder Queue) for final rendering using presets and settings specified in Adobe Media Encoder.
Queue in AME button in the render queue (Window > Render Queue) for rendering a draft copy of your composition using the render settings specified in the rendering queue, while you continue to work on the composition.

For information about using Adobe Media Encoder for rendering, see Encode video or audio items in Adobe Media Encoder .

Note:

Last updated 3/8/2018

Rendering and exporting

The output module settings, such as format settings or color channel selection, are not transferred to Adobe Media Encoder when you choose the Queue in AME option. The output filename and location are transferred, however, Adobe Media Encoder does not use the filename and location templates, which may result in image sequence numbering mismatch.

Add a composition directly to Adobe Media Encoder

To add a composition to Adobe Media Encoder, do the following:

Drag the After Effects project containing the composition you want to encode into the Encoding Queue in Adobe Media Encoder.

You can add a composition to Adobe Media Encoder from After Effects. Do one of the following:

Choose Composition > Add To Adobe Media Encoder Queue

Choose File > Export > Add to Adobe Media Encoder Queue

Press Ctrl+Alt+M (Windows) or Command+Option+M (Mac OS)

The Import After Effects Composition dialog box opens. Choose the composition you want to encode.

Encode the file as you normally would by choosing presets and an output location in Adobe Media Encoder.

Add a composition from render queue to Adobe Media Encoder

To add a composition to the Adobe Media Encoder with render settings for draft rendering:

Choose Composition > Add to Render Queue or press the keyboard shortcut Control + M (Windows) or Command + M (Mac).

In the Render Queue panel, click the Queue in AME button.

Choosing formats and output settings

After Effects provides various formats and compression options for output. Which format and compression options you choose depends on how your output will be used. For example, if the movie that you render from After Effects is the final product that will be played directly to an audience, then you need to consider the medium from which you'll play the movie and what limitations you have on file size and data rate. By contrast, if the movie that you create from After Effects is an intermediate product that will be used as input to a video editing system, then you should output without compression to a format compatible with the video editing system. (See Planning your work.)

Aharon Rabinowitz provides an article on the Creative COW website about planning your project and deciding what formats and settings to use for final output.

Keep in mind the fact that you can use different encoding and compression schemes for different phases of your workflow. For example, you may choose to export a few frames as full-resolution still images (for example, TIFF files) when you need approval from a customer about the colors in a shot; whereas you may export the movie using a lossy encoding scheme (for example, H.264) when you need approval for the timing of the animation.

Supported output formats

You can add the ability to export other kinds of data by installing plug-ins or scripts provided by parties other than Adobe. For example, Paul Tuersley provides a script on the AE Enhancers forum with which you export After Effects composition data as Cinema 4D project data. Mark Christiansen provides an article on the ProVideo Coalition website that links to scripts and plug-ins for exporting from After Effects for use in Cinema 4D, Maya, Lightwave, and other 3D applications. (See Plug-ins.)

Unless otherwise noted, all image file formats are exported at 8 bits per channel (bpc).

519

Rendering and exporting

Video and animation formats

QuickTime (MOV)

Video for Windows (AVI; Windows only)

To create an animated GIF movie, first render and export a QuickTime movie from After Effects. Then import the ▪ QuickTime movie into Photoshop and export the movie to animated GIF.

Video project formats

Adobe Premiere Pro project (PRPROJ)

Still-image formats

Adobe Photoshop (PSD)

Cineon (CIN, DPX)

Maya IFF (IFF)

JPEG (JPG, JPE)

OpenEXR (EXR)

PNG (PNG)

Radiance (HDR, RGBE, XYZE)

SGI (SGI, BW, RGB)

Targa (TGA, VBA, ICB, VST)

TIFF (TIF)

Audio-only formats

Audio Interchange File Format (AIFF)

MP3

WAV

Collect files in one location

The Collect Files command gathers copies of all the files in a project or composition into a single location. Use this command before rendering, for archiving, or for moving a project to a different computer system or user account.

When you use the Collect Files command, After Effects creates a new folder and the following information is saved in the new folder:

A new copy of the project

Copies of the footage files

Proxy files as specified

A report describing the files, effects, and fonts necessary to re-create the project and render the compositions.

After you collect files, you can continue making changes to a project, but be aware that those changes are stored with the original project and not with the newly collected version.

Choose File > Dependencies > Collect Files.

In the Collect Files dialog box, choose an appropriate option for Collect Source Files. **All** Collects all footage files, including unused footage and proxies.

Rendering and exporting

For All Comps Collects all footage files and proxies used in any composition in the project.

For Selected Comps Collects all footage files and proxies used in compositions currently selected in the Project panel.

For Queued Comps Collects all footage files and proxies used directly or indirectly in any of the compositions with a Queued status in the Render Queue panel.

None (Project Only) Copies the project to a new location without collecting any source footage.

Select other options, as appropriate:

Generate Report Only Selecting this option does not copy the files and proxies.

Obey Proxy Settings Use this option with compositions that include proxies to specify whether you want the copy to include the current proxy settings. If this option is selected, only the files used in the composition are copied. If this option is not selected, the copy contains both proxies and source files, so you can later change proxy settings in the collected version.

Note: If you choose For Queued Comps in the Collect Source Files dialog box, After Effects uses the proxy settings from the render settings, not the composition.

Reduce Project Removes all unused footage items and compositions from the collected files when the following options are chosen in the Collect Source Files menu: For All Comps, For Selected Comps, and For Queued Comps.

Change Render Output To Use to redirect the output modules to render files to a named folder in the collected files folder. This option ensures that you have access to your rendered files when you're rendering the project from another computer. Rendering status must be valid (Queued, Unqueued, or Will Continue) for the output modules to render files to this folder.

Enable 'Watch Folder' Render You can use the Collect Files command to save projects to a specified watch folder and then initiate watch-folder rendering over a network. After Effects also includes a render control file called *[project name]_RCF.txt*, which signals to watching computers that the project is available for rendering. After Effects and any installed render engines can then render the project together across a network. (See Set up watch-folder rendering .)

Maximum Number Of Machines Use to specify the number of render engines or licensed copies of After Effects that you want to allocate to render the collected project. Below this option, After Effects reports how many items in the project will be rendered using more than one computer.

Note: If rendering time is unusually long, you may have set Maximum Number Of Machines too high, and the network overhead required to track rendering progress among all computers is out of proportion to the time spent actually rendering frames. The optimal number depends on many variables related to the network configuration and the computers on it; experiment to determine the optimal number for your network.

To add your own information to the report that will be generated, click Comments, enter your notes, and click OK. The comments appear at the end of the report.

Click Collect. Name the folder and specify a location for your collected files.

Once you start the file collection, After Effects creates the folder and copies the specified files to it. The folder hierarchy is the same as the hierarchy of folders and footage items in your project. The new folder includes a (Footage) folder and may include an output folder (if you selected Change Render Output To).

The names of these folders appear in parentheses to signal to any attending render engines that they should not search these folders for projects.

Carl Larsen demonstrates the use of the Collect Files command and the Consolidate All Footage command in a video tutorial on the Creative COW website that shows how to organize, consolidate, and archive project files and footage.

521

Rendering and exporting

David Torno provides a script on the After Effects Scripts website that exports specified information about a project.

Specify filenames and locations for rendered output

You can locate a previously rendered item or check the destination of a queued render item by expanding the Output ▪ *Module group in the Render Queue panel and clicking the underlined file path, or by right-clicking (Windows) or Control-clicking (Mac OS) the Output Module heading.*

Specify the filename and location for a single render item

To manually enter a filename and destination folder, click the underlined text next to the Output To heading.

To name a file using a file naming template, click the triangle next to the Output To heading, and choose a template from the menu.

Create and use a custom file naming template

You can use custom templates to name the output according to properties of the composition and project.

To make a file naming template the default template, hold down Ctrl (Windows) or Command (Mac OS) as you choose ▪ *the template from the Output To menu.*

In the Render Queue panel, choose Custom from the Output To menu.

If you want to base the new file-naming template on an existing template, choose the existing template from the Preset menu.

Click in the Template box where you want to insert a file-naming rule, and do any of the following:

To add a preset property to the filename, choose the property from the Add Property menu.

Enter text in the Template box.

Note: *Make sure that the insertion point is outside the square brackets [ ] of preset properties.*

Do any of the following:

To save the file-naming template as a preset for future use in the Output To menu, click the Save button ▣ . In the Choose Name dialog box, enter a name for the file-naming template, and click OK.

To always use the selected file-naming template, select Default.

To apply the selected file-naming template to the current Output Module, click OK.

Name output files automatically

The Use Default File Name And Folder preference ensures that all compositions added to the render queue are automatically assigned a unique output filename (except for files created by saving previews, which still use the composition name). When this option is selected, each render item is assigned the same folder name as the previous render item until you change the path. If a composition is rendered more than once, After Effects adds a number to the filename (for example, composition_name_1).

Note: *Avoid using high-ASCII or other extended characters in filenames for projects to be used on different platforms or rendered using a watch folder.*

Choose Edit > Preferences > Output (Windows) or After Effects > Preferences > Output (Mac OS).

Select Use Default File Name And Folder.

Rendering and exporting

Support for paths in templates

You can add paths to templates. Absolute paths can be defined in a template. For example, you can define and save a template that always places rendered files in E:\Output\[compName].[extension]. See the File Name and Location templates section in What's New in After Effects CC 12.2 for information about the new templates in After Effects CC 12.2 release.

Render settings

Render settings apply to each render item and determine how the composition is rendered for that specific render item. By default, the render settings for a render item are based on the current project settings, composition settings, and switch settings for the composition on which the render item is based. However, you can modify the render settings for each render item to override some of these settings.

Render settings apply to the root composition for a render item, as well as all nested compositions.

Note: *Render settings only affect the output of the render item with which they're associated; the composition itself is not affected.*

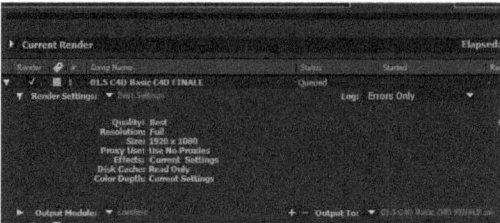

Render settings

Change render settings

To change render settings for a render item, click the render settings template name next to the Render Settings heading in the Render Queue panel, and choose settings in the Render Settings dialog box.

To apply a render settings template to selected render items, click the triangle next to the Render Settings heading in the Render Queue panel, and choose a template from the menu. You can choose a custom render settings template or one of the preset render settings templates:

Best Settings: Often used for rendering to final output.

Draft Settings: Often appropriate for reviewing or testing motion.

DV Settings: Similar to Best Settings, but with Field Rendering turned on, set to Lower Field First.

Multi-Machine Settings: Similar to Best Settings, but with Skip Existing Files selected to enable multi-machine rendering.

Note: *The default render settings template is assigned to a render item when it is created. To change which render settings template is the default, hold down Ctrl (Windows) or Command (Mac OS) as you choose a render settings template from the menu.*

Rendering and exporting

Create, edit, and manage render settings templates

You perform the following tasks in the Render Settings Templates dialog box. To open the Render Settings Templates dialog box, choose Edit > Templates > Render Settings, or click the triangle next to the Render Settings heading in the Render Queue panel and choose Make Template.

To make a new render settings template, click New, specify render settings, and click OK. Enter a name for the new template.

To edit an existing render settings template, choose a template from the Settings Name menu, click Edit, and specify render settings.

Note: Changes to an existing template do not affect render items that are already in the render queue.

To specify a default render settings template to be used when rendering movies, individual frames, pre-rendered movies, or proxies, choose a template from a menu in the Defaults area of the Render Settings Templates dialog box.

To save all currently loaded render settings templates to a file, click Save All.

To load a saved render settings template file, click Load, select the render settings template file, and then click Open.

Render settings reference

Each of these settings overrides composition settings, project settings, or layer switch settings.

Log You can choose how much information After Effects writes to a render log file. If you choose Errors Only, After Effects only creates the file if errors are encountered during rendering. If you choose Plus Settings, a log file is created that lists the current render settings. If you choose Plus Per Frame Info, a log file is created that lists the current render settings and information about the rendering of each frame. When a log file has been written, the path to the log file appears under the Render Settings heading and Log menu.

Quality The quality setting to use for all layers. (See Layer image quality and subpixel positioning.)

Resolution Resolution of the rendered composition, relative to the original composition dimensions. (See Resolution.)

Note: If you render at reduced resolution, set the Quality option to Draft. Rendering at Best quality when reducing resolution produces an unclear image and takes longer than Draft quality.

Disk Cache Determines whether the disk cache preferences are used during rendering. Read Only writes no new frames to the disk cache while After Effects renders. Current Settings (default) uses the disk cache settings defined in the Media & Disk Cache preferences. (See Disk cache .)

Proxy Use Determines whether to use proxies when rendering. Current Settings uses the settings for each footage item. (See Placeholders and proxies.)

Effects Current Settings (default) uses the current settings for Effect switches * . All On renders all applied effects. All Off renders no effects.

Solo Switches Current Settings (default) uses the current settings for Solo switches ◌ for each layer. All Off renders as if all Solo switches are off. (See Solo a layer.)

Guide Layers Current Settings renders guide layers in the top-level composition. All Off (the default setting) does not render guide layers. Guide layers in nested compositions are never rendered. (See Guide layers.)

Color Depth Current Settings (default) uses the project bit depth. (See Color depth and high dynamic range color.)

Frame Blending On For Checked Layers renders frame blending only for layers with the Frame Blending switch ▣ set, regardless of the Enable Frame Blending setting for the composition. (See Frame blending.)

Field Render Determines the field-rendering technique used for the rendered composition. Choose Off if you are rendering for film or for display on a computer screen. (See Interlaced video and separating fields.)

Rendering and exporting

3:2 Pulldown Specifies the phase of 3:2 pulldown. (See Introduce 3:2 pulldown.)

Motion Blur Current Settings uses the current settings for the Motion Blur layer switch ✐ and the Enable Motion Blur composition switch. On For Checked Layers renders motion blur only for layers with the Motion Blur layer switch set, regardless of the Enable Motion Blur setting for the composition. Off For All Layers renders all layers without motion blur regardless of the layer switch and composition switch settings. (See Motion blur.)

Time Span How much of the composition to render. To render the entire composition, choose Length Of Comp. To render only the part of the composition indicated by the work area markers, choose Work Area Only. To render a custom time span, choose Custom. (See Work area.)

Frame Rate The sampling frame rate to use when rendering the movie. Select Use Comp's Frame Rate to use the frame rate specified in the Composition Settings dialog box, or select Use This Frame Rate to use a different frame rate. The actual frame rate of the composition is unchanged. The frame rate of the final encoded movie is determined by the output module settings. (See Frame rate.)

Skip Existing Files Lets you rerender part of a sequence of files without wasting time on previously rendered frames. When rendering a sequence of files, After Effects locates files that are part of the current sequence, identifies the missing frames, and then renders only those frames, inserting them where they belong in the sequence. You can also use this option to render an image sequence on multiple computers. (See Render farming - Render a still-image sequence with multiple computers.)

Note: The current image sequence must have the same name as the existing image sequence, and the starting frame number, frame rate, and time span must be the same. You must render to the folder that contains the previously rendered frames.

Output modules and output module settings

Output module settings apply to each render item and determine how the rendered movie is processed for final output. Use output module settings to specify file format, output color profile, compression options, and other encoding options for final output.

You can also use output module settings to crop, stretch, or shrink a rendered movie; doing this after rendering is often useful when you are generating multiple kinds of output from a single composition.

Output module settings are applied to the rendered output that is generated according to the render settings.

For some formats, an additional dialog box opens when you choose the format in the Output Module Settings dialog box. You can modify these settings and use settings presets to specify format-specific options, such as compression options.

You can apply multiple output modules to each render item, which is useful when you want to make more than one version of a movie from one render. For example, you can automate the creation of a movie and its alpha matte, or you can create high-resolution and low-resolution versions of a movie.

Note: *Before rendering, check the Audio Output settings in the Output Module Settings dialog box to ensure that they are correct. To render audio, Audio Output must be selected. If your composition does not include audio, do not select Audio Output, so that the size of the rendered file does not increase needlessly.*

Rendering and exporting

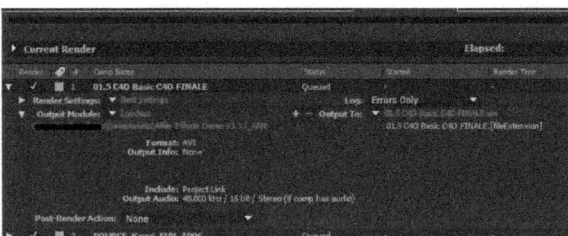

You can set the output module of multiple render queue items at the same time. Select the render queue items, and then choose an output module template from the Output Module Settings menu for one of the items.

You can drag an output module to the Project panel to import the finished movie or a placeholder into the project for use as a footage item. (See Import footage items.)

Andrew Kramer provides a video tutorial with tips for working with proxies, output modules, and output module templates on the Video Copilot website.

Change output module settings

To change output module settings for a render item, click the underlined output module settings template name next to the Output Module heading in the Render Queue panel, and choose settings in the Output Module Settings dialog box.

To apply an output module settings template to selected render items, click the triangle next to the Output Module heading in the Render Queue panel, and choose a template from the menu.

You can choose a custom output module settings template or one of the preset output module settings templates. Several templates are provided, including the Lossless template for creating movies for transfer to video, film, or an NLE system.

Note: *The default output module settings template is assigned to a render item when it is created. To change which output module template is the default, hold down Ctrl (Windows) or Command (Mac OS) as you choose an output module template from the menu.*

To change output module settings for multiple output modules at once, select the output modules and then choose an ▪ output module template. The template is applied to all selected output modules.

Create, manage, and edit output module templates

You perform the following tasks in the Output Module Templates dialog box. To open the Output Module Templates dialog box, choose Edit > Templates > Output Module, or click the triangle next to the Output Module heading in the Render Queue panel and choose Make Template.

To make a new output module settings template, click New, specify output module settings, and click OK. Enter a name for the new template.

To edit an existing output module settings template, choose a template from the Settings Name menu, click Edit, and specify output module settings.

Rendering and exporting

Note: *Changes to an existing template do not affect render items that are already in the render queue.*

To specify a default output module settings template to be used when processing movies, individual frames, previews, pre-rendered movies, or proxies, choose a template from a menu in the Defaults area of the Output Module Templates dialog box.

To save all currently loaded output module templates to a file, click Save All.

To load a saved output module template file, click Load, select the output module template file, and then click Open.

Add output modules to and remove output modules from render items

To add a new output module with default settings to a single render item, click the plus (+) sign to the left of the Output To heading of the last output module for the render item.

To remove an output module from a render item, click the minus (-) sign to the left of the Output To heading of the output module.

To add a new output module with default settings to selected render items, choose Composition > Add Output Module.

To duplicate selected output modules, press Ctrl+D (Windows) or Command+D (Mac OS).

Output module settings

For information on using controls in the Color Management area of the Output Module Settings dialog box, see Assign an output color profile.

Format Specifies the format for the output file or sequence of files.

Include Project Link Specifies whether to include information in the output file that links to the source After Effects project. When you open the output file in another application, such as Adobe Premiere Pro, you can use the Edit Original command to edit the source project in After Effects.

Include Source XMP Metadata Specifies whether to include XMP metadata in the output file from the files used as sources for the rendered composition. XMP metadata can travel all the way through After Effects from source files, to footage items, to compositions, to rendered and exported files. For all default output module templates, Include Source XMP Metadata is deselected by default. (See Exporting XMP metadata from After Effects.)

Post-Render Action Specifies an action for After Effects to perform after the composition is rendered. (See Post-render actions.)

Format Options Opens a dialog box in which you specify format-specific options.

Channels The output channels contained in the output movie. After Effects creates a movie with an alpha channel if you choose RGB+Alpha, implying a depth of Millions of Colors+. Not all codecs support alpha channels.

Note: All files created with a color depth of Millions of Colors+, Trillions of Colors+, or Floating Point + have labeled alpha channels; information describing the alpha channel is stored in the file. Therefore, you do not have to specify an alpha interpretation each time you import an item created in After Effects.

Depth Specifies the color depth of the output movie. Certain formats may limit depth and color settings.

Color Specifies how colors are created with the alpha channel. Choose from either Premultiplied (Matted) or Straight (Unmatted). (See Alpha channel interpretation: premultiplied or straight.)

Starting # Specifies the number for the starting frame of a sequence. For example, if this option is set to 38, After Effects names the first frame *[file_name]*_00038. The Use Comp Frame Number option adds the starting frame number in the work area to the starting frame of the sequence.

Rendering and exporting

Resize Specifies the size of your output movie. Select Lock Aspect Ratio To if you want to retain the existing frame aspect ratio when resizing the frame. Select Low Resize Quality when rendering tests, and select High Resize Quality when creating a final movie. (See Scaling a movie downand Scaling a movie up.)

Crop Used to subtract or add rows or columns of pixels to the edges of the output movie. You can specify the number of rows or columns of pixels to be added or subtracted from the top, left, bottom, and right sides of the movie. Use positive values to crop, and use negative values to add rows or columns of pixels. Select Region Of Interest to export only the region of interest selected in the Composition or Layer panel. (See Region of interest (ROI).)

By adding one row of pixels to the top and subtracting one row from the bottom of a movie, you can change the field ▪ order.

Audio Output Specifies the sample rate, sample depth (8 Bits or 16 Bits), and playback format (Mono or Stereo). Choose a sample rate that corresponds to the capability of the output format. Choose an 8-bit sample depth for playback on the computer, and a 16-bit sample depth for CD and digital audio playback or for hardware that supports 16-bit playback.

Note: The specifications for some formats impose limits on audio parameters. In such cases, audio options may be unavailable for modification in the Output Module Settings dialog box. Also, audio options for some formats are set in the export settings dialog box for that format. For example, to set audio output options for Windows Media, click Format Options in the Output Module Settings dialog box.

Warning for mismatch in frame rate or dimensions

Some formats enforce constraints on frame dimensions and frame rate.

If you choose such a constrained output format, and your composition, its render settings, or its output module settings don't match the constraints, then After Effects shows a yellow warning icon ⚠ and the message "Settings mismatch" at the bottom of the Output Module Settings dialog box.

Click the warning icon to see a detailed message that describes how the output file will be modified to meet the format constraints. You can go back and change composition settings, render settings, and output module settings if you don't want After Effects to make the changes automatically in the output module.

For more information about output module constraints and the warnings for mismatches in frame rate, dimensions, and pixel aspect ratio, see the Adobe website.

Encoding and compression options for movies

Compression is essential for reducing the size of movies so that they can be stored, transmitted, and played back effectively. Compression is achieved by an encoder; decompression is achieved by a decoder. Encoders and decoders are known by the common term *codec*. No single codec or set of settings is best for all situations. For example, the best codec for compressing cartoon animation is generally not efficient for compressing live-action video. Similarly, the best codec for playback over a slow network connection is generally not the best codec for an intermediate stage in a production workflow. For information on planning your work with final output in mind, see Planning your work.

After Effects uses an embedded version of the Adobe Media Encoder to encode most movie formats through the Render Queue panel. When you manage render and export operations with the Render Queue panel, the embedded version of the Adobe Media Encoder is called automatically. The Adobe Media Encoder appears only in the form of the export settings dialog boxes with which you specify some encoding and output settings.

Note: The embedded version of the Adobe Media Encoder used to manage export settings within After Effects output modules does not provide all the features of the full, stand-alone Adobe Media Encoder application. For information about the full, stand-alone Adobe Media Encoder application, see Adobe Media Encoder Help .

For most output formats, you can specify format-specific encoding and compression options. In many cases, a dialog box opens and presents these options when you choose a format to export to or click the Format Options button in the Output Module settings dialog box. (See Output modules and output module settings.)

QuickTime (MOV) encoding and compression settings

In the Render Queue panel, click the underlined name of the output module.

Choose QuickTime from the Format menu.

Click Format Options in the Video Output section.

In the QuickTime Options dialog box, choose a codec and set options according to the specific codec and your needs:

Quality A higher Quality setting produces better image quality but results in a bigger movie file.

Key Frame Every In QuickTime terminology, the term *key frames* refers to something different from the change-over-time keyframes placed in the After Effects Timeline panel. In QuickTime, key frames are frames that occur at regular intervals in the movie. During compression, they are stored as complete frames. Each intermediate frame that separates them is compared to the previous frame, and only changed data is stored. Using key frames greatly reduces movie size and greatly increases the memory required to edit and render a movie. Shorter intervals between key frames enable faster seeking and reverse playback, but can significantly increase the size of the file.

Frame Reordering Some codecs allow for frames to be encoded and decoded out of order for more efficient storage. **Note**: For more information on QuickTime, see the Apple website.

Click OK.

Specify other settings in the Output Module Settings dialog box.

Post-render actions

You can use post-render actions to automate simple tasks that occur after a composition is rendered.

A common example of the use of post-render actions is with pre-rendering: Choosing Composition > Pre-render adds the selected composition to the render queue and sets the Post-Render Action option to Import & Replace Usage.

Note: You choose Post-Render Action options in the Output Module group, so be aware that changing the Output Module template could also change the Post-Render Action option. (See Output modules and output module settings.)
Expand the Output Module group in the Render Queue panel by clicking the arrow to the left of the Output Module heading.

Choose one of the following from the Post-Render Action menu: **None** Performs no post-render action. This option is the default.

Import Imports the rendered file into the project as a footage item when the rendering is complete.

Import & Replace Usage Imports the rendered file into the project and substitutes it for the specified item. Drag the pick whip to the item to replace in the Project panel to specify it.

Use the Import & Replace Usage option to create a chain of dependent render items. For example, you can set one ● render item to use a watch folder and multiple computers to create a still-image sequence, and then the next render item can render a single movie file from that still-image sequence. (See Network rendering with watch folders and render engines.)

Set Proxy Sets the rendered file as a proxy for the specified item. Drag the pick whip to the item in the Project panel item to specify it.

Rendering and exporting still images and still-image sequences

Render and export a sequence of still images

You can export a rendered movie as a sequence of still images, in which case each frame of the movie is output as a separate still-image file. When you render one movie using multiple computers on a network, the movie is always output as a still-image sequence. Many 3D animation programs accept sequences of still images. Sequences of PNG files are often a good choice for transfer of visual elements from After Effects to Flash Professional.

If you are creating a movie for transfer to film, you will need to create a sequence of still images that you can then transfer to film using a film recorder.

Creating a sequence of PSD files is a good way to transfer frames to Photoshop for touchup and editing. You can then import the image sequence back into After Effects.

When specifying the output filename for a still-image sequence, you actually specify a file-naming template. The name that you specify must contain pound signs surrounded by square brackets ([#####]). As each frame is rendered and a filename created for it, After Effects replaces the [#####] portion of the name with a number indicating the order of the frame in the sequence. For example, specifying mymovie_[#####].tga would cause output files to be named mymovie_00001.tga, filmout_00002.tga, and so on.

The maximum number of frames in a still-image sequence is 32,766.

Render and export a single frame of a composition

You can export a single frame from a composition, either as an Adobe Photoshop (PSD) file with layers intact or as a rendered image. This is useful for editing files in Adobe Photoshop, preparing files for Adobe Encore, creating a proxy, or exporting an image from a movie for posters or storyboards.

The Photoshop Layers command preserves all layers from a single frame of an After Effects composition in the resulting Photoshop file. Nested compositions up to five levels deep are preserved in the PSD file as layer groups. The PSD file inherits the color bit depth from the After Effects project.

In addition, the layered Photoshop file contains an embedded composite (flattened) image of all the layers. This feature ensures that the file is compatible with applications that don't support Photoshop layers; such applications display the composited image and ignore the layers.

A layered Photoshop file saved from After Effects may look different from the frame viewed in After Effects if the frame uses features that Photoshop doesn't support. For example, if the frame contains a blending mode that isn't available in Photoshop, a blending mode that most resembles it is substituted in the layer, but the embedded composite image (viewable only by applications that don't support Photoshop layers) looks the same. Alternatively, you can render the frame using the Composition > Save Frame As > File command to export a flattened and rendered version of the file to the PSD format.

PSD files generated by Save Frame As > Photoshop Layers have the sRGB IEC61966-2.1 ICC color profile embedded if color management is disabled for the project (the project's working color space is set to None). If color management is enabled for the project (the project's working color space is set to something other than None), then PSD files generated by Save Frame As > Photoshop Layers have the color profile embedded that corresponds to the project's working color space. (See Color management and color profiles.)

Go to the frame that you want to export so that it is shown in the Composition panel.

Do one of the following:

To render a single frame, choose Composition > Save Frame As > File. Adjust settings in the Render Queue panel if necessary, and then click Render.

To export a single frame as an Adobe Photoshop file with layers, choose Composition > Save Frame As > Photoshop Layers.

To change the default output settings for the Save Frame As > File command, change the settings for the Frame Default ▪ render settings template (See Create, edit, and manage render settings templates.)

Export an After Effects project as an Adobe Premiere Pro project

You can export an After Effects project as an Adobe Premiere Pro project without rendering.

Note: Projects created using the latest version of Adobe After Effects and saved as Adobe Premiere Pro projects can be opened by the latest version of Adobe Premiere Pro.

When you export an After Effects project as an Adobe Premiere Pro project, Adobe Premiere Pro uses the settings from the first composition in the After Effects project for all subsequent sequences. Keyframes, effects, and other properties are converted in the same way as when you paste an After Effects layer into an Adobe Premiere Pro sequence. (See Importing from After Effects and Adobe Premiere Pro .)

Choose File > Export > Adobe Premiere Pro Project.

Specify a filename and location for the project, and click Save.

Note: You can also import Adobe Premiere Pro projects and sequences into After Effects, copy and paste between After Effects and Premiere Pro, and use Dynamic Link to exchange data between After Effects and Premiere Pro.

Converting movies

Convert footage items between video formats

You can use After Effects to convert one kind of video to another. When converting video, keep in mind the following guidelines:

Changes in resolution may result in a loss of picture clarity, especially when up-converting from a standard-definition format to a high-definition format.

Changes in frame rate may require the use of frame blending to smooth out the interpolated frames. For longer footage items, the use of frame blending can result in very long render times.

Import the footage you're converting into a composition using the preset of the format you're converting to. Example: if you're converting NTSC to PAL, add your NTSC footage item to a composition with the appropriate PAL composition settings preset.

Select the layer with the footage to be converted and choose Layer > Transform > Fit To Comp Width (or Fit To Comp Height).

Note: For converting between two formats with the same frame aspect ratio, either of these two Fit commands does the same thing; if the frame aspect ratios differ (for example, going from 4:3 to 16:9), fitting to width or height chooses between cropping or letterboxing the resulting image.

Do one of the following:

If your footage has no scene cuts, choose Layer > Frame Blending > Pixel Motion. Pixel Motion provides the best results for interpolation of frames, but may require long rendering times.

If your footage has scene cuts, or if you want to sacrifice quality for shorter rendering times, choose Layer > Frame Blending > Frame Mix.

Choose Composition > Add To Render Queue.

In the Render Queue panel, next to Render Settings, choose the appropriate preset from the menu. For example, if you're converting to DV footage, select DV Settings from the menu.

In the Render Queue panel, next to Output Module, choose the appropriate output module preset from the menu, or choose Custom to enter custom settings. For example, if you're converting to DV PAL, choose the D1/DV-PAL output module preset with the audio sampling rate that you require.

Click the name of the output module preset that you chose in step 6 to select additional Format Options.

Specify a name and destination for the output file using the controls to the right of the Output To heading in the Render Queue panel. (See Specify filenames and locations for rendered output.)

Click the Render button to render your movie.

Convert DV footage from PAL to NTSC using pulldown

Because After Effects can easily convert film (24 fps) to video (29.97 fps) using 3:2 pulldown, you can perform a clean PAL-to-NTSC transfer by setting up 25-fps PAL video to act like 24-fps film. This lets you apply 3:2 pulldown to the footage when converting to 29.97 fps. This technique works especially well for progressive (noninterlaced) PAL video.

Create a new composition with the DV NTSC or DV NTSC Widescreen preset.

Import your DV PAL footage into the new composition.

Select the layer with the DV PAL footage, and choose Layer > Transform > Fit To Comp Width (or Fit To Comp Height).

Do one of the following:

To preserve audio synchronization but slightly lower the pitch, choose Layer > Time > Time Stretch, and then enter 95.904 in the Stretch Factor box.

To preserve audio pitch but not synchronization, or for clips without audio, right-click (Windows) or Control-click (Mac OS) the footage item in the Project panel, select Interpret Footage > Main, select Conform To Frame Rate, and then enter 23.976 in the Conform To Frame Rate box.

Choose Composition > Add To Render Queue.

Choose Custom from the Render Settings menu.

In the Render Settings pane, enable Field Rendering (choose the field order required by your output type), select any option from the 3:2 Pulldown menu, and then click OK.

Choose the output type from the Render Queue Output Module menu (for example, Microsoft DV NTSC 32 kHz).

Specify a name and destination for the output file using the controls to the right of the Output To heading in the Render Queue panel. (See Specify filenames and locations for rendered output.)

10 Click the Render button to render your movie.

Scaling a movie down

Several methods exist for producing a reduced-size movie from your composition, each with tradeoffs between speed and quality:

Nest the composition Create a new composition at the smaller dimensions, and nest the large composition inside it. For example, if you create a 640x480 composition, place it in a 320x240 composition. Use the Fit To Comp command to scale the composition to fit the new smaller composition size: Press Ctrl+Alt+F (Windows) or Command+Option+F (Mac OS), and then collapse transformations by choosing Layer > Switches > Collapse. The resulting composition rendered at full resolution and best quality will have excellent image quality, better than if you had rendered using a reduced resolution.

Resize the composition This method produces the highest quality reduced-size movie but is slower than nesting. For example, if you create a 640x480 composition and render it at full resolution, you can set the Resize value in the Output Module Settings dialog box to 50% to create a 320x240 movie. For a composition rendered at full resolution, the image quality is excellent when the Resize Quality is set to High.

Note: Do not use resizing to change the vertical dimensions of a movie when field rendering is on. Resizing vertically mixes the field order, which distorts motion. Use either cropping or composition nesting if you need to vertically resize a field-rendered movie.

Crop the composition This method is ideal for reducing the size of a movie by a few pixels. Use the Crop options in the Output Module Settings dialog box. Remember that cropping cuts off part of the movie, so objects centered in the composition may not appear centered unless the movie is cropped evenly on opposite edges.

Note: In some special cases, After Effects will automatically crop rather than scale when creating an output movie with dimensions that don't match the dimensions of the composition. For example, when creating a 720x480 movie with a pixel aspect ratio of 0.91 or 1.21 from a 720x486 composition, After Effects will crop instead of scale.

Crop to a region of interest To render just a portion of the composition frame, define a region of interest in the Composition panel. Then, select the Region Of Interest option in the Output Module Settings dialog box before rendering. (See Region of interest (ROI).)

Rendering and exporting

Note: *Cropping an odd number of pixels from the top of a field-rendered movie reverses the field order. For example, if you crop one row of pixels from the top of a movie with Upper Field First field rendering, the field-rendering order then becomes Lower Field First. Remember that if you crop pixels from the top of the movie, you need to add to the bottom row of the movie to maintain the original size. If you don't mind losing one scan line, this technique gives you a way to output two movies from one render, each with a different field order.*

Render the composition at a reduced resolution This method is the fastest for creating reduced-size movies. For example, if you create a 640x480 composition, you can set the composition resolution to one half, reducing the size of the rendered composition to 320x240. You can then create movies or images at this size. The reduced resolution reduces the sharpness of the image and is best used for creating preview or draft movies.

Note: *When rendering at reduced resolution, set the quality of the composition to Draft. Rendering at Best quality while reducing resolution does not produce a clean image and takes longer to render than rendering at Draft quality.*

Scaling a movie up

Increasing the size of the output from a rendered composition reduces the image quality of a movie and is not recommended. If you must enlarge a movie, to maintain highest image quality, enlarge a composition that was rendered at full resolution and highest quality using one of the following methods:

Nest the composition Create a new composition at the larger dimensions and nest the smaller composition inside it. For example, if you create a 320x240 composition, you can place it in a 640x480 composition. Resize the composition to fit the new larger composition size, and then collapse transformations by choosing Layers > Switches > Collapse. The resulting composition rendered at full resolution and best quality will have better image quality than if you had resized the movie. However, this method also renders slower than if you created a composition and resized it.

Note: To create a draft movie with specific dimensions, use both the Resize option and reduced resolution in the rendered composition.

Resize the composition For example, if you create a 320x240 composition and render it at full resolution, you can set the Resize value in the Output Module Settings dialog box to 200% to create a 640x480 movie. For a composition rendered at full resolution, the image quality is usually acceptable.

Note: Do not use resizing to change the vertical dimensions of a movie with field rendering. Resizing vertically mixes the field order, which distorts any motion. Use either cropping or composition nesting if you need to vertically resize a field-rendered movie.

Crop the composition To enlarge a movie by a few pixels, increase the size using negative values for the Crop options in the Output Module Settings dialog box. For example, to increase the size of a movie by 2 pixels, enter −2 in the Cropping section of the Output Module Settings dialog box. Remember that negative cropping adds to one side of a movie, so objects originally centered in the composition may not appear centered when the movie is cropped.

Note: Adding an odd number of pixels to the top of a field-rendered movie reverses the field order. For example, if you add one row of pixels to the top of a movie with Upper Field First field rendering, the field-rendering order then becomes Lower Field First. Remember that if you add pixels to the top of the movie, you need to crop from the bottom row of the movie to maintain the original size.

Adobe Photoshop provides fine control over resampling methods used for scaling of images. For fine control of resampling, you can export frames to Photoshop to change the image size and then import the frames back into After Effects.

For a list of plug-ins that provide high-quality scaling—including some designed to create high-definition images from standard-definition sources—see the Toolfarm website.

For a script that scales multiple compositions simultaneously, see the AE Enhancers forum.

Create a composition and render source footage items simultaneously

You can simultaneously create a composition from source footage and prepare it for rendering. This process is useful when you want to change some characteristic of the source footage, such as frame rate or compression method, and have that rendered version available in your project.

Drag one or more footage items from the Project panel to the Render Queue panel, or select the footage items in the Project panel and do one of the following:

Choose Composition > Add to Render Queue.

Press Ctrl+Shift+/ or Ctrl+M(Windows) or Command+Shift+/ or Command+M (Mac OS).

Note: If the Use System Shortcut Keys option is enabled in General preferences (Mac OS), the shortcut is Ctrl+Cmd+M.

After Effects creates both a new item in the render queue and a new composition in the Project panel for each footage item.

Adjust the render settings as desired, and click Render.

Introduce 3:2 pulldown

If you are creating output for film that's been transferred to video, or if you want to simulate a film look for animation, use 3:2 pulldown. Footage items that were originally film transferred to video and had 3:2 pulldown removed when imported into After Effects can be rendered back to video with 3:2 pulldown reintroduced. You can introduce 3:2 pulldown by choosing one of five different phases. (See Remove 3:2 or 24Pa pulldown from video.)

Note: It is important to match the phase of a segment that had 3:2 pulldown removed if it will be edited back into the video footage it came from.

In the Render Queue panel, select the render item and then click the underlined text next to the Render Settings heading.

For Field Render, choose a field order.

For 3:2 Pulldown, choose a phase.

Select other settings as appropriate, and then click Render.

Chris and Trish Meyer provides an overview of 3:2 pulldown in an article on the Artbeats website.

Test field-rendering order

When you render a composition containing separated footage, set the Field Rendering option to the same field order as your video equipment. If you field-render with the incorrect settings, the final movie may appear too soft, jerky, or distorted. A simple test can determine the order in which your video equipment requires fields.

Note: The field order might get altered if you change the hardware or software of your production setup. For example, changing your device control software or VCR after setting the field order can reverse your fields. Therefore, any time you change your setup, test the field-rendering order.

The test takes about 15 minutes and involves creating two movie versions of the same composition (one rendered with Upper Field First and one with Lower Field First), and then playing the movies to see which choice looks right.

Create a simple composition with the correct frame size and frame rate. Choose an NTSC or PAL preset in the Composition Settings dialog box, and make the composition at least 3 seconds long.

Within the composition, make a layer that is a small rectangular solid. The layer can be any color as long as it contrasts sharply with the composition background. You may want to add a title (such as "Upper Field First") to the solid to make identification of the movie easier.

Apply some fast movement to the solid using keyframes in its Position property. Set keyframes from the upper-left of the Composition panel to the lower-right for 1 second.

Save the project, and then drag the composition to the Render Queue panel.

Click the underlined Render Settings name, and then choose Upper Field First from the Field Render menu.

Click OK, and then click Render to make the movie.

In the composition, change the color of the solid in the Composition panel, and add a new title, such as "Lower Field First", to identify it.

Render the composition again, choosing Lower Field First from the Field Render menu in the Render Settings dialog box.

Record both movies to the same device.

10 Play both movies.

One movie will look distorted and have jumpy horizontal motion or shape distortion during vertical motion. The other movie will play back smoothly, with sharply defined edges. Use the field order for the smooth-playing movie whenever you render movies with that particular hardware configuration.

Automated rendering and network rendering

Automating rendering with aerender

The executable file aerender.exe is a program with a command-line interface with which you can automate rendering. The executable file is located in the same folder as the primary After Effects application. The default locations for this file are:

Windows: \Program Files\Adobe\Adobe After Effects CC\Support Files

Mac OS: /Applications/Adobe After Effects CC

You can use the aerender application to perform rendering operations on multiple computers as part of a render farm, or you can use the aerender application on a single computer as part of a batch operation.

You use the program by entering the command aerender on the command line (or in a batch script), followed by a series of optional arguments. Some of the arguments are simple options that take no arguments of their own (for example, - reuse), whereas others take arguments of their own (for example, -project project_path).

Enter the command aerender -help to show usage information.

The version and build number of the application are written to standard output (stdout).

The render may be performed either by an already running instance of After Effects or by a newly started instance. By default, aerender starts a new instance of After Effects, even if one is already running. To instead use the currently running instance, use the –reuse argument.

This example command tells After Effects to render frames 1 through 10 of Composition_1 in project_1.aep to a numbered sequence of Photoshop files using a multi-computer render:

aerender -project c:\projects\project_1.aep -comp "Composition_1" -s 1 -e 10 -RStemplate "Multi-Machine Settings" -OMtemplate "Multi-Machine Sequence" -output c:\output\project_1\frames[####].psd

To render just Composition_1 to a specified file, enter this command:

aerender -project c:\projects\project_1.aep -comp "Composition_1" -output c
:\output\project_1\project_1.avi

To render everything in the render queue with current settings in the project file, enter this command:

aerender -project c:\projects\project_1.aep

Argument	Description
–help	Print usage message.
–version	Display the version number of aerender to the console. Does not render.
–v verbose_flag	verbose_flag specifies the kind of messages reported: ERRORS: Reports only fatal and problem errors. ERRORS_AND_PROGRESS: (default) Reports errors and progress of rendering.
–reuse	Reuse the currently running instance of After Effects (if found) to perform the render. When an already running instance is used, aerender saves preferences to disk when rendering has completed, but does not quit After Effects. If this argument is not used, aerender starts a new instance of After Effects, even if one is already running. It quits that instance when rendering has completed, and does not save preferences.

-mem_usage image_cache_percentmax_mem_percent	image_cache_percent specifies the maximum percentage of memory used to cache already rendered images and footage. max_mem_percent specifies the total percentage of memory that After Effects can use. For both values, if installed RAM is less than a given amount (n gigabytes), the value is a percentage of the installed RAM, and is otherwise a percentage of n. The value of n is 2 GB for 32-bit Windows, 4 GB for 64-bit Windows, and 3.5 GB for Mac OS.
-project project_path	project_path is a file path or URI specifying a project file to open. If this argument is not used, aerender works with the currently open project. If no project is specified and no project is open, the result is an error.
-comp comp_name	comp_name specifies a composition to render. If the composition is in the render queue already, then the first instance of that composition in the render queue is rendered. If the composition is in the project but not in the render queue, then it is added to the render queue and rendered. If this argument is not used, aerender renders the entire render queue; in this case, only the −project, −log, −output, −v, −mem_usage, and −close arguments are used, and all other arguments are ignored.
-s start_frame	start_frame is the first frame to render. If this argument is not used,

	aerender uses the start frame in the file.
–e end_frame	end_frame is the last frame to render. If this argument is not provided, aerender uses the end frame in the file.
–i increment	increment is the number of frames to advance before rendering a new frame. A value of 1 (the default) causes normal rendering of all frames. Higher values render a frame and use it increment times in output, and then skip ahead increment frames to begin the cycle again. Higher values result in faster renders but choppier motion.

⊢OMtemplate output_module_template	output_module_template is the name of a template to apply to the output module. If the template does not exist, using this argument causes an error. If this argument is not used, aerender uses the template already defined for the output module.
⊢RStemplate render_sett ings_template	render_settings_template is the name of a template to apply to the render item. If the template does not exist, using this argument causes an error. If this argument is not used, aerender uses the render template already defined for the item.
⊢output output_path	output_path is a file path or URI specifying the destination for the final output file. If this argument is not used, aerender uses the path defined in the project file.
⊢log log_file_path	log_file_path is a file path or URI specifying the location of the log file. If this argument is not used, aerender uses standard output (stdout).
⊢sound sound_flag	If sound_flag is ON, a sound is played when rendering is complete. Default is OFF.
⊢close close_flag	close_flag specifies whether to close the project when rendering is complete, and whether or not to save changes: DO_NOT_SAVE_CHANGES: (default) The project is closed without saving changes. SAVE_CHANGES: The project is closed

	and changes are saved. DO_NOT_CLOSE: The project is left open if using an already-running instance of After Effects. (New instances of After Effects must always quit when done.)
-rqindex index_in_render_queue	-rqindex works just like -comp, except that it won't create a render item from the composition automatically.
-mp	More processes may be created to render multiple frames simultaneously, depending on system configuration and preference settings. (See Memory & Multiprocessing preferences .)
-continueOnMissingFootage	The render operation continues even if a source footage item is missing.

Lloyd Alvarez provides a script on his After Effects Scripts website that takes items that are ready to render in the render queue and sends them to render in the background using aerender.

Network rendering with watch folders and render engines

You can render one or more compositions from a project using multiple computers over a network in a fraction of the time that a single computer would require. Network rendering involves copying the project and source files to a networked folder, and then rendering the project. A network of computers used together to render a single composition is sometimes called a render farm.

Render farming is when a network of computers is used together to render a single composition. You can set this up to work with render-only versions of After Effects called render engines.

You can install render engines in the same manner as the full version of the application. You run the render engine using the Adobe After Effects Render Engine shortcut in the Adobe After Effects CC folder. For more information, see same composition Setup and installation .

You cannot use a watch folder and multiple render engines to simultaneously render a single movie file. However, in render farming, you can use multiple render engines to render a movie as a sequence of still-image files. You can then use a post-render action to create a single movie file from that still-image sequence. For more information, see Post-render actions .

Network considerations

When working with multiple render engines on multiple computers, keep in mind the following guidelines:

When possible, identify folders using absolute file paths so that the paths are correctly identified for all render engines. Identifying folders using absolute file paths may mean mapping network drives to a particular drive letter on all computers (for example, H:\renders\watch\). Avoid using relative paths (for example, \\renders\watch).

Each Macintosh computer monitoring the watch folder must have a unique name. Because the default names of computers are often identical, you should rename your computers to not use the default name.

Make sure that all servers and clients (computers monitoring the watch folder) have hard drives with unique names.

Do not use the same computer to serve a watch folder and to run After Effects in Watch Folder mode. Use a dedicated server that's accessible to all render engines to serve your watch folder.

Do not render to or initiate Watch Folder mode on the root of a volume or a shared folder that appears as the root when viewed from another computer. Specify a subfolder instead. Also, avoid using high-ASCII or other extended characters and slashes in filenames. For multiple-computer rendering, After Effects includes the Multi-Machine sample template that you can use as a starting point.

When rendering across a network that includes volumes using different network or operating systems, such as Windows, Mac OS, Novell, and UNIX, make sure that you specify output files using a file-naming convention that's compatible with all rendering or destination volumes.

Project considerations

Make sure that you install all fonts, effects, and encoders (compressors) used in the project on all computers monitoring the watch folder. If a computer monitoring the watch folder can't find fonts, effects, or encoders used in a project, the render fails.

When you install an After Effects render engine on a computer, it contains all the plug-ins included with After Effects. If a composition uses a plug-in from another manufacturer, the plug-in must be present on all computers to render the composition. However, support for network rendering varies among plug-in manufacturers. Before you set up a network to render effects created by third-party plug-ins, see the documentation for your plug-ins or contact the plug-in manufacturers and get answers to the following questions:

Does the license agreement for the plug-in allow installing multiple copies on a network for the purposes of rendering?

Are there any other limitations or tips that apply to using the plug-in for network rendering?

Collect Files folder considerations

When you use the File > Collect Files command, files relevant to a project are copied to a single folder. This folder includes a copy of the project file, a *render control file* (RCF), and other files, depending on the options you choose in the Collect Files dialog box. If you save the Collect Files folder to a networked computer other than a server, don't run a render engine on that computer. Avoid saving the Collect Files folder to a local disk, the root level of a disk (such as

in Windows or the Macintosh HD in Mac OS), or a shared folder, all of which can signify different locations to each render engine. All render engines must interpret the path in the same way.

Once the collected files appear in the watch folder, all monitoring render engines start rendering automatically. If you . prefer, you can use the Collect Files command to store compositions and their source footage to a specified location and then initiate the watch-folder rendering process later. Doing so renders the projects in alphabetical order, rather than the order in which they were saved to the location.

Track dependencies of a watch-folder render

You can track render dependencies when you render over a network by setting Post-Render Action options. When you set these options, After Effects confirms that all of the items that have to be rendered are ready and available. For example, if one item depends on another to render, and the first has not finished rendering or has received an error, the second does not render.

You can use this process to render a single QuickTime or AVI movie from a watch-folder render. The movie is created on only one computer.

Note: This procedure assumes that you have already created a multiple-computer watch-folder.

In the Render Queue panel, drag the output module to the Project panel. After Effects creates a placeholder for that item's output.

Drag the placeholder back to the Render Queue panel.

Set the render settings and output module settings for the placeholder, and click Render.

Start in watch-folder mode

Watch-folder mode applies only to rendering from a folder on your local computer.

To start After Effects in watch-folder mode automatically, save a project with the filename Watch This Folder.aep. After Effects watches the folder containing the project if you open that project.

To start After Effects in watch-folder mode when you start your computer, create a shortcut (Windows) or alias (Mac OS) to the Watch This Folder.aep project and move it to your Startup folder (Windows) or your Startup Items folder (Mac OS). After Effects watches the folder containing the project if you open that project.

(Windows only) To start After Effects in watch-folder mode from the command line, choose Start > Run, and then enter the following, modifying the application path to the exact name of the folder in which you installed After Effects, and replacing C:\[temp] with the path to your watch folder: "C:\Program Files\Adobe\Adobe After Effects CC\Support Files\afterfx.exe" -wf C:\[temp]

To start the After Effects render engine rather than the full version of After Effects, use the -re option with the command.

Note: *You can also use this command line in batch files.*

Render farming - Render a still-image sequence with multiple computers

Render farming is when a network of computers is used together to render a single composition. You can set this up to work with render-only versions of After Effects called render engines. Render farming helps reduce the time a single machine takes to export a composition. You can use multiple computers and multiple copies of After Effects to render a composition across a network. You can use multiple computers to render only still-image sequences; you cannot use multiple computers to render a single movie.

Aharon Rabinowitz provides a video tutorial on the Creative COW website that goes through and explains the steps for rendering a still-image sequence with multiple computers.

Set up the network

Follow the process illustrated in the image to understand the requirements to set up the network.

Rendering and exporting

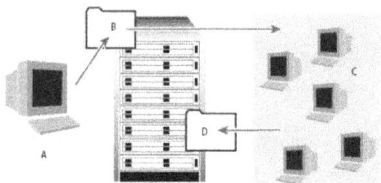

A Computer with full version of After Effects *B* Save a project and all source files to a folder on a server *C* Computers with the render engine installed *D* Open the project and render a still-frame sequence to a designated output folder on the server

You can use any number of computers for rendering; in general, the more computers, the faster the rendering. However, if too many computers are used across a busy network, network traffic may slow down the entire process. You can detect network slowdown by observing the time spent in the Compressing & Writing stage in the Current Render section of the Render Queue panel.

Note: Adobe does not provide technical support for general network configuration; consult your network administrator.

Render a still-image sequence with multiple computers

Important points in the process of rendering a still image sequence with multiple computers:

To render a still-image sequence with multiple computers, you can use any number of computers.

When you render a still-image sequence with multiple computers, rendering in each copy of After Effects starts at approximately the same time.

If your queued render items are set to Skip Existing Files (a Render Settings option), the render process skips the existing frames or frames in progress.

Multiple computers can render the project simultaneously, writing the still-image sequence to a single folder.

To render a still-image sequence, follow these steps:

Install After Effects on each computer that is used to render the project. Make sure that you have the same fonts installed on each computer.

Note: *Do not share plug-ins across a network. Make sure that you have a copy of the plug-ins folder on each computer that is running After Effects. When using third-party plug-ins, also be sure that the same plug-ins are available on all computers and that you have sufficient licenses for the plug-ins.*

Open the project on one computer and select Composition > Add To Render Queue.

In Render Queue panel, specify a format in the Output Module area, and specify a folder in the Output To area. This folder must be available for all the computers that are rendering.

In the Render Queue panel, select Skip Existing Files (allow multi-machine rendering) in the Render Settings section so that multiple computers do not render the same frames. Do not use multiple output modules for one render item when using skip existing files.

Save the project on the computer where you opened it in step 2.

On each computer that will be rendering, open and save the project. Saving the project ensures that After Effects records the new relative paths to each computer in the following step.

Unless the network can handle large file transfers rapidly, copy the project file and all its source footage to each rendering computer.

Open the Render Queue panel on each computer and click Render. You do not need to start rendering on each computer simultaneously, but to ensure equal workloads, start them at approximately the same time. As each computer finishes rendering a frame, After Effects searches the Output folder for the next unrendered frame and starts rendering again.

You can stop and start any computer at any time. However, if you stop a computer without starting it again, the frame that it was rendering may not be finished. If one or more computers stop during rendering, starting any one computer ensures that all frames in the sequence get rendered.

Run aerender in non-royalty bearing mode

After Effects CS5.5 had to be serialized on render-only machines due to licensing issues. In After Effects CS6 and later, you can now run aerender or use Watch Folder in a non-royalty bearing mode, so serialization not required.

To ensure that After Effects is running in non-royalty bearing mode, place a blank file named ae_render_only_node.txt into the following location:

Install After Effects on the render-only machine.

Mac locations: /Users/<username>/Documents/ /Users/Shared/Adobe/

Windows locations: C:\Users\<username>\Documents
C:\Users\Public\Documents\Adobe

Segment settings

Segment settings are in the Output preferences category.

Choose Edit > Preferences > Output (Windows) or After Effects > Preferences > Output (Mac OS).

After Effects can render sequences and movie files into segments that are limited to a specified number of files or by file size. This is useful when preparing a movie for a medium such as CD-ROM, for which file or folder size may need to be limited to chunks of 650 MB or less. Use the Segment Video-only Movie Files At value to set the maximum size for segments in megabytes. Use the Segment Sequences At value to set the maximum number of still-image files in a folder.

If you are exporting a movie that is larger than the maximum file size for your hard disk formatting scheme, then you can set the Segment Video-only Movie Files At value to a value under this maximum. Hard disks formatted for Windows can be formatted using the FAT, FAT32, or NTFS scheme. The maximum file size in the FAT scheme is 2 GB, and the maximum file size in the FAT32 scheme is 4 GB. The maximum size for a file for NTFS is large (approximately 16 terabytes), so you are unlikely to reach this limit with a single movie.

Only movies that do not contain audio can be segmented. If an output module includes audio, the Segment Video-only Movie Files At preference is ignored for that item.

The Segment Sequences At preference is ignored for any render item for which Skip Existing Files is selected in the render settings. (See Render settings reference.)

Note: *After Effects won't render and export a segmented movie to the root directory (e.g., C:\). To render and export a segmented movie, choose an output directory other than the root directory. (See Specify filenames and locations for rendered output.)*

Using the GoPro CineForm codec in After Effects

About the GoPro CineForm codec

The GoPro CineForm codec is a cross-platform intermediate codec that is commonly used in film and television workflows that use HD or higher resolution media.

In the latest version of After Effects CC and Adobe Media Encoder CC, the GoPro CineForm codec can be used to natively decode and encode QuickTime files (.mov). Hence you do not need to install additional codecs to create and use QuickTime files.

GoPro CineForm codec settings

There are five compression quality settings and two pixel format settings that you can use to adjust your output when using the GoPro CineForm codec. To export your After Effects projects with the GoPro CineForm codec, do the following:

Select a project in the Render Queue and click the Output Module setting.

Choose QuickTime as the output format in the Format drop-down list and click Format Options.

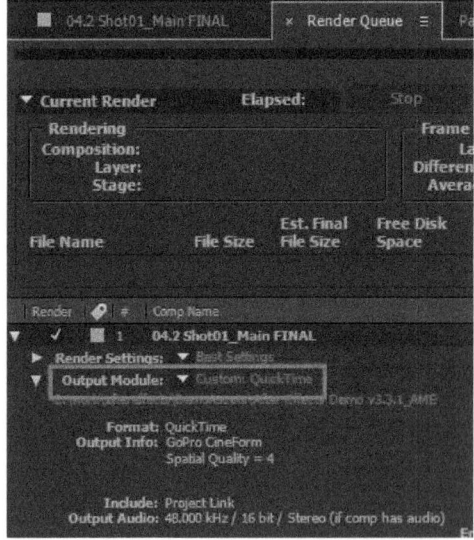

Rendering and exporting

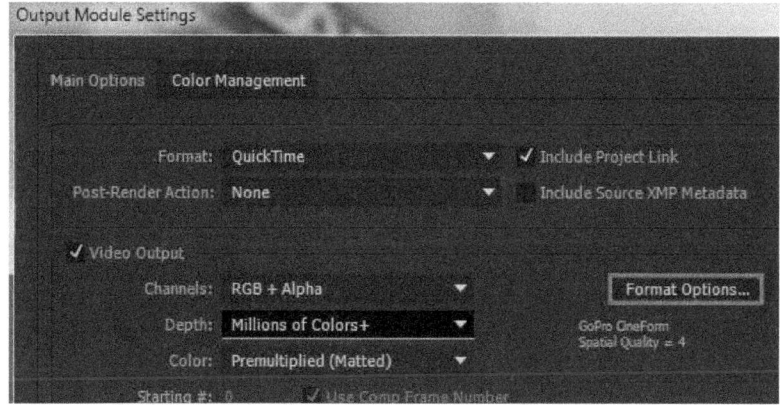

Choose GoPro CineForm as the video codec in the QuickTime Options dialog box. Adjust the compression settings using the Quality slider under the Basic Video Settings. The slider can be moved from a range of 1 to 5, with 1 for the Low setting and 5 for Film Scan 2 setting. The default value is 4 (Film Scan).

Low

Medium

High

Film Scan

Film Scan 2

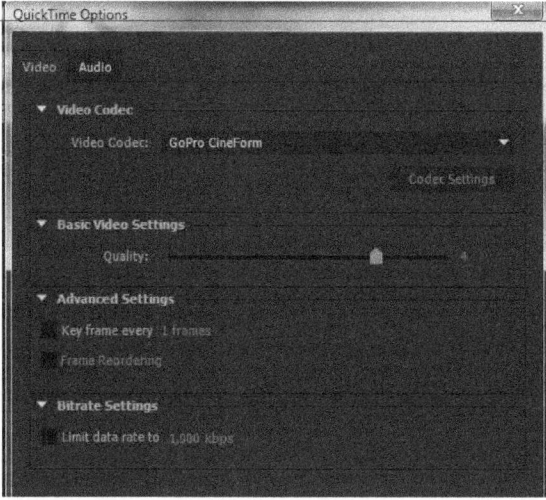

See the Understanding CineForm Quality settings article on the CineForm website for detailed information about this setting.

The GoPro CineForm codec can encode pixels in YUV 4:2:2 at 10 bits per channel, or RGBA 4:4:4:4 at 12 bits per channel.

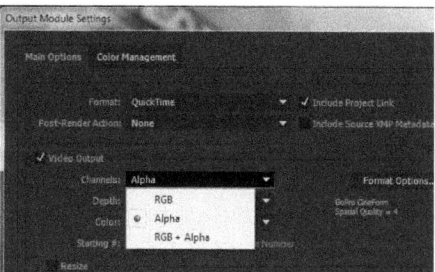

The encoded pixel format is based on the color depth and alpha channel settings that you choose in the Output Module Settings dialog box. There are three Channels settings that can be set, RGB, Alpha, and RGB+Alpha:

Set Channels to RGB or Alpha to encode to 10bpc YUV. In this case, Depth can only be set to Millions Of Colors.

Set Channels to RGB+Alpha to encode to 12bpc RGBA. In this case Depth can be set to Millions of Colors+ or Trillions of Colors+.

Note: After Effects renders the composition at the color depth specified in the Project and Render Settings, and the GoPro CineForm encoder will resample the frames to 10-bit YUV or 12 bpc RGBA as appropriate.

Click Render in the Render Panel to begin rendering your project with the GoPro CineForm settings.

GoPro CineForm settings in Adobe Media Encoder

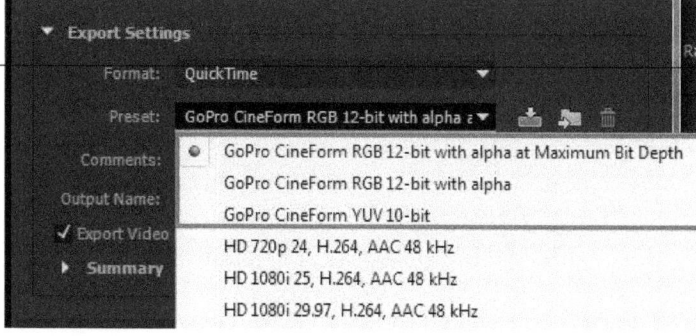

When you want to output to QuickTime format in Adobe Media Encoder using the GoPro CineForm encoder, there are three presets that you can use in the Export Settings dialog box:

GoPro CineForm RGB 12-bit with alpha at Maximum Bit Depth

GoPro CineForm RGB 12-bit with alpha

GoPro CineForm YUV 10-bit

Note: The frames may be rendered at a higher or lower quality by Adobe Media Encoder, depending on the sources in use and whether the Maximum Bit Depth option is enabled. The GoPro CineForm encoder will resample the frames to 10 bpc YUV or 12 bpc RGBA as appropriate.

Other considerations

You can edit the basic video settings, such as Frame Rate and Aspect ratio by unchecking the boxes next to each of these settings. For unsupported sizes such as GoPro 2.7K, change the resolution settings and down-scale to 1080,2K, or 4K or upscale to 6K.

Due to the frame size limitations, frame width sizes should be divisible by 16, and frame height sizes should be divisible by 8, regardless of bit depth. For example, the frame size of GoPro 2.7 is 2704x1524 and hence this is currently not supported as its width of 1524 results in a partial frame size of 95.25.